Protomusic
The Role of Prosodic Modulation in the Emergence of Language

Alessandra Anastasi
University of Messina, Italy

Series in Language and Linguistics

Copyright © 2023 Vernon Press, an imprint of Vernon Art and Science Inc, on behalf of the author.

All rights reserved. No part of this publication may be reproduced, stored in a retrieval system, or transmitted in any form or by any means, electronic, mechanical, photocopying, recording, or otherwise, without the prior permission of Vernon Art and Science Inc.

www.vernonpress.com

In the Americas:
Vernon Press
1000 N West Street, Suite 1200
Wilmington, Delaware, 19801
United States

In the rest of the world:
Vernon Press
C/Sancti Espiritu 17,
Malaga, 29006
Spain

Series in Language and Linguistics

Library of Congress Control Number: 2022945865

ISBN: 978-1-64889-639-2

Also available: 978-1-64889-152-6 [Hardback]; 978-1-64889-548-7 [PDF, E-Book]

Product and company names mentioned in this work are the trademarks of their respective owners. While every care has been taken in preparing this work, neither the authors nor Vernon Art and Science Inc. may be held responsible for any loss or damage caused or alleged to be caused directly or indirectly by the information contained in it.

Cover design by Vernon Press using elements designed studiogstock / Freepik and pch.vector / Freepik.

Every effort has been made to trace all copyright holders, but if any have been inadvertently overlooked the publisher will be pleased to include any necessary credits in any subsequent reprint or edition.

CONTENTS

LIST OF FIGURES — v

ACKNOWLEDGEMENTS — vii

PREFACE Music, Musicality, and the Nature of Human Language by Alessandra Falzone — xi

INTRODUCTION — xv

Chapter 1 MUSIC, LANGUAGE, AND COGNITIVE SCIENCES — 1
 1.1 Natural History, Music History — 1
 1.2 The Language of Sounds — 7
  1.2.1 Phonetic-phonological level — 9
  1.2.2 Syntactic-structural level — 11
  1.2.3 Musical Semantics — 13
 1.3 Towards a Theory of Musical Language — 15
 1.4 Cognitive Linguistics and Music Cognition — 20
 1.5 Revisiting Darwin's Theory on Musical Protolanguage — 29

Chapter 2 MUSIC FIRST, WORDS LATER — 37
 2.1 Parental Care: A Brief Overview — 37
 2.2 Prehistoric Mothers: The Biological Role of Maternal Singing — 41
 2.3 Motherese: A Comparative Perspective — 46
 2.4 From Sound to Speech: Prosodic Bootstrapping Hypothesis — 50
 2.5 The Adaptive Function of Speech — 54

Chapter 3 THE ROOTS OF MUSICAL COMMUNICATION — 61
 3.1 Musical Communication in Non-Human Animals — 64
  3.1.1 Birdsongs — 65

	3.1.2 Singing in the trees	*70*
	3.2 Learning or Imitation?	74
	3.3 Species-Specific Traits of Musicality	82
Chapter 4	**BIOLOGICAL FOUNDATIONS OF MUSIC AND LANGUAGE**	**87**
	4.1 Music, Language, and Performativity	87
	4.2 Vocal Performativity: Morphological Aspects and Biological Constraints	92
	4.3 Music as Adaptation	95
	4.4 Music as Exaptation	103
	4.5 Music as a Natural Precursor of Language	105
	CONCLUSION	**109**
	BIBLIOGRAPHY	**115**
	INDEX	**159**

LIST OF FIGURES

Figure 2.1	Spectrogram of an indri song	56
Figure 2.2	Ventral and dorsal streams	60
Figure 3.1	Syrinx	75
Figure 3.2	Diagram of the song system	77

ACKNOWLEDGEMENTS

This book is the result of studies that I made in recent years. For this reason, I would like to recall the scientific and human debt I owe many people during this book's writing. I wish to begin by giving special thanks to Alessandra Falzone. To her, I owe my scientific growth. She is, for me, a reference point within academia, and this book would not have had life without her valuable suggestions.

I would also like to express my gratitude to Marco Gamba. The encounter with him was so important during my PhD and it allowed me to explore a topic I love.

I would like to take this opportunity to thank the Department of Cognitive Sciences - University of Messina - and its young researchers and professors who have contributed to my academic background. A collective thanks to my friends for supporting my book project.

I also wish to thank my family for their unwavering support.

To Francesco and his sparkle

PREFACE
Music, Musicality, and the Nature of Human Language by Alessandra Falzone

The nature of human language and its evolution is one of the most challenging topics in cognitive science in recent decades. The centrality of this issue has not always been so evident in the history of scientific and philosophical studies on the human mind. On the contrary, for more than a century, from the edict of the Société de Linguistique de Paris in the mid-nineteenth century until the late 1880s, scientific discussion around the topic of evolutionary processes that enabled language and how much these could determine the nature of human language was simply bracketed, if not, in some cases, opposed.

For years, the main challenge of proponents of language evolution has been to show that even this refined and very peculiar ability of *Homo sapiens* was not the result of a qualitative leap (as asserted, for example, in the more classic Chomskyan position on the nature of human language, see Chomsky 1966), but that it was rooted in a history of changes that led to the current linguistic capability.

The embodied approach of the cognitive sciences and the accumulation of a staggering amount of data on the functioning of language and animal and human communication systems have put evolutionary processes back at the centre of the debate, so much so that several scholars are now arguing that evolution determines the nature of human language and, consequently, human nature per se. In 2003, Christiansen and Kirby argued that "To understand ourselves, we must understand language. To understand language, we need to know where it came from, why it works the way it does, and how it has changed." (2003, 1)

Today, even the most stubborn sceptics will admit to some form of evolution for language function, albeit adopting the theoretical strategy of identifying some "special, unique" component of sapiens (such as recursion, see Hauser, Chomsky, Fitch 2002).

Indeed, understanding the evolution of human language has been considered by some to be "the hardest problem of science" or even a real "mystery" (Hauser et al. 2014). Without going into the details of the debate, the thesis of linguistic discontinuity - that is, of a qualitative difference, a leap, between human language and other forms of animal communication - resurfaces periodically. The goal of the proponents of the discontinuity thesis is to demonstrate that all the scientific data that is constantly being collected by psychologists, biologists, ethologists, geneticists, linguists, and paleoanthropologists do not, in the least, scratch the gap present between *Homo sapiens*, birds, and nonhuman primates about language. According to Hauser and colleagues, for example, the identification only in *Homo sapiens* of the anatomical foundations of language, particularly the conformation of the supralaryngeal vocal tract, would be concrete evidence of this unbridgeable gap, and thus of the qualitative difference between sapiens and other nonhuman animals. Trying to understand the evolution of language would, consequently, be a futile effort, just as it would be futile to ask whether the faculty of language actually evolved.

On several occasions, I have been able to show how precisely the identification of morphological traits that enable articulate language has made it possible to overcome the discontinue position. The supralaryngeal vocal tract, the structures of auditory perception as well as the brain areas that coordinate auditory-vocal feedback, in fact, are not the guarantee of qualitative difference in human language but are the biological signs, the morphological constraints, that enable sapiens to have articulate verbal language. As the most recent studies in evolutionary developmental biology (EVO-DEVO) have shown, morphological constraints can never come out of nowhere in any species but are the result of a complex process of genetic variation and selection and species form (Falzone 2019).

It is these morphological constraints that enable sapiens to produce and perform the articulate voice, and therefore it is these biological constraints that reveal the evolutionary continuity of the voice and determine its social cognitive dimension (Falzone 2014; 2020).

Alessandra Anastasi's book ranks among the contributions in favour of the continuity thesis of human vocality. In the wake of Patel's (2007) hypothesis, Anastasi argues that music is a cognitive competence of sapiens, a capacity on par with reading and writing, but, unlike Patel, Anastasi considers music, like all cognitive capacities, a biological capacity constrained by morphological structures.

The author's main goal is to demonstrate, building on the distinction made by Honing and colleagues (2015), that musicality is part of the biological make-up of *Homo sapiens*, while music as a syntactically organized system is the socio-cultural expression of musicality. This is a very interesting thesis for several reasons.

First, to conceive of musicality as constrained by "natural" components is to recognize its status as a biological function, that is, a universal function: in the case of sapiens, musicality is realized through the morphological constraint of the supralaryngeal vocal tract, our "musical organ." The voice is the first instrument of communication for sapiens. It is no coincidence that the author devotes ample space to the musicality of sapiens, infants, and in particular, to so-called prosodic modulation. Even before understanding the meaning of words, from the very first interactions with caregivers of infants, the sounds of the mother tongue are perceived as a kind of constant and pleasant musical variation. An impressive body of studies has shown that every adult of our species addresses, in an automatic way, the young with the so-called "motherese language" (Falk 2009), that is, a prosodic mode marked by certain characteristics, such as exaggeration of intonational contours, redundancy of both modulatory peaks and words, and amplification of rhythmic temporality (Mehler et al. 1988). Rhythmicity and melodic modulation produce prosodic patterns that foster the development of metric competence, a kind of melodic storytelling pattern that attunes child and caregiver and facilitates the development of skills to manipulate such patterns (Ferald-Simon 1984). This type of vocality and its rhythm forms the basis for the development of many cognitive functions, following a pattern known as prosodic bootstrapping (cf. Pennisi and Falzone 2016). From a neurocognitive perspective, motherese language activates pleasure and reward circuits in both the adult and the infant (particularly the paleocortex and subcortical circuits involved in the attachment process, cf. Cozolino 2006), who begins to select motherese language phonons on the basis of prosodic musicality (Kuhl et al. 2006). Moreover, the arousal produced by motherese language vocal patterns in the infant determines the activation of attention circuits by promoting dialogic turn-taking, a form of vocal protonarration.

Another interesting and original aspect of the hypothesis formulated in this book is the continuity of musicality, and consequently, of voice, throughout evolutionary history: indeed, numerous data is presented on the musical-vocal abilities of different animal species, from those closest to us evolutionarily, such as nonhuman primates, to those more distant, such as birds or fish.

Musicality, thus, is presented as a form of protolanguage, an evolutionary precursor to the articulate human voice and articulate language. Anastasi does not consider music a byproduct of other evolutionary processes or even an "evolutionary cheesecake" (Pinker 1997) i.e., an "evolutionary frill," but an object of sexual and natural selection.

The merit of Alessandra Anastasi's book is that it explicitly argues for the key role of musical communication in all animal species that communicate through voice: as a universal interspecific component that has had groundbreaking consequences in the evolutionary history of human beings.

INTRODUCTION

The intention behind this book is to make us understand how music, identified by most as an art capable of evoking different states of mind, is not just a mere pastime for our ears. Music is most certainly more. Its ability to be as expressive as language has been the focus of the main studies on the brain for the longest time. The fact that that simple sequence of notes, once it is in our heads, activates the same areas of the brain as the language (cerebral cortex), in addition to the motor and auditory cortex, has in recent years opened a debate about whether music can or cannot be defined as language. And if it is a language, how exactly should its processing be interpreted?

Before delving into theoretical matters, I would like to clarify right away the type of eyes through which I decided to look at this issue. I realise that defining music is not so straightforward. Being both a natural and cultural trait means that the level of investigation that needs to be used must be multidisciplinary, and for this reason, this text will contain music, musicality, and singing terminology. In terms of defining music and musicality, the recent distinction by Honing and colleagues (2015) seems as comprehensive as ever. Scholars have defined musicality as a natural and spontaneous set of traits that are based on and limited by our biological and cognitive systems (attention, memory, and expectations). On the other hand, music is understood as the social and cultural expression grounded in musicality. By combining these distinctions, components of musicality such as relative pitch[1] and rhythmic perception[2] (Honing 2013) traced in the natural history of vocal and acoustic communication of related or different species represent the evolutionary starting point of music and language.

For this reason, musicality in this book is understood as biological because representing the natural set of functional traits that have bound our biological and cognitive body gives music itself a clear biological matrix. Applying this theoretical principle, the study of species-specific vocal communication systems becomes crucial in identifying the evolutionary and morphological bases (articulation, hearing and brain) that allow our species' vocal and musical performativity. Singing, on the other hand, will be defined here as the musical output of our phonatory organ. This means that the voice can be seen

---

[1] Being able to recognize a melody regardless of the tempo and pitch in which it is sung.
[2] The perception of regularity in a varying rhythm.

as the oldest "musical instrument" and it has become a part of our biological and mental structures through natural evolution (Anastasi 2016).

Through a critical analysis of the phylogenetic and ontogenetic aspects that distinguish the emergence of language, this book will intend to clarify which components have distinguished language. In this study, music plays a cognitively and evolutionarily important role since demonstrating a biological predisposition characterised by a strong phylogenetic value supports the hypothesis of its involvement in communicative functions. In this sense, nature has given us a musical instrument, our voice, whose functioning is provided by the behaviour of the whole of each component of our phonatory system. The voice and the articulate voice have always been the "qualitative" difference between the capacities defined as uniquely human, but to understand it in this way would mean denying that it has its own evolutionary history.

As you can see in these pages, many species, both phylogenetically closely and distantly related to *Homo sapiens*, use the voice to communicate, which is the evolutionary guarantee of the articulate voice. Therefore, my goal is to describe the voice as an evolutionary anchor of linguistic articulation and a cognitive capacity at the base of a musical capacity also present in sapiens. This is also traceable in elementary forms in phylogenetically preceding species. Debunking the hypothesis of primate "mutism", i.e., the inability to produce more or less articulate sounds because they are bound to a set of phonatory equipment that prevents them from possessing a referential system of communication (cf. Premack 1986), provides the possibility of building an evolutionary bridge leading to the natural history of the voice (Anastasi 2016).

For this reason, I will not be applying a monodisciplinary approach to music, but I intend to bring together studies in music and language. It is my aim, therefore, to accompany the reader in the discovery of what music is to me, and in doing so, it will be necessary to take account of the formal aspects and the emotional-affective dimension made possible precisely by that musicality that characterises the voice.

The idea will therefore be to trace the origins of music as a precursor of articulated language, whose appearance would be marked by a path such as: sound/signal, syntax, and semantics. Reconstructing the main stages, it is possible to hypothesise that everything began with vocal learning and the execution of complex vocal signals, which subsequently were assigned the hierarchical and compositional structure (the syntax) that allowed us to transform sounds into a language. The endpoint of such a language evolution does not culminate in syntax, as many may believe, but in semantics, which manifests clear, communicative intention (cf. Fitch 2010; 2011).

Introduction

Naturally, against the background of a broader analysis of linguistic structures and a comparison of verbal and nonverbal systems, it seems inevitable to place pragmatics alongside syntax and semantics. But it's important to note that this reconstruction is not about the possibility of musical pragmatics. Pragmatics is seen here as a way to improve language, but it doesn't have to come from musical semantics (Meyer 1956; Huron 2008).

Applying this perspective makes it possible to place a transitional linguistic phase between the hypothetical communication system shared by anthropomorphic apes and our common ancestor and the linguistic-propositional system: the protolanguage (Brown 2000). The transition from the production of vocalisations to the musical protolanguage would have been made possible precisely by musicality, which, probably taking advantage of the emotional and prosodic flow of the voice, becomes the narrative foundation for the establishment of the protolanguage and is therefore prior to language itself (Trehub 2006).

The similarities found in music and language allow for the hypotheses addressed in this book, namely that the origin of the musical (and prosodic) communicative system may lie in the communication between mothers and their children (Roederer 1984; Hodges 1989; Falk 2004). When mothers sing melodies to their infants, they communicate emotional information that the child perceives. Mother-infant co-voicing marks the quality of their bond and the optimal environment for brain development (Feldman 2007; Brandt et al. 2019). During this communication, in addition to incurring emotional sharing, there is a transmission of information that may have been crucial to survival. Clearly, we are not talking about uniquely human communication. In fact, the acoustic structure of the phrasing produced by mothers of the human species is quite like that emitted by the mothers of some non-human primates, such as rhesus monkeys (*Macaca mulatta*) (see Whitam et al. 2007).

The union between sound and voice would have resulted in a kind of special language, linguistically and emotionally rich (Dissanayake 2004; Newman 2004; Falk 2009), characterised by prosodic exaggerations, onomatopoeia, rhythmic and melodic aspects, with the prerogative of being able to capture the attention of the listener precisely because of the musicality that distinguishes it. The ability to modulate the prosodic characteristics of a given signal is, therefore, to be understood as one of the possible traits we share with our ancestors. Through these co-vocalisations, also known as motherese, mother and child create an emotionally charged communicative link that allows the mother to convey actual emotional states through parameters such as intensity, shape, and duration that we typically find in music (Stern 1985; Hatfield et al. 1994). Motherese creates a communicative routine that reinforces the linguistic dimension and communication in general.

From the harmony of the sounds made by the mother and the child as a prosodic component, it would be possible to go from understanding single words to understanding and building sentences, which are more difficult tasks. Although motherese might seem unusual, it is also present in mammals as a form of vocally expressed communication (cf. Newman 2004). The songs and vocalisations used by mothers to attract the attention of their young have the same function as human motherese, and the parts of the brain used for their execution are the same as those used for language.

It is clear at this point that communication is not only based on representation and the need to have a semantic reference but has its roots in the ability to establish and maintain social ties (see Dissanayake 2004). The idea that the origins of musical behaviour and human communication lie in the mother-child dynamics opens multiple perspectives on how linguistic ability evolved. A we will see later, this will allow me to support the hypothesis that verbal and musical language is part of an integral system in which vocality represents the trigger of their evolution.

To support this hypothesis, it is necessary to move away from those theories according to which modern man, with his syntactically articulated symbolic language, would have suddenly made an evolutionary leap that distanced him from all other living species (cf. Tattersall 2012). An evolutionary leap that, to this day, remains unexplained, even in Chomskyan hypotheses. Because of this, I think that the best way to explain where music and, by extension, the language came from is not to focus only on the mental and cognitive processes involved in the musical or linguistic capacity per se but rather to explain how the biological evolution of some unique parts of our bodies has allowed this ability to take root.

The hypothesis that the first expressions uttered by hominids were musical in form, even though they lacked any combination of the parts of the signal and those of the external reference (Jespersen 1922), leads us to question how the formation of a musical protolanguage came about. If, on the one hand, the phylogenetic reconstruction of the origin of language leads us to consider language as the child of a slow and continuous progression of the structures that make its execution possible, the linguistic function, on the other hand, is to be understood as the overall framework of operations made possible by lexicon, syntax, and semantics, which made their appearance through phonetic segmentation (cf. Wray 2002). Compositional language is thought to have started with the splitting up primate protolinguistic signals, which were initially not put together in a certain way.

This reconstruction could also call into question of the role played by emotional configurations in the onset of the human language system. The relationship between phonetics, emotional configurations, and the involvement of parts of the mouth, shows that linguistic phenomena do not reside entirely in the systems deputed to acts and actions, but perceptual systems and emotional-affective systems also come into play, which contributes to the formulation and understanding of locutions (Glenberg and Gallese 2011; Jablonka et al. 2012; Ma et al. 2019). The reinforcement and refinement of vocal emotional expression made possible by the prosodic richness of voice, rhythm, and melody could thus be understood as music's inheritance from language.

Within modern hypotheses on the evolution of language, Darwin (1871) unwittingly pioneered the idea that emotional expressions may have been influential at two times in the development of communication: first as an adaptive function, and second when the need to regulate intraspecific communication emerged (see Griffiths 1997). According to the Darwinian hypothesis, music would have developed by natural selection as part of the mating rituals performed by nonhuman animals. Darwin's insight (1871) applies to the assumptions of genetics that if an organism must reproduce to pass on its genes, the qualities found attractive by the mate are exactly those that will be encoded in the genome (Levitin 2006). Musical notes produced through singing would have been how to increase the reproductive fitness of a species.

Certainly, since Darwin, the hypotheses about the origin of music have multiplied. Another one of the issues addressed in this text will be to determine whether or not human music has links with the songs produced by some animals. The issue is certainly complex, but if we start from the idea that music has its own evolutionary foundation and is not just composed of a succession of pleasant notes, we will soon realise that it is able to pave the way for linguistic prosody, even before the brain is ready to process phonetics (Fernald and Simon 1984; Fernald and Kuhl 1987; Levitin 2006; Cozolino 2014). In this sense, the rhythmicity and melodic modulation of the voice are the basis for the development of many cognitive functions, for example, prosodic bootstrapping (Gleitman and Wanner 1982) regarding the use of prosodic and acoustic signals useful for the understanding of grammatical information inherent to the native tongue.

From this, we can deduce that the first aspect of vocal control was probably the prosodic language, which constitutes the basis of primitive singing. The latter, which is difficult to define since it took a central role in sapiens culture, can nevertheless be approached within a prelinguistic context as a precursor to language itself (Anastasi 2018). Species phylogenetically related to humans share some of our abilities. They thus provide good models on which to make possible comparisons. Indeed, it is precisely by examining the evolutionary convergence[3] between species we can identify the biological constraints and selective pressures that enabled a particular function.

While animal songs have remained strictly connected to natural and sexual selection and continue to be constrained by these forces, human language has been distinguished both by the production of formant frequencies and by the ability to consistently emit a wide range of frequencies. Comparative studies within an interdisciplinary research framework can provide interesting data on the functional role of prosodic modulation in human and non-human animals (Anderson and Adolphs 2014) while simultaneously allowing for a deep understanding of evolutionary roots and interactions in humans. The investigation of prosodic-musical modulation allows me to arrive at a theoretical paradigm in which it is possible to hypothesize what the linguistic preconditions were that triggered the evolution of language at both phylogenetic and ontogenetic levels. Based on the elements explained so far, the passage from musical protolanguage to the language-cognition interface will be understood as the turning point of the species-specificity of our language.

Given these premises, this volume is not intended to be a book on the history of the philosophy of music or musical aesthetics. However, there is no lack of references. My attention is focused on identifying those elements that have made music (and singing) not an accessory or side element in the history of man but that have made it a fundamental component in the linguistic history of the human being. Just as Darwin's scientific naturalism (1871) was created to clarify the mystery of nature and the origin of life, in the same way, musicological sciences (or musical positivism), once music was freed from the concept of metaphysics of art, relied on a scientific methodology as well as was empirically founded (Comte 1830). Thus, musical positivism becomes the key to studying the complexity of music by applying an objectivist and empirical attitude to grasp its specificity and nature. The main areas through which it is considered possible to investigate the scientific nature of music are (Migliaccio 2009):

a) the study of the acoustic, physiological, and psychoacoustic components of music;

b) the psychology of music is understood as the study of the psychic components of musical reception;

c) the study of the origins of music in evolutionary terms;

---

[3] Convergent evolution is the process whereby organisms not closely related, independently evolve similar traits as a result of having to adapt to similar environments or ecological niches.

d) the sociology of music;

e) the theory of musical formalism.

This type of approach allows those dedicated to studying music to investigate its function within human activities (Cross 2003) and try to understand its role in the human mind. The existence of a non-verbal, pre-linguistic, musical mode of communication undoubtedly leads to discussing the role of human vocality, starting with the structures of vocal articulation and thus the species-specificity of language. In this scenario, a comparative perspective was essential to guarantee the accuracy of voice communication data. The incentive for this reconstruction is precisely that predisposition to using a proto-musical language that appeared in the first hominids and probably derived from the rhythms and sounds that evolved in our primate ancestors.

Considering this, a theoretical framework supporting the role of music within the cognitive sciences will be introduced in the first chapter. The links between music and cognitive science are certainly manifold and can be identified in these three elements:

a) the growing understanding that music is a universal, biological, and cultural trait;

b) music presents itself as the perfect marriage between the complementary aspects of phylogeny and ontogenetic development;

c) from the perspective of studying the human mind, the cognitive processing of music involves most perceptual, cognitive, and emotional processes.

Music allow us the opportunity to accommodate different interpretations to demonstrate how the elements that distinguish it are polyvalent and biologically and culturally significant. To provide a complete picture of the dialogue between music, language, and cognitive science and to obtain a clearer understanding of the concept of the origin of the protolanguage, it was, therefore, necessary to resume and implement some points of Darwinian theory.

Darwin's intuition, based on the concept of emotional communication, is clearly a cornerstone of the evolutionary theory of communication and the paradigm from which my hypothesis takes its cue. By virtue of the scenarios analysed, as much as the theories on protolanguage may appear speculative, they represent a model through which to abolish the dichotomy between music and language, showing that it is a fallacious dichotomy given by the ontological and epistemological dualism in which this issue has been bound, and that must be dismantled. When a behaviour or trait is widely spread among members of a species, we infer that it is encoded in the genome. This leads one to think that skills such as music cannot be defined solely in terms of productive competence (Cross 2001) since every individual can listen to and understand music.

For this reason, beyond its history and anatomy, it is necessary to understand how music was selected and how much the need to communicate contributed to making it an evolutionarily grounded trait. Helping to shed light on this reconstruction, there could be the prosodic interactions that, besides having triggered the first vocalic utterances, would have had undeniable effects in terms of sexual selection, territorial defence, and sociality. The strong point of this thesis comes both from the need for communicative coordination and prosody characteristics. In fact, we should not forget that a prosodic pattern can exist even without having a sequence to be segmented; think, for example, of the mooing produced with the mouth closed when we reproduce a melody.

In the second chapter, we will examine prosodic skills and, in particular, the role of prosodic modulation in the origin and acquisition of language. It is well known that children have a certain sensitivity to intonation and prosody from the first months. Therefore, the segmentation of acoustic sequences seems to facilitate the language acquisition process. The protolinguistic signals produced by both small sapiens and non-human animals are united by their non-compositional nature. The presence of similar or homologous vocal skills in other animal species shows that the related mechanisms involved in this phase are rooted in a communication system defined by Mithen (2005) as holistic and manipulative. The basic idea is that, just as with children, when they resort to segmentation of phonetic units during language acquisition, early hominids would have fragmented holistic expressions into distinct units, each with referential and combinable meaning.

The trigger for this mechanism may have been the prehistoric mothers themselves. Mothers, driven by the need to calm their infants or to communicate with them when distant, may have filled this gap using primitive vocalisations. These interactions, already present in the world of non-human primates and representing yet another piece of evidence in favour of vocal continuity, would also be, according to some excellent studies (cf. Maestrepieri and Call 1996), at the basis of cooperative breeding. Vocal signals, as well as tactile and visual signals, are species-specific and characterise the parental care of non-human primates, whose vocalisations, among other things, seem to contain a great deal of information that varies according to the socio-ecological context. To explore the value of the prosodic traits of spoken languages, in the second part of this chapter, we will proceed with the analysis of motherese and the emotional, cognitive, and acoustic-phonological requirements that would have facilitated the process of language acquisition.

In the third chapter, the origins of musical communication will be investigated. The similarities in communication between human and non-human primates suggest the existence of deep evolutionary roots that can be found in the prosodic-musical components of speech. Comparative studies of the language of non-human primates have certainly highlighted their ability to use formants as an element to identify individuals within the group. The fact that forms of learning by imitation are documented in species such as birds or cetaceans clearly prompts us to formulate testable hypotheses about the adaptive function of vocal mimicry. This is more evidence that to understand how language has changed over time, we need to look at how it has changed in other living species. This protects us from making mistakes in our reconstructions if we only look at fossils, and it also lets us see if there is a possible line of vocal continuity.

Observations on the species-specificity of musical communication allow us to see that even though the evolutionary pathways are no longer phylogenetically crossed, the appearance of music in animals probably preceded that of humans. Therefore, the bifurcation that allowed the transition from musical protolanguage to a language-cognition interface would be the true turning point of species-specific language. Within this chapter, a review will be made of the main causes of musical animals that have been shown to possess vocal and instrumental capabilities. Therefore, we can say that species-specific vocal communication, a shared biological basis, and learning through building relationships within a single group are the three things on which not only the whole hypothesis of musical protolanguage but also the development of skills like linguistic performativity can be based.

Finally, in the fourth and final chapter, the evolutionary perspective will be applied to the concept of vocal performativity. We will then discuss the performative value of the body as a means by which to manifest linguistic function. I will focus on the morphological structures used in vocal performance because they represent the constraints that allow the vocal performance of a given species in relation to the environment in which it lives. In this project, vocal communication takes on a privileged role through which we can explain the appearance of music and, more specifically, singing. Understanding music as a biological and cognitive trait is based on structures that originated for different purposes but were reassigned for communication. It is precisely on these structures that articulated language would have taken root. The main evolutionary perspectives will be examined to identify the elements that have made the appearance of musical protolanguage possible. The theses discussed here sometimes disagree with each other but will be grouped here in three major theoretical postulates: sexual selection, kin selection, and group selection. In the three models, it will be possible to see the different ways that adaptation could have led to the development of music.

The hypothesis of an evolutionary path with several stages that would have led to verbal communication will be analysed here, starting from the first model of protolanguage, the prosodic-musical one. This preverbal communicative system includes at least two fundamental structural features of today's languages: the auditory-vocal channel and the complex structures that allow learning and subsequent cultural transmission (cf. Fitch 2005a). From this scenario, we can talk about the parts of vocal continuity by describing the change from a prosodic protolanguage to a propositional protolanguage. This change can be seen in melodic units that have a complex structure but don't have any semantic or referential meaning.

Chapter 1

MUSIC, LANGUAGE, AND COGNITIVE SCIENCES

1.1 Natural History, Music History

What is music? My task should be to provide a comprehensive answer to the question that opens this chapter. For the sake of clarity, I should clarify from the outset that I do not believe there is any definition that can be comprehensive. In fact, the variety of forms and analyses that distinguish music within the humanities make it impossible to give a description that can satisfy each of the aspects that distinguish it. For this reason, the purpose of this text will not be to provide a definition of music but to tell the imprint it has had during the evolution of language. Thus, regardless of its presence within different cultures (Merriam 1964; Blacking 1995; Cross 2001; 2003; Wallaschek 2010), music will be recounted in these pages as something embedded in our biological, linguistic, and cognitive functions.

Since its inception, music has proven to be a complex phenomenon to study, so approaching it through a sectoral study would only be an understatement. Whatever opinion you have about it, talking about music as a universal activity is not the same as having a real knowledge of what it is and what it is really for (see Ball 2010). What we can do, in my opinion, is to try to get away from the manic search for a definition and try to dismantle some of the prejudices within which it has been bound. Music is not only the notation and development of rhythm and harmonic structures but also the result of a perfect union between art and biology. Therefore, one may think that its history deserves to be narrated by applying an interdisciplinary approach through which it is possible to create a certain harmony between the different fields of knowledge.

The history of musical thought has put us in front of a philosophical vision that can be summarised into two major schools of thought. On the one hand, we have those who have dwelt on the concept of music in terms of rhythm and pitch (Hamilton 2007; Kania 2013); on the other hand, we have the attempt to explain it in terms of aesthetics and experience (Levinson 1990; Scruton 1997). The main problem with the first type of condition is that every sound seems capable of being included in musical performance and characterising it. If we lean toward the second school of thought, the aesthetic condition, it would be appropriate to distinguish between aesthetically organized sounds and sound arts (Anastasi 2021).

It is evident that for those who deal with philosophy, music represents a fertile ground for discussion. As opposed to other types of art, one of the main debates involved the difficulty of finding its representational dimension (cf. Bertinetto 2012). According to philosophical reflection, music, being the most abstract of the arts, does not possess a representative capacity because it is only the art of sounds. The turning point in this sense comes with the advent of the metaphysics of art (Gentile 1931), thanks to which art becomes the means to represent reality and the only organ capable of telling the truth of existence[1]. Therefore, understood as a science in which the acoustic dimension was not so essential, music undergoes a clear change within philosophical thought from the moment it becomes part of the fine arts system (see Kristeller 1951; Vattimo 2010).

Above all, Schopenhauer (1819) comes to give music not only a decisive role within the world of the arts but also places it in an apex position within his metaphysical system. The philosopher raises a series of comments that are nothing but a severe criticism of language and its ability to capture the truth. Language is compared to a telegraph because it is limited to transmitting concepts that are not helpful in understanding reality; concepts, according to Schopenhauer, are forms of our being trapped in a merely phenomenal world. Music, on the other hand, as the enemy of the concept, is alien to language, which gives it the ability to embody moods, emotions, and affections in their pure essence and paradigmatic order.

Therefore, the idea emerges through what we can define as the romantic music paradigm. Thanks to its indeterminacy, music can express the inexpressible (Jankélévitch 1961). The search for truth through art will also characterise the philosophical studies of the young Nietzsche (1872), who considers the excellence of music the origin of every inspiration of man. For Nietzsche, music is Dionysian; it is based on melody, not rhythm. Through it, it is possible to forget the boundaries between individuals and return to primal unity. Therefore, music does not need to join images and concepts because it already owns the keys to the world within itself.

This romantic vision of Nietzsche changed a few years later (1878) when he overturned his own idea and defined music not as the means to reach the absolute truth but as the immediate language of feeling. In Nietzsche's new enlightenment vision, music is now intertwined with concepts and feelings,

---

[1] Gentile (1931) understands art as a spontaneous expression of subjectivity, in which the creative capacity and free nature of the ego is revealed.

allowing for a quick understanding of musical symbolism. If we want to make an intellectual effort in the philosopher's words, it seems that music has become a sort of "second nature" (Dewey 1925) because it is shaped by culture and by the experience of the human being.

A strong dichotomy between music and language is created within philosophical thought. It reached its peak in 1866 when the Linguistic Society of Paris decided to ban any meeting with the origin of language as its theme. This decision ended what could be understood as a parallel theme to language, the origin of music. The evolution of language, which became part of the scientific debate only in the last decades of the last century, is still the subject of completely different answers. Similarly, philosophical reflection on music has never ceased to ask the question of how it is possible that these "Sound Forms in Motion" (Tönend bewegte Formen), (Hanslick 1854) could somehow be of help to understand the nature of the human language fully.

Contrary to what one may think, these two forms of communication have many common characteristics: sound. Despite the specific nature of each, sound represents the basic element on which musical and verbal language are based. Clearly, the articulation of sounds varies in pitch and duration (melody and rhythm) because if every word is an articulated, rhythmic sound, every rhythmic sound (with its respective articulation in successions of sounds ordered by pitch and duration) is music (Patel 2003; Jackendoff 2009; Hausen et al. 2013). Therefore, we can consider sound, melody, and rhythm as the fundamental elements of music and language. Since these are both ways to communicate, it makes sense to ask what makes it possible to make and combine sounds, which in the case of language will also be given a referential meaning.

In the next few chapters, I'll talk a lot about the theories about how language and music changed over time, and I'll also explain my own ideas about this. However, for now, I'd like to focus on the thing that, in my opinion, shows the close connection that music has with the body and with biological and cognitive processes (Imberty 1986; Imberty and Buzzanca 2000).

Actions such as reading a book or humming a tune are among those communicative acts in which the voice, or if you prefer, the vocal expression, has a certain pitch and a minimum rhythmic articulation (Stefani 1982). The voice is to be understood not only as a means of communication through which a message is conveyed, but also as the symbol through which we distinguish our social life. Using voice and sounds, human beings (as well as animals) can manipulate the reactions of the individuals they address. Therefore, it is possible to define spoken language and singing as forms of social production of sound (Ostwald 1973). The use of voice assumes a crucial existential function made possible by the biologically rooted components that distinguish the phonetic gesture (cf. Saltzman and Munhall 1989; Mattingly 1990; Munhall and Löfqvist 1992).

The appearance of the tongue, laryngeal, and auditory structures has anatomically provided the individual with the physiological ability to speak and listen. Every vocal action produced by the individual is to be understood, at least for the voice phenomenology (Merleau-Ponty 1945), as a trivial physiological event in which thought and language, as well as singing, become metaphysical activities without which there would be a dumb culture (Tarasti 2002). This metaphysical endeavour that would enable communication's origin allowed our bodies to create a figurative and meaningful sense of verbal gesture. For this to occur, the verbal gesture must occur within a community of speakers capable of using the established alphabets of significance and understanding them (cf. Merleau-Ponty 1945).

The theory of the phenomenology[2] of language (Saussure 2002), intended to put in the foreground *langue* rather than *parole* (Saussure 1955), provides us with a vision of the voice placed at the service of semantics, which would lead us to a positive conception of the voice (Lagaay 2008). Yet, if we think of the voice in its simplest and most immediate manifestation, namely that which precedes the institution of language (Bologna 1992), what we get is an empty voice, in no way able to convey a concept or meaning. In this sense, the voice that characterises the human being and that can signify nothing reaches its maximum representation in singing because in the singing voice, the communicative and semantic part is reduced, letting the matter of which the voice is made emerge, and that is its bodily nature (Barthes 1982; Muscelli 2017).

Indeed, distinguishing the history of the voice from the history of vocal music is by no means simple. In this regard, the essay of Roland Barthes (1982) on the "grain of the voice" (grain de la voix) enhances the importance of understanding sound, whether it is linguistic or musical, but has also created a dichotomy since it suggests a division between geno-song and pheno-song. The term geno-song indicates the physiological aspect of the act of singing, the vocal technique and therefore the body's involvement. Pheno-song, on the other hand, refers to all factors related to the structure of the language, the genre, and the encoded forms. Our impression is that philosophical reflection cannot detach itself from the idea of sound construction. In fact, it seems that

---

[2] In Saussure's view, language is a phenomenon since it represents the exercise of a faculty. He develops a distinction between *langue*, that is, the set of conventions adopted by speakers to communicate with each other, and *parole*, that is, the individual act of speaking consisting of the individual productions of the speaker.

elements such as style, technique, or expressiveness must be involved to talk about the singing or speaking voice.

Studies of the voice based on facts show that we can't just say that everyone has a unique voice (Tarasti 2002). Speech has its own influence on the vocal dimension of singing, which has contributed to sparking the interest of music scholars in the means of sound production from an anatomical and physiological point of view (Seashore 1938; Sundberg 1987). Thus, the need emerges from comparing the means of sound production that call into question both human and animal vocality. This need is certainly not recent, as the first anatomical comparisons between man, the lower animals, and insects were dated in 1650 by Athanasius Kirchner, a Jesuit historian who had noticed some similarities in the means of sound production possessed by animals and humans.

When Sundberg (1987) made the distinction between voice and sound, he did so not only by examining the production of voice in different registers (chest, middle, and head), but he also paid particular attention to the functioning of the phonatory apparatus and the muscular contractions of the larynx. The most important thing is that the phonation system can be trained. Singers use a type of proprioceptive memory to do this. The basic idea is that the phonation system can act as a stylistic device when you want to exaggerate the articulation to give a certain nuance to the pronounced words. Think of the muscular effort made by a soprano (Joliveau et al. 2004) who finds herself having to contract the larynx muscles to change the tone of voice. The frequency of the formants will determine the quality of the voice and its timbre (Sundberg 1974), which will influence how words are understood and how the voice manages to project itself beyond the musical accompaniment.

At this point, music has an organic nature, and our body and voice are the means through which we can give life to it. This does not mean that music can be defined only when the voice is used. There is also instrumental music, and in this sense, the discovery of a bone flute in the Hohle Fels cave in Germany dating back to about 40,000 years ago (Conard et al. 2009) is certainly evidence of the widespread diffusion of musical practices far back in time. However, this does not imply that the two forms of music (vocal and instrumental) followed different paths or that the presence of one excludes the other. Together, these two forms suggest the presence of music within human evolution.

Certainly, the appearance of music is older than the German flute since it is quite unlikely that the flute was one of the first instruments. On the contrary, it is possible to argue that the earliest adopted instruments were percussion instruments such as drums, proto-maracas, and rattles. Similarly, I agree with Levitin (2006) in arguing that sung music may contain the appearance of at least the flute, which is why considerable emphasis will be given within this book to the evolution of singing, starting with the hypothesis that it evolved multiple times in different animal species such as crickets, birds, marine mammals, and all monogamous primates (Haimoff 1986; Anastasi 2017a).

Thinking about the role of music as a form of communication and not only as the ability to produce musical sounds or notes opens an evolutionary scenario that, although complex, allows us to formulate several hypotheses about the close link between music and language. Like language, music has facets and represents a powerful communication device to which, arguably, language has clung to manifest itself in its most complex form (Huron 2001; Cross 2003; Bannan 2012; Anastasi 2014). Referring to music and language as communication systems assimilated from a common origin has prompted academics to create an all-encompassing term, namely, protolanguage. Clearly, this did not solve the problem of the origin of language; rather, it extended it. In fact, identifying the exact nature of protolanguage has become the most important goal facing anyone attempting to understand how language evolved (Mithen 2005).

In this sense, many philosophers of music have tried to apply the classical communication model (Jakobson 1963), according to which speech is accomplished by assigning six functions to musical communication: expressive, poetic, conative, factual, metalinguistic, and referential. For communication to be successful, there must be a full sharing of the communicative code by the sender and receiver. If Jakobson's model can work at the level of linguistic communication in terms of musical communication, it encounters some obstacles, especially if we fall into the error of understanding music as a model of unidirectional communication. Because of this, it is important to look at how linguistics can be used in music.

The study of the elaborative processes that characterise music and the comparison with those that characterise language can therefore represent a significant step forward for current neuroscientific research. What should be clear from the outset is that to understand music, we need to rely on meta-musical codes and, in the most common cases, on language (Bertirotti 2003). The elements of music are cognitively also elaborated thanks to the intervention of language that completes the underlying musical meanings of music itself with as many linguistic meanings, the result of ideologies and cultures.

A dual threat, therefore, links music and language, and for this reason, I believe that the question about their origin can be addressed by highlighting similarities and differences between the two types of language, firstly by applying a study of the formal aspects that distinguish them.

1.2 The Language of Sounds

The topics reviewed in this paragraph are of fundamental importance to understanding the usefulness of examining music in relation to language. In fact, if we look at the formal differences between the two ways of communicating, we can describe the rules that both language and music are based on.

The first thing we can see when we apply the study of music from the structural point of view is that it can be divided internally into substructures or, in other words, into musical phrases. This approach, which is visually depicted with tree diagrams, was shared with the structural linguistics of the twentieth century (Saussure 1955; Bloomfield 1933) and is, in turn, the result of the need for a trend such as positivism to achieve a highly taxonomic study of the different fields of knowledge. The use of linguistic models in musical analysis began thanks to the union between semiotics and structuralism that allowed the development of a structuralist philosophy based on two factors (Boudon 1968): to verify the theory of the object studied and, therefore, its structural description, and to establish the definite or indefinite character of the object of study (cf. Nattiez and Faroldi 2000).

Since the 1950s, music has become an object of study of structuralism thanks to the intrinsic characteristics that make it permeable to the linguistic model. In this regard, numerous works published by musicologists have celebrated the successful encounter between music and linguistics (Deliége 1965; Ruwet 1967; Nattiez 1972; Stefani 1976). Beyond the enthusiastic tones with which this union has been treated, it is inevitable to note that musical language does not possess the same status as verbal language. Music, in abstract terms, is certainly capable of conveying effective and emotional meanings. However, it is not at the level of the supporting units that it is organized syntactically. The study of the structure and its organization is only possible at the level of discrete units (Nattiez and Faroldi 2000). This principle is also true if you want to study music analysis using a linguistic model that is not just structuralist.

The radical way of approaching the problem of the description of language starting from its structure (Chomsky 1957; 1965), as well as being a great stimulus for the birth of psycholinguistics, has been at the same time the trigger for the birth of a generative grammar of music based on the writings of the musicologist Schenker (1935). The standard theory of Chomsky (1965) intended to discuss the universals of language and linguistic competence and introduced the notions of surface structure and deep structure, paying particular attention to the descriptive function of grammatical rules. Some musicologists found this approach to be inspiring, and it did lead to a thorough review of Chomskyan generativism.

Although Schenker's (1935) theory may appear to most experts on the subject not as a theory of analysis of music but of composition, it is relevant that his idea of hierarchical development of musical structure has shaped the assumptions in the years to come about the concept of the grammar of music. The application of his harmonic analysis model has revealed several similarities with Chomsky's standard model which I think is worth contemplating. While Chomsky argues that all-natural languages have the same structure at a deep level, which can tell us something universal about the intellect (cf. Sloboda 1985), Schenker identifies a deep level, a middle level, and a surface-generating level in musical structure. Schenker's (1935) postulate, based in part on the way tonal melodies tend to reflect the tonal hierarchy, is that any musical sequence can be simplified. To get to the deep structure, i.e., the *Ursatz* of the piece, it is therefore sufficient to eliminate what is considered a mere stylistic embellishment. This means that while in verbal language, the deep structure represents the point of arrival, in musical language, it is the point of departure.

The theoretical parallelism drawn unintentionally by Chomsky and Schenker has led linguists and musicologists to identify some similarities between music and language that I will summarize below.

a) Music and language are universal characteristics of human beings. However, at the same time, I would define them as being species-specific. Even though there is no animal whose way of communicating is as complicated as human language, we can't deny that some animal songs and calls have a musical element (see chapter 3 for more information).

b) Music and language can generate an unlimited number of phrases and melodies.

c) Language and songs appear in the first mother-infant interactions: motherese language.

d) Music and language are processed through the auditory-vocal channel, and by sharing many of the neural mechanisms useful for recognizing the stimulus received.

e) It is possible to decompose the theoretical structure of music and language by analysing the formal components: phonology, syntax, and semantics.

What can be deduced - from this brief synthesis is that there are not only significant similarities through which it is possible to draw a comparison between musical language and verbal language but that it would be appropriate to consider the two elements contiguous instead of similar, primarily if these two communicative forms are understood as an integrated system. To compare the different linguistic and musical processing levels, it is necessary to resort to a theoretical framework of reference that allows us to make this comparison. If we put aside the phylogeny that affects music and language, the only other way we can stick to give a view of their similarities that is tangible is to examine the organization of sounds, whether musical or linguistic, that are characterised by their structure.

1.2.1 Phonetic-phonological level

Musical notation is based primarily on two recognized parameters: the pitch of the sound (space) and its duration (in time). These parameters, however obvious they may seem in music, are not only essential in language but are often used similarly. Think about the emotional content of a spoken or musical sentence: If the intent is to express joy or happiness, the sentence will be pronounced quickly, at a fast pace; in the case of a musical piece, the same logic will be applied. This calls into question the studies on the relationship between acoustic parameters and emotions conveyed in music and in the language in which various authors have noted how prosodic-intonative characteristics (such as tone, intensity, rhythm, and pauses) are to be placed in relation to paralinguistic elements that concern the communication of the emotions of the individual (cf. Scherer 1991; Anolli and Ciceri 1992; Juslin and Laukka 2003; Magno Caldognetto et al. 2004).

At a phonetic level (production and perception of sounds), the two main phenomena involved in music and language are categorical perception and phonemic restoration (Aiello 1994). The phenomenon of phonemic restoration[3] occurs when replacing a part of the emitted linguistic signal i.e., a phoneme, with noise or silence. In this case, if the subject realises that the signal has been modified, he will claim to have perceived a noise simultaneous to the music or the word heard. This shows that semantic-lexical or musical expectations take over the acoustic analysis and fill in the missing information (Schön et al. 2007).

The phenomenon of categorical perception, on the other hand, is related to the fact that a sound continuum, whether linguistic or musical, is perceived as being segmented into discrete units, i.e., phonemes, notes, or words. For instance, studies using *Mismatch Negativity* of evoked potentials (ERPs) as an index of pre-attentive categorization of phonemes have shown how phonological

---

[3] Phonemic restoration demonstrates that phenome perception is influenced by the lexical context and demonstrates an interaction between syntax, semantics, and phonology. In music perception is determined by an interaction between knowledge of musical structure and incoming musical imput (Krumhansl 2000; Bowers and Davis 2004; Prinz 2005).

representations are formed in children during the first year of life (Dehaene-Lambertz and Baillet 1998) and how these representations guide categorical perception of linguistic sounds (Dehaene-Lambertz 1997; Näätänen et al. 2007). Similarly, regarding the categorical perception of melodies, the study conducted by Schellenberg and Trehub (1999) demonstrated how prototypical representations of musical melodies are formed by exposure throughout development and guide the perception of melodies.

Although the categorical perception of music is not considered absolute or universal, as it is in language, it nonetheless plays a fundamental role. Since the 1970s, much research has shown that skilled musicians are able to identify peaks of discrimination within category boundaries or to distinguish intervals between musical notes, whether these are performed synchronously or diachronically, in categorical tasks assigned to them (Locke and Kellar 1973; Siegel and Siegel 1977; Burns and Ward 1978; Zatorre and Halpern 1979). Although the ability to categorize musical intervals seems to depend on the degree of musical education of the subjects, it is also true that there are tasks in which the performance of musical and non-musical subjects is comparable because they demonstrate the ability to represent the relevant elements of the tonal system (Deutsch 1999). The assessment tasks, in this case, were structured so that subjects could estimate the ability to adapt individual notes to previously presented musical contexts. This procedure, also known as the probe tone method, has shown that when a musical context is established, intervals assume a more important role by being more salient than others (Jordan and Shepard 1987; Krumhansl 1985).

Beyond having a good musical ear, we must not forget that there are substantial differences between phonemes and notes of a musical scale. For this reason, the idea that the phoneme represents the categorical unit of perception is countered by several arguments in favour of a more extended unit such as the syllable (Albano Leoni 2009; Kazanina et al. 2018; Grimaldi 2019). Syllables are functional units of prosodic structure and thus are much less variable than phonemes. This allows access to language properties through the acoustic signal, which appears to contain more stable information at the level of syllable cores. This is not to say that phonological representation is a secondary or even nonexistent process; instead, it highlights the hypothesis that phonological entities are necessary to explain the phonological processes of a language. Units conditioned as a function of the production of an adjacent sound are always phonological segments that undergo some modification of their characterizing properties (Grimaldi 2019).

1.2.2 Syntactic-structural level

The idea that all-natural languages have syntactic structure has led to linguistic syntax being innate and universal (Chomsky 1988). The Chomskyan generative approach not only opens up many arguments for or against universal grammar but also inevitably leads to a discussion of the existence of music grammar, given its analogy with language. In fact, the syntax of the linguistic system is comparable to the harmonic rules of the diatonic system in that it possesses an organisation based on useful rules to give it formal construction. In both domains, syntactic rules and harmonic rules generate expectations in listeners about words or notes (Patel et al. 1998).

The principles of the generative theory were applied to music (GTTM) by Lerdhal and Jackendoff (1983). The scholars created a theory of musical grammar that formalizes the relationship between the listener and the structure of a given musical work. Having examined the fact that syntax is a closed system since it is aimed at the sole purpose of generating sequences that will be considered grammatical (Sloboda 1985), one of the issues discussed was to understand musical syntax as a universal system on par with language. Just as in language, it is possible to communicate and be understood without using correct grammar; similarly, this happens in music. Specifically, the multitude of styles that music can have means that its grammar has a system of rules that assigns each piece of music a precise analysis (Sloboda 1985; Anastasi 2017b). GTTM suggests four types of hierarchical structure associated with a tonal piece in this regard:

a) grouping structure;
b) metrical structure;
c) reduction in time periods;
d) reduction in extensions.

This grammatical structure seems to have the advantage of being able to apply regardless of compositional styles and is defined as idiom-independent. Some rules that compose it appear as "universal" to musical perception and could be used to represent the innate aspects of musical cognition (Bent and Drabkin 1980). GTTM is articulated through a formal procedure to achieve the reduction of pitches, to reach the deep structure of each piece of music. The result will be applying a tree structure whose main branches end on the notes considered most significant and the shorter ones on the embellishments (Schenker 1935).

Just as language can produce related sentences in which some elements can be legitimately changed, just as one does with a verb or noun, similarly, notes and chords can be substituted for each other in different positions (Ball 2010).

This mechanism finds its major limitation in that the grammatical rules envisaged by GTTM are only usable on tonal music (Lerdhal and Jackendoff 1983).

Despite the similarities, it should not be forgotten that there are also differences between music and language. Syntactic processes undoubtedly represent the shared aspect of musical and linguistic syntactic processing. However, while the hierarchical structures of music bear a strong relationship to the affective-gestural system that defines the social-intentional system, the hierarchical structures of language are embedded in a conceptual system that gives rise to compositional meaning (Asano and Boeckx 2015). Next, we add that the rules of musical grammar are more flexible than those of language, which instead give little wiggle room. Finally, while the communicative function of language allows for syntactic stability, the ambiguity that distinguishes music can be understood as an aesthetic determining element (Schön 2007).

In studying musical syntax, the question is, what body of music do we want the syntax to explain? Musical forms change rapidly. Therefore, there are no clearly defined syntactic functions, as is the case in the language. Sundberg and Lindblom's (1976) study on writing a complete generative grammar for eight-beat melodies shows that the key element is the prominent contour beyond the constituent structure (the syntax). This is the same contour used in speech to assign accents, rhythm, and pitch to phrases, while in music, it is used to generate suitable chords and durations.

The model of the Shared Syntactic Integration Resource Hypothesis (Patel 2003) is particularly promising in this area of formal analysis. Using the contribution of cognitive neuroscience, Patel hypothesises that incongruous chords in a harmonic sequence can give rise to the same detectable signals in brain activity that occur in a violation of linguistic syntax. These musical errors would be quite like when we hear a sentence without full meaning. The proof would be provided by the garden path phenomenon, a typical case of the linguistic labyrinth in which the reader can get lost in linguistic or musical comprehension due to the variation of the reading rhythm. This means that our brain, when listening to an off-key chord will react the same way as when it recognizes a syntactic error of a linguistic nature (Patel 2008).

Musical syntax located in the frontal lobes of both hemispheres is overlapped with those regions that process speech syntax, such as Broca's area, and is visible independently of the listeners' musical knowledge (Levitin 2006). The brain area dedicated to the syntactic integration of individual language units is thus responsible for processing both musical and lexical units (cf. Zatorre et al. 2002). This means that the cognitive mechanism underlying syntactic processes in both domains is structural integration (Patel, 2003), and the two syntaxes can interact at a neuronal level (Koelsch et al. 2005).

Therefore, just as combining words within a sentence can change its meaning, in music, the process of integration finds its expression in the perception of pitches and chords. Each chord, just like words, will be associated with another based on a precise structural relationship (Patel 2008). Regardless of the specifics of processing and comprehension, music and language share the ability to recognize syntax, although they use it differently. Moreover, because of this, it's important to remember that both language and music are based on learned sound categories: language on sound categories made by timbral contrasts, which lead to vowels and consonants, and music on sound categories made by pitch contrasts, which lead to intervals and chords (Patel 2003).

A few years later, Perruchet and Poulin-Charronat (2012) extended the interaction between music and language to include the semantic maze, thus challenging the assumption that the element in which the interaction is played out was a single processor dedicated to syntax. This led the way to the hypothesis that the interaction was internal to the context of the language maze per se, regardless of whether it was syntactic or semantic. The more likely hypothesis is that different types of linguistic manipulation require different attentional resources for resource modulation and, therefore, processing of the musical message.

1.2.3 Musical Semantics

Defining music as being self-referential (Jakobson 1973; Meyer 1956) is one of the considerations one can come across when dealing with the structural analysis of music. The reason is quickly stated: music has no arbitrary rules that associating meaning with sounds. After Hanslick (1854), one of the biggest mistakes made by linguists and musicologists was to reduce music to a condition of simple aesthetic reception and, therefore, totally devoid of concepts. The theoretical line argues that music does not mean anything outside of itself (Eco 1973). This approach over the years has certainly favoured the study of the syntax of music, to the detriment of the semantic one with its meanings and significance (cf. Stefani et al. 1990).

Yet, the possibilities offered by the perspective of a semiotic study of music show us that since music is a communication system, it cannot be interpreted as a self-referential form. Music, unlike language, escapes the arbitrary rules that associate every meaning to a sound. During the music listening process, the meaning emerges, which happens because the interpretation of the information takes place (Schön et al. 2007; Koelsch 2011). Looking for possible musical meanings as one does in an ordinary language only generates misunderstandings. I believe the semantic aspect of music can be encapsulated in Meyer's (1956) thought, for which two meanings can be traced. A designatory meaning refers to something external to music that does not belong to the musical domain. An embedded meaning in the sense that a piece of music can have for the listener not only in terms of its own structure but also in terms of the listener's own musical knowledge and expectations.

There are many theories about what music really means (see Reybrouck 2021 for an overview of multiple approaches to musical meaning), but the possibility of discussing musical meaning emerges uniquely in the figure of Nattiez (1987) and his anthropological and cultural approach to musical semiotics. Nattiez (1987) questions the possibility that music, like verbal language, is also constituted by a symbolic system endowed with expressive and communicative capacity. In his perspective, music becomes a form of meta-language whose semiological analysis depends on the ability of verbal discourse to mediate knowledge of music and, thus, to pass musical knowledge through linguistic analysis. Therefore, the scholar uses the model of semiological tripartition, arguing the need to analyse not only works and styles but also harmony, melody, rhythm, meter, and in particular, any form of discourse about music in which it is possible to highlight those aspects that in musical language correspond to the grammar of a natural language.

From the first comparison between verbal language and musical language, it is obvious that, on the level of semantics, the meaning in music has a different status from the one intended in language. Music can clearly convey emotional, imaginative, or imitative meanings, but this does not happen at the level of the syntactically organized units, but at the level of discrete units (Nattiez and Faroldi 2000). For this reason, the model of semiological tripartition (Molino 1975; Nattiez 1975) is more relevant than the one proposed by Jakobson (1963) derived from communication theory. In the semiological tripartition, three dimensions or levels, one can recognise the following.

1. The poetic process is related to the creation of the work.
2. The esthetic process is related to the perception of the work.
3. A neutral process that serves as the glue between the previous two levels.

According to this perspective, the sender (poetic process) and the receiver (esthetic process) activate a process of understanding the message that can influence the meaning in unison. The receiver is not a passive subject who simply collects the message but is an active subjective who will not necessarily come to decipher the message of the sender (or composer). For this reason, Molino (1975) identifies a neutral level through which an objective and immanent description of the musical material can be provided by analysing its imminent properties and configurations.

According to Nattiez (1975), this occurs when we talk about music, we tend to create superstructures that have nothing to do with the music itself. Even if music is intended as a symbolic system, it has rules, conventions, social functions, and expressive creativity that vary and evolve according to the socio-cultural context in which it is practised. The musical sign, therefore, assumes a sense when it is related to other signs and a context of reference. At the same time, its meaning arises from its relationship with a reference (Imberty 1986).

A solution that can be reached at this point is to understand language as a communication system composed of signs in which the syntactic and semantic dimensions are integrated with the pragmatic dimension. This implies that a communicative meaning governs communicative interaction in each context alongside a strictly linguistic meaning. According to Morris (1938), the same logic will allow us to qualify a music as a language since it is constituted by recognized syntactic rules, whose elements are organized according to principles capable of expressing meaning from time to time.

As for the pragmatic dimension, however, the value of musical signs must be sought in the different social contexts in which they are produced and enjoyed. The existence of musical pragmatics is demonstrated through the habit and ritual many individuals have when they come together to listen to or produce music (cf. Maeder and Reybrouck 2015). In the view of Morris (1946; 1975) and Peirce (1960), this can be traced to the roles of interpreter and interpretant. The interpreter is the organism to which the sign is directed; the interpreter can be defined as the dress the organism wears since it changes depending on the sign system used during communication.

1.3 Towards a Theory of Musical Language

Research in the field of music and language, therefore, arises differently by the type of theoretical approach that is intended to support. If we lean towards a purely cognitive approach, the musical ability will be understood as a mechanism of assimilation and accommodation and, therefore, the result of the ability to acquire new skills (Piaget 1945; Langer 1969). On the other hand, if we use Chomsky's theory as a guide, we will see that the human body is biologically set up to be good at a few specific cognitive skills, especially verbal language (Chomsky 1957).

Nevertheless, just like the development of language, the development of music is the result of a complex neuronal activity, so structured and organized as to make music the human prerogative. For this reason, it is necessary to investigate music from a biological and cognitive point of view. Gardner and

Wolf (1983) argued that the two perspectives should not cancel each other out. Instead, they should be used to understand how human development is characterised by the distinct acquisition of specific abilities made possible by basic biological mechanisms and common structural elements, which tend to make each new acquisition build on the ones that came before.

Language and music exhibit a wide sphere of structural similarities, and both are connoted by forms of sound such as accent, pitch, duration of sounds, the overall speed of vocalisations, intensity and pitch, timbre, and articulation (Patel 2008; Lerdahl 2013). We know that motor control of sound production makes it possible, just as in other species. For example, in most songbird species, the modulation of frequency, duration of sounds, amplitude, and rhythmic patterns (see Mol et al. 2017). Using these acoustic parameters, in addition to the presence of discrete notes, it is possible to identify a somewhat musical scenario in the speech we proffer. Once we note that music and language is a human activity, it can be assumed that it comes with a structure that our minds allow us to produce.

Music, just as language can produce related sentences with some elements, can be legitimately changed. Just as one does with a verb or noun, similarly, notes and chords can be substituted for each other in different positions (Ball 2010). Clearly, there are also inconsistencies: while the temporal structure and rhythmic organization play a crucial role in both codes, the metrical aspect of sound sequences constitutes a specific aspect of musical language that does not find the same correspondence in the less specific and more variable prosodic aspect of language.

At the same time, the segmentation of the sound continuum with discrete elements, which allows the formation of scales of sounds and distinguishes the music structure, finds interesting correspondences in the prosodic aspect of spoken language. The discrete units that constitute speech, i.e., phonemes, morphemes, and syllables, while having their own meaning, tend to group and recombine to create new locutions (Wray 1998), just as music recombines its notes during the construction of a song. In this regard, it should be pointed out that in sound processing, segments such as consonants and vowels take on different roles in categorizing the flow of sounds. While consonants are better suited to identify discrete units, vowels are endowed with the ability to convey prosodic information (e.g. pitch and its extension). They are linked to the syntactic structure of patterns that characterize the distribution of sounds (Toro et al. 2008).

On the other hand, as far as the recognition of the musical contour, i.e., the melody, is concerned, it is comparable to the identification of the prosodic aspect of a sentence (Aiello 1994; Jackendoff 2009; Heffner and Slevc 2015). In this regard, many composers are attracted by the prosodic properties of speech have attempted to implement a transcription of prosodic speech references through the use of musical instruments (Glaser 2000). To date, however, being able to realistically translate sound's spectral and temporal evolution has not yet achieved the desired results.

To formulate a real theory of musical language, it is necessary to call into question the bio-cognitive elements that not only determine the concept of music itself but also allow us to identify the similarities with the prosodic language. An exhaustive and at least complete definition comes from Doolittle (2007), who identified the following bio-cognitive capabilities:

a) ability of vocal control;
b) modulation of frequency, duration, and amplitude of sounds;
c) rhythmic structuring;
d) connection of sounds to an emotional state;
e) organisation of a sequence of sounds in structural units.

These components determine a functional definition of the concept of music in which it is possible to highlight an evolutionary continuum between music, prosodic modulation, and verbal language.

In discussing the relationship between music and language, conflicting hypotheses emerge. Patel (2008), for example, identifies the lack of a stable structure in the intervals between notes as the key element in the divergence between music and discursive prosody. Returning to the *Autosegmental-metrical* paradigm[4], Patel (2008) argues that although sound frequencies in discursive prosody lack a regular structure (i.e., the specific regular intervals found in music grammar) in which to contextualise note recognition, it is still possible to isolate certain discrete notes in the sound continuum of prosodic modulation.

Yet, despite the lack of specific scales within which to steer the perception and production of notes, it is possible to identify a musical scenario in our speeches (cfr. Chow and Brown 2018). We should not forget that while music

---

[4] One of the greatest difficulties encountered in the study of the sounds of languages is being able to establish boundaries between segments and represent these, in a multilinear manner. In addition to the segmental level where consonants and vowels of an utterance are represented, additional levels must be added to the representation, each indicating a specific aspect of sound. On these levels, traits such as nasality and intonation are represented, which are named autosegments (Nespor 1993). Taking this approach again, it is possible to hypothesize that acoustic parameters such as frequency modulation, the duration of sounds and the amplitude of rhythmic patterns, together with the presence of discrete notes make the sounds we utter "musical".

uses a structure of discrete notes, prosodic language has a modulatory intonational continuum with ascending and descending movements (Jackendoff 2009). This means that, just as in language, there is a natural tendency to impose an order on the flow of words; in melodies also, our mind tries to establish an ordered sequence when it perceives a sequence of notes.

The second term of comparison between music and prosody concerns emotional solicitation and, in particular, frequency pitch. If it is high, it is less pleasant in music and more pleasant in language. The emotional range of signals is rendered, as much in music as in the vocal expression, by the modulation of specific acoustic parameters (time, timbre/frequency, amplitude) capable of transferring certain basic emotions. Through the modulation of rhythm, intensity, and pitch of speech, it is possible to ascertain the evocative power of certain systematic vocal patterns (cf. Balconi 2008) distinguishable into two acoustic classes:

- a class characterized by high fundamental frequency, high intensity, and speed;
- a class characterized by low fundamental frequency, little pitch variation, weak intensity, and low speed.

Analyzing the emotions, the pattern consisting of the combination of high frequency, high volume, and high speed corresponds to emotions such as joy, anger and fear, which require a high degree of activation. On the other hand, the second pattern is typical of emotions with low activation levels, such as boredom, sadness, and apathy (Davidson et al. 2003).

Certainly, there is numerous research starting from Darwin's (1872) studies that support the existence of a phylogenetically traceable link between music and vocal expression of effect (Scherer et al. 2002; Juslin and Laukka 2003). Therefore, it is possible to hypothesize that some animal species and humans, to adapt to the environment, have acquired the ability to decode vocal messages with respect to their emotional content. This leads us to reiterate that it is precisely from the development of expressive patterns traceable in pre-verbal vocal affective manifestations that the evolution of music, now governed by specific laws inherent in harmony, pitch and melodic progression, began (Ilie and Thompson 2006; cf. Fritz et al. 2009).

The studies inherent in the compositional music techniques (Cook 1994) and those inherent in music semiotics (Nattiez 1973; Reybrouck 2001), while representing the foundations of the theoretical approach to music, still lack a common understanding. In the absence of a unified theoretical framework on the semiotics of music, the idea of Seifert and colleagues (2013), certainly not only linguistic, aims to consider the four axes that would correspond to the factors that have contributed to its creation.

1) World axis: describes the relationship between the internal world, that is, the ability of music and language to trigger emotions (and probably, its embodiment, perception, and cognition) and the external, social world.
2) Affective-propositional axis: from affective to propositional meaning.
3) The sensorimotor-symbolic axis is based on levels that extend from sensorimotor processing to conceptual and symbolic processing.
4) Structure axis: considers the structure that extends from a small scale (such as a sentence in language) to a large scale (such as a narrative or speech).

It can be concluded that music can boast the ability to modify its meaning according to several factors, ranging from those related to the social and cultural context to the mechanisms involved in the production and perception of musical processing that affect its semio-aesthetic and linguistic fruition (Tarasti 1994; Nieminem et al. 2012). My intent, however, is not to create separations between the two modules (music and language) but to bring together the data described so far. To this end, I believe that Greimas's (1966) thesis, also known as the elaborated generative path model, is helpful in this reconstruction. His thesis should be credited with reconciling both the syntactic aspect of sense production and the semantic aspect as it considers the formation of meanings from the moment one proceeds from the deep level to the surface level of the text. According to this model, the deepest level consists of logical-semantic instances that are transformed into semantic-syntactic planes placed at a more superficial level until the discursive structure is reached. Greimas's model is clearly a generative model of semiotics that constitutes, according to Tarasti (1994), the necessary condition for the analysability of musical discourse.

Currently, studies on musical ability and the prosody to transfer information with possible emotional content have specifically highlighted the different meanings of expression, determined by the acoustic qualities of the signal itself, regardless of its syntactic structure. It emerged that beyond the shared cognitive aspects, music and verbal language show crucial differences on the semantic-morphological level (Koelsch et al. 2004; Steinbeis and Koelsch 2008). From the combinatorial nature of the constituent elements of melodies, it does not result, as in words, in a meaning that is clearly identifiable. Moreover, melodies don't have the properties of double articulation, the ability to refer unambiguously to events or things, and the random connection between signifiers and meanings that make words unique (Hauser et al. 2002; Carapezza 2005).

Beyond the theoretical framework, one decides to support it. However, the question remains open as to how the emission of a holistic signal may have affected the evolution of the syntactic and semantic structure of language. This important evolutionary step allowed us to move from prosodically modulated sound sequences to propositional language.

1.4 Cognitive Linguistics and Music Cognition

Discussing the nature of language requires not only considering its role in human cognition but also inevitably brings us into the debates following the linguistic turning point carried out by Richard Rorty (1967). According to the hypothesis of the American philosopher, the analysis of language is the method for solving all philosophical problems. This conception, even though it has not been accepted and developed in a univocal and uniform way by philosophers, especially analytical philosophers, still represents a substantial problem for cognitive science (see Tomasello 1999). When one assumes that there are communicative antecedents in the evolutionary history of the human species, one must also consider the forms of cognition that have made language development possible. Obviously, the problem arises when we try to attribute the role of a useful tool for the origin of culture and human sociality to language (see Tomasello 1999; 2008), ignoring or denying its biological nature. Certainly, this is not the idea being put forward in this book.

I believe articulated language should be understood as a species-specific activity made possible by peripheral (phonatory apparatus) and central (auditory cortex) structures selected during evolution. Human and animal cognitive activity, made possible by cognitive, perceptual, and motor systems that perform specific tasks useful for the species' survival, plays a decisive role in this scenario (see Hauser and Spelke 2004). As argued by Elizabeth Spelke (2009), the cognitive abilities of all animals depend on the close relationship between infant development and the domain-specific knowledge systems inherent in language use and learning. According to this hypothesis, better known as *core knowledge*, there are specific and highly specialized foundational knowledge cores that we share with different animal species (Spelke and Kinzler 2007). In this book, sapiens' social and linguistic knowledge begins as our linguistic and musical history. For many scholars, this is where the world of non-human animals and the world of sapiens diverge.

In fact, with the cognitive explosion, as supported by the reconstruction of Mithen (1999), the barriers between different forms of intelligence fall, allowing their integration through the development of *cognitive fluidity*. Therefore, if we want to compare similarities and differences, sapiens' cognition is not the ability to relate to and understand social structures but the ability to combine abilities present in other animal species in a new and flexible way. This combinatorial ability is given by language, an element that has constrained humans in communication with its conspecifics (see Pennisi 2014; Falzone and Cardella 2014; Anastasi 2016).

The mechanism through which our vocal capabilities have developed is linked to fine control of the organs involved, but at the same time, it is also sensitive to aspects of an emotional nature: tonal variations in speech or manifestations of stereotyped non-linguistic vocalisations such as laughter or crying. According to Deacon (1997), this sort of dichotomy between vocal motor control and emotional control results from a slow overlap between intentional cortical motor mechanisms and subcortical autonomous vocal behaviours. This would explain how the parts of the brain that control speech have changed throughout *Homo sapiens'* evolution.

While with regards to the mechanisms that regulate sound production, we can confirm that musculoskeletal control allows for vocal flexibility and intentional control of speech production (cf. Ghazanfar and Rendall 2008; cf. Pomberger et al. 2018), the issue becomes thornier when cognition is called into question. The cognitive correlates of language are often the boundary on which various scholars tend to mark the stark and unbridgeable difference with the rest of the living things. In fact, the vision of structural continuity now supported that language as a form of species-specific cognition could represent a means by which human cognition has undergone a clear enhancement.

In this perspective, the principle of segmentation (which we will discuss further in the following chapters) is involved. Phonetic segmentation, which made it possible for compositional language to develop, would have slowed down other cognitive processes (Wray 2002; Carruthers 2002), making holistic communication (Mithen 1999) a unique trait.

Despite the evidence, the debate on the evolution of language is not only still heated, but it is possible to read discontinuous hypotheses in which it is emphasized how special the cognitive capacity of human beings is (see Penn et al. 2008). Discussions of this kind today have probably become anchored in a first group that includes sceptics and pessimists and a second group that, on the contrary, advocates a strong adaptationist approach according to which language has been gradually shaped by selective pressures (Pievani 2014). In this sense, the Evo-Devo perspective[5] has demonstrated the decisive role of growth time adjustments of biological and genetic mechanisms involved in the

---

[5] Evo-Devo stands for evolutionary developmental biology. It is a conceptual paradigm intended to understand the variety of life forms. It studies the constraints that have structurally conditioned the evolution of species by explaining in fact, their morphological variations. Some of its leading experts include Sean B. Carroll (2005).

evolution and how their remodulations are often a source of innovation (cf. Gould and Eldredge 1977). The relationship between structure and function is then revised in the light of data showing that organisms can respond to selective pressures by co-opting already existing traits created for a certain function (or none) in favour of another, even very different from the first (cf. Gould and Vrba 1982).

Typical human cognitive abilities have been immediately identified through language skills, and the reason for this association is quickly stated: language is the most obvious manifestation of human differentiation from non-human animals (Whitaker 1998; Pennisi and Falzone 2010). The reconstruction data made possible by a young discipline like paleoneurology today has increased neuroscientific knowledge about the actual organization of brain functions from an anatomical and functional point of view. We know that the development of our cognitive functions results from the species' evolution. We have evolved, transformed as organisms, and modified the environment we have lived in by responding effectively to our goals and needs (Johnson 1987).

To explain how human and animal cognition acts, it is not necessary to illustrate the mechanisms that affect individual mental processes. However, it is appropriate to identify what allows us to describe our mental and cognitive capacity as a unitary process (see Gazzaniga 2009). Considering an ecological perspective can be useful to understand how the different cognitive domains (language, perception, action) are not independent systems but are part of a single multifunctional cognitive system. According to the definition proposed by Gibbs (2003), cognition occurs when the body interacts with the physical and cultural world, so it should be studied considering the interactions between the individual and the environment. However, we must not forget that it is the body that over-determines the cognitive possibilities of the individual and not mental procedures or environmental inputs alone (Pennisi and Falzone 2017).

The challenge of modern cognitive sciences is to illustrate the dynamics through which human beings organize their experience and behaviour, so language, as an integral part of cognition, assumes a central role. This approach, typical of cognitive linguistics, bases its theoretical framework on the concept of the embodied mind, conditioned in its processes, both general and linguistic, by the biological structure of the body, physically and culturally located (Lakoff and Johnson 1999). The uniqueness of this perspective is to consider the body and its sensorimotor activities as real constraints on cognitive activity (cf. Menary 2010).

The cognitive evolution, according to the French paleoanthropologist, Leroi Gourhan (1964), is the result of a complex transformation not only of the brains but of the whole organism starting from the musculoskeletal apparatus; the cognitive revolution begins with the acquisition of bipedalism followed by a series of cascade events that will bind the human being in their possibilities: the liberation of the hands, enlargement of the cortical fan with the consequent growth of the brain mass, formation of a vocal tract ready for formant modulation. In this scenario, what emerges is that there has been a slow evolution of bodies followed by a real cognitive explosion. Our cognitiveness is tied to the evolution of our bodies and their functional possibilities. Without a vocal tract functionalised for communicative purposes, there would have been no linguistic brain. Without a musculoskeletal system that made possible the functional liberation of the upper limbs, we would not have had a sensorimotor brain. These aspects are merely stages in the biological evolution that led *sapiens to* their current form (Pennisi 2016; 2020).

Considering this, we can say that the linguistic complexity of human beings would have been cognitively insignificant if there had been no selection of specialized structures to control language. The question of the nature of language must be addressed, keeping in mind the constraint of evolutionary plausibility. Therefore, it becomes necessary to understand the substantial impetus for the appearance of language. Cognitive linguistics, interested in our knowledge of the world and how language contributes to it, allows us to advance the idea that language contributes to making our cognition different. What makes it different would not be the relational abilities and understanding of social systems but the ability to combine those abilities also present in other animal species (Thompson 1995).

Nonhuman primates, spontaneously or through learning, of categorizing sounds, understanding their use, associating them with meanings (Cheney and Seyfarth 1997), and even understand novel meanings generated by different syntactic combinations of the same words, are a clear example of this. Although, according to some studies (Fischer and Price 2017; Proust 2016), vocal communication does not allow the sender to manipulate the different levels of intentionality attributable to nonhuman primate behaviour and affect the behaviour of conspecifics; protolinguistic expressions are intended to induce a behavioural reaction in the receiver (Wray 2002).

Speaking at this point of a language-cognition co-evolution could be a viable way to explain how much language has helped shape the brain. However, it is good to clarify that this does not mean that biologically we are monkeys and cognitively we are special beings. The most likely hypothesis is that the language circuit (Broca's area) that we use is not only used to communicate between conspecifics using vocal articulation but also has a higher function: to allow the representation of reality mediated by language (Hagoort et al. 2004). Human cognitiveness, strongly conditioned by the linguistic mode of data processing, shows us how the co-evolutionary relationship between linguistic abilities and cognitive abilities should be understood from a naturalistic-continuist perspective. This doesn't mean we should ignore how sapiens think; instead, it shows how language, a real cognitive process, ties us together as a species in the way we think and organise linguistic and nonlinguistic elements.

The question arises at this point as to what role music plays in human cognition. As argued in this book, the prosodic-musical ability would have played a crucial role in the emergence of linguistic and musical abilities (see Bryant 2013), and several theories of language (Darwin 1871; Jespersen 1922; Livingstone 1973; Brown 2017) have identified early protomusical forms as the trigger for the emergence of language. In this reconstruction, evidence of cognitive processes shared by music and language leads me to believe that the two skills were linked. This is also supported by ethological data showing musical behaviours in animals that are not closely related to us (Nottebohm 1975; Rendall et al. 2009; Berwick et al. 2011), which will be discussed in this text.

Humans are known to produce music. They do it using musical instruments, but they started all this using their vocal cords. What about the brain? What has been its role in all this? Current data from psychobiology and psychophysiology provide an interesting picture. While listening to music, the brain seems to have a certain preference for consonant musical intervals, which would reside in the fact that consonant intervals are also present in the acoustic spectrum of our vocalisations (Schwartz et al. 2003; Mado Proverbio et al. 2016). Seen this way, the brain seems to be shaped precisely by the ability to use musical sounds to communicate through song, and this would have its roots in the very earliest forms of communication used by hominids. Thus, musical protolanguage was the means to create bonds, signal danger and cooperate before the appearance of articulated language. These capacities were not lost with the emergence of sapiens and articulate language. Indeed, the emergence of articulate language opened a myriad of singing and musical possibilities, which were made possible by equally massive brain development (cf. Arbib and Iriki 2013; Mado Proverbio 2019).

By that, then, can seven simple notes explain what happens in our brain? The cognitive processes involved in musical elaboration affect the whole brain; therefore, we can start by excluding that there is a single centre of language and a single centre of music. Our brains have undergone a gradual evolutionary process in which brain structures, already present to some extent in other animals, have been refunctionalised for a different and more complex use, and music is among them (Patel 2014; Honing et al. 2015; Anastasi 2016).

To process music, our brain employs a system of detectors to analyse specific aspects of the musical signal: pitch, timbre, and timing. Musical processing has some points in common with the operations necessary for understanding and processing verbal language. In fact, to understand a speech, it is necessary to segment a sequence of sounds into words, sentences, and periods and capture any nuances (Levitin 2006). For this to happen, our brain must analyse the perceived sound and implement recognition. The auditory faculties required to process and appreciate any form of sound-musical activity consist mainly of the ability to perceive sounds and tonal relationships, not only the specific acoustic properties of a given note (Hanson 1944).

Of course, the brain's response to music does not consist only in automatically distinguishing patterns and regularities at the level of pitch and rhythm. When the primary auditory cortex receives a musical signal, the subcortical part, the oldest part of our brain, is activated and triggers a series of circuits. The cerebellum will be called upon to analyse tempo and rhythm; the thalamus, placed in close contact with the amygdala, produces an emotional response if needed and otherwise starts the detailed decomposition of the sound. The hippocampus is stimulated to give possible memories based on how the music goes. The prefrontal cortex does the delicate work of anticipating and expecting, and Broca's area, which is involved in language processing, analyses the syntactic parts of the music (Altenmüller et al. 2000; Zatorre 2003; Levitin 2006; Critchley and Henson 2014).

In nature, the recognition of sounds represents a valid survival tool: think of the cercopithecus (*Cercopithecus*), able to distinguish between three different alarm calls (Seyfarth and Cheney 1980), or of the red-bellied lemurs (*Eulemer rubriventer*) able to recognize the acoustic properties of the signal produced and to identify which species the emitter belongs to (Gamba and Giacoma 2005; Gamba et al. 2012). Even if the recognition mechanism is performed by the primary auditory cortex, which once analyses the frequency intervals of the signal and decides whether the perceived sound is a linguistic sound or of another nature, the key element seems to remain the resonance of the vocal tract.

The auditory cortex certainly represents the primary means of processing sounds (cf. Falzone 2012a; cf. Anastasi 2018). It is essential for sound localization and discrimination, vocalisation recognition, learning, and auditory memory (Schindler et al. 2009). Specifically, recognition of calls occurs through a mechanism of dynamic processing of vocalisations made possible by prefrontal auditory neurons carrying the correlated signal (Plakke and Romanski 2014).

The ability to recognize and discriminate sounds by their prosodic patterns (Patel et al. 1998) certainly reinforces the evolutionary hypothesis that music and language share a similar biological background that converges in their structural and functional form. Whether we are dealing with linguistic sequences or musical sequences, what is certain is that a "melodic-rhythmic" structure must contain three essential elements: the lexical tone, i.e., the intonation by which meaning is conveyed; the rules by which the combination of short sequences is formed; and the expressive mechanisms that modulate acoustic properties in order to assign the right emphasis, e.g., fast rhythms to communicate happiness and slow rhythms to communicate sadness (Brown 2000; cf. Narmour 1990).

Regarding the ability to discriminate between different languages based on prosodic features, the study by Ramus and collaborators (2000) appears significant. Using the head movement of cotton-haired tamarins (*Saguinus oedipus oedipus*) and the frequency of pacifier sucking for infants as parameters for recognition, the authors subjected the two groups to listen to sentences uttered in two different languages, Japanese and Dutch. Three different experimental conditions were applied.

 a) The same sentences but uttered by people of different genders.

 b) Using only the prosodic line of these sentences, artificially extracting it from lexical or phonetic information.

 c) Reproducing the sentences in reverse.

From this study, it was possible to observe in both species: a similar ability to recognize the rhythm, even when it was the rhythm of a spoken language, and the failure in the third condition, that is, the reproduction of sentences on the contrary. It is concluded that humans and tamarins use prosodically regulated information patterns in discriminating natural, historical languages.

Studies of this type validate the hypothesis that certain cognitive traits sensitive to the auditory perception of prosodic information from the vocal signal are common to the two species. The presence of cognitive skills that are similar, or homologous, in other animal species, demonstrates that the relevant recognition mechanisms are rooted in the biological correlates that distinguish them (Ramus et al. 2000; cf. Toro et al. 2003; cf. Naoi et al. 2012). But it's still not clear what role phonetic values, especially prosodic properties like the length and pitch curve of sounds, play in propositional rhythm.

Regarding propositional rhythm, Wittgenstein's (1975; 2012) observations on the fusion of the musical-syntactic and semantic aspects of articulated propositions (i.e., the backbone of language) show how the sound and rhythm of propositions sometimes constitute the crucial component for their understanding. Wittgenstein (2012, 82), says this is why "everyday language has a propositional rhythm, but not everything with this rhythm is a proposition."

Therefore, from these considerations, it is possible to frame the reflections regarding the musical nature of communication. We certainly know that specimens of different species can extract a wide range of information useful to them from their conspecifics' voices and expressive behaviour (Ohala 1996), whether the signal is a short alarm call or an elaborate song. The pitch of sounds, which is useful in the distant calls of non-human primates and conversations, is a tool for conveying meanings in addition to the more immediate ones contained in individual words (Brown 2000).

That music and language share specific neural resources is an indisputable fact: all natural-historical languages use prosodic modulation to transfer information of a different nature, and about half use tonality to mark lexical distinction (see Brown 2017). According to some studies, the use of tonal languages seems to possess a greater chance of developing a musical ear (Bidelman et al. 2013). The latter consideration would be due to the merit of tonal languages that, as they are rich in tones, allow one to switch between high and low tones, changing the meaning of a word. Tonal and non-tonal languages represent a great example of how musicality can convey the meaning of words. The tone changes the meaning of a word in languages with tones, but in languages without tones, it can change the meaning of the whole sentence, giving it an expressive tone and making it sound like a question or a yes.

The fascination of tonal languages lies in the musicality of the elements. They use vowels, consonants, and tones. All these elements bind the speaker to use the dynamics and the intonation of the sound; therefore, it is a bit like singing instead of speaking. The musical properties of tonal languages have been confirmed by a study conducted by the Max Plank Institute. The heat and humidity of some countries allow a wide variation of intonation of the vocal cords easily. The mucous membranes by which these are covered change their balance and increase their elasticity, so that language development based on this possibility has a much better chance of spreading due to a greater propensity for vocal oscillation (Everett et al. 2015). Although the climate-language correlation might seem unusual, we are dealing with a specific linguistic trend passed down from one generation to the next that has nothing to do with cultural diversity. It is a clear example of the human body's adaptation to the place where it lives.

Another example comes from the whistled languages (Meyer 2004) typical of some mountainous areas, such as the region of Oaxaca in southwestern Mexico, where it is possible to hear whistled communications. Obviously, it is not a real language, and it is not intended to replace the spoken one, but it has a complexity that can be used as a form of parallel communication. It is a form of communication at a distance that serves to stay in contact. Whistling is most often done with two fingers placed between the lips when high levels of power are desired for long-distance speech or directly with the lips for short-distance discussions, and sometimes the use of a leaf is employed. Whistling can reach an amplitude of 130 dB, and changes in amplitude levels roughly follow those of frequency. This means that you have to raise the air pressure from the whistle to make it sound louder (see Busnel and Classe 1976; Meyer 2015).

The structural properties of this type of language in terms of the way it is made are certainly reminiscent of the long-distance calls produced by non-human primates (Mitani et al. 1994; Kulahci et al. 2015; Arlet et al. 2015; Oliveira and Ades 2004), birds (Bhatt et al. 2000; Cornec et al. 2017), and some marine mammals (Stafford et al. 1998; Tyack and Clark 2000). Further similarity can then be identified with so-called talking musical instruments[6] (TMI) (e.g. flutes, guitars, harps, gongs, drums and khens) typical of Chinese and African cultures (see Stern 1957). Whether whistles or sounds were produced by means of instruments, data of this type not only shows us a different perspective but could positively influence further studies on language. Let's take the whistle produced by a human being as an example, which usually has a frequency of between 1000 and 3000 Hz and compare it with any vocalisation produced by another animal. The only differences we may notice will be the frequency level or the degree of frequency modulation (Meyer 2004).

In both cases, we have a signal created and produced to overcome certain natural barriers which contain relevant information. The whistles that follow the melodies conveyed in a spoken sentence allow them to convey a certain meaning, just like if it were a tonal language that changes the inflexion of syllables changes the meaning of a sentence (cf. Duanmu 2004; Best 2019). It should also be added that whistles travel farther than spoken language and have significantly more communicative power than gestural communication.

Whistled languages are an original adaptation of spoken language and arose with the clear function of solving the communicative needs of isolated human groups. Sound contact surrogates physical contact. Therefore, it is not a fallback of verbal language rather than a communicative strategy produced by human cognition, and therefore it is a fundamental part of cultural heritage. Meyer (2004) and Meyer (2015) say that these and other languages are still used by millions of Mexicans, Chinese, Turks, Africans, and people from Papua New Guinea, showing that they developed separately.

The study of whistled languages can therefore represent a further step towards understanding better the role and status of prosody in the faculty of

---

[6] The sound of TMIs and similarly whistled languages can be regarded as an abridgment of speech (Meyer 2004: 409). Questi suoni ricoprono un ruolo chiave nelle cerimonie popolari di alcune comunità della Cina meridionale. Esse hanno lo scopo di rappresentare la memoria di qualcuno attraverso la cultura orale. Ad esempio, quando qualcuno muore o nasce, sono usati per raccontare la vita dei morti o degli antenati del neonato in altri villaggi (Xian-Ming 2002).

language and some elements of its evolution related to musical aspects. Besides representing a sort of modern protolanguage, these languages at the border between spoken and sung are a valid tool to understand how our brain elaborates on this kind of language. Current studies show that biaural listening to these whistles involves the activation of both cerebral hemispheres and of the right hemisphere, which is particularly interested in the processing of rhythm and melodies (cf. Carreiras et al. 2005; Güntürkün et al. 2015).

Humans seem to show certain ease in recognising those melodies that follow a kind of arc motion, i.e., that move up or down (cf. Ball 2010; Patel and Demorest 2013). To make this possible, a specific role is played by relative intonation (Lee et al. 2011) as a fundamental component of musical perception that has obvious symmetries in both prosody and music (cf. Proto 2015; McDermott and Oxenham 2008). Music and language are thus based on a well-structured system made of prosodic and suprasegmental traits: tones, intonational profiles, accents, and rhythms (Giannattasio 1998), whose combination generates a complex system resulting from two evolutionary lines that must be probed as a univocal domain, i.e., as human cognition in the strict sense (cf. Boeckx 2012). The two systems should therefore be understood in a relationship of contiguity and not similarity.

The idea of complementarity between musicality and language creates the conditions for the musicality inherent in communicative competence to have been the basis of pre-linguistic forms. It is no coincidence that during the preverbal phase, the sound-musical component of motherese can replace the momentary lack of spoken language. In the maternal language, the use of empty words (articles, prepositions, pronouns, conjunctions) allows these words to be fixed in the cerebellum, and this would indicate that empty words are managed by neurological processes different from those that are represented in the cortex in an almost automatic way, but that makes possible the linguistic architecture (Balboni 2006). The brain networks that deal with linguistic processing are therefore sedimented on top of those used for music. This may support the idea that the brain has developed two distinct but complementary neural systems (Albouy et al. 2020).

1.5 Revisiting Darwin's Theory on Musical Protolanguage

Initially, it was singing. These simple words were enough to summarise the Darwinian theory that the production of sounds through singing caused the appearance of language. As we have seen in the previous pages, the Darwinian assumption starts from the idea that sexual selection was the impetus through which the proto-musical abilities of our ancestors manifested themselves. According to Darwin (1871), these musical expressions would have taken on a biologically adaptive role, considering the observations he made in the field:

mating calls, alarm signals, and signals for the defence of territory. Cognitive ethology (Griffin 1992; Bekoff 1995; Kingstone et al. 2008) has generally agreed with the data, which is what made this book possible. This has sparked new interest in the evolutionary processes that led to the development of propositional language.

In the wake of Darwin, the data collected by comparative studies have contributed to adding relevant information about the communicative capacity of the animal kingdom and, therefore, the evolutionary role it has played. To reconstruct this phylogeny of music, we must refer to the animal species closest to us, although there are exceptions. In the case of songbirds, for example, it is possible to identify interesting homologies at the level of brain circuits involved in learning and performing vocalisations (Jarvis et al. 2005; Dugas-Ford et al. 2012). If we assume that music is part of human nature, the recognition of its function is biological and not cultural.

The study of the biological basis of music has led some scholars (Zatorre and Peretz 2001; Peretz 2006) to propose the existence of a *core mechanism* that would give humans, regardless of their musical training, the ability to sing a melody, move in time with music, and feel emotions, simply by listening to it. Peretz and Coltheart (2003) described these mechanisms as a system of modules, each of which would be dedicated to the analysis or processing of specific musical aspects, such as melodic control, intervals, and rhythm. Here again, opinions are divided. Some understand musical ability as a trait shaped by natural selection (Christiansen and Kirby 2003), and others see it as a by-product of natural selection (Pinker 1997). If, as Darwin (1871) and Miller (2000) both said, singing was a way to find a partner, then musical ability itself would have helped people get pregnant and strengthened relationships within the group (Hauser and McDermott, 2003).

What should be pointed out is that singing not only conveys a message of courtship but also the musicality inherent in vocal cadences has the primary purpose of expressing emotions (Fitch 2009; Honing 2019). As we shall see later, musicality is expressed ontogenetically very early on; just think of the ability to hear in utero and then manifest the ability to produce baby talk in the first months of life (cf. Fernald 1991; Trainor et al. 2000; Matsuda et al. 2014) by which some phonological aspects may have gradually been strengthened into a complex grammatical structure.

The same mechanism would also have occurred in phylogenetically distant species but endowed with the capacity for vocal learning and imitation (Fernandez and Knörnschild 2020; Tyack 2020; Tchernichovski and Marcus 2020). From the moment we accept the idea that there is a biological inclination for musical ability even in nonhuman animals (Wallin 1991; Marler 2000; Doolittle and Gingras 2015; Hoeschele et al. 2015), it is important to explain how the emergence of a communication system that is not yet referential but like singing, has conditioned the nature of our language. The hypothesis supported here is that the vocalisations produced by early hominids were made possible using an apparatus common to all mammals. Therefore, precisely morphological variations would have bound us first to a form of musical vocalisation and then to propositional language.

To encourage this hypothesis of mine, the scientific literature inspired by Darwinian theory (Owings and Morton 1998; Mithen 2005; Fitch 2009; Boë et al. 2017) has been essential; in fact, it has put before us the evidence that, in nature, there are songs and calls, more or less complex, in which through its structure is possible to distinguish different levels of melodiousness. The ability to exploit the prosodic contour not only in an emotional but also in a communicative perspective (think of group coordination activities and mother-child interactions) in early hominids as well as in different animal species show how prosodic modulation has a clear adaptive value and therefore has been crucial in the emergence of language (Pell et al. 2011; Langus et al. 2012; Ravignani et al. 2014; Filippi 2016). It is precisely by starting from the referential value of prosody that Darwinian theory must be updated. As Darwin (1871) said, it is not enough to explain emotions as a simple rule of association based on how tone and rhythm work together.

We know that prosody comprises a set of non-verbal acoustic signals (e.g., intonation, rhythm, and use of pauses) that specify the meaning and intention of verbal production. The idea that the use and forms of intonation are biologically conditioned finds its counterpart in the melodic analogies of languages, as interlingual studies show (Vaissière 1995; Gussenhoven 2004; Jun 2007). Such biologically and naturally conditioned analogies are true universal traits because they are related to the prelinguistic use of frequency modulations to signal status, emotions, and attitudes, just like animals do (Bryant 2013, Wakefield 2020, Filippi 2020).

From the ethological perspective, melodic variations are interpreted exclusively as an index of the way the transmitter feels about the linguistic content or the situation and never as a vehicle of linguistic meanings. Many animal calls are emotional, not symbolic, and this, says Marler (2000), can be used as a starting point to look at what sounds and music have in common: both have emotional meanings, but in general, neither the animal call nor the human call can be seen to have a symbolic meaning.

Studies conducted in the field of communication ethology now offer us the opportunity to implement traditional theories of animal communication whose focus has always been on the role of semantics, i.e., the meaning of signals within the communication system (Scarantino and Clay 2015; Gill and Bierema 2013; Townsed and Manser 2013; Seyfarth et al. 1980). Vocal communication is understood here as a central aspect of language evolution and should not be based solely on a signal-response model; animal vocalisations may or may not intentionally trigger a reaction (Sievers et al. 2017). Some signals may provide the recipient with specific information (Smith 1977); others may seem vague and contentless (Seyfarth and Cheney, 2017), and in this, prosodic modulation is crucial.

In human language, we know that prosodic modulations allow us to access the verbal content of a sentence in some sense. Think of modulation to mark a question's intonation or provide salient information (Rialland 2007; Mitterer et al. 2016). Prosody, or speech melody if you prefer, thus serves linguistic and emotional functions in speech communication. Because it is so important to communication, talking about its role in adapting may give us more information about how musical protolanguage came to be (Zimmermann et al. 2013).

The study of prosody is in a delimited space, on the one hand, by psychoacoustics, and the other, by communicative relevance (Hart et al. 2006), which can make it difficult to analyse it both because of the physical variables that determine it (time and intensity for rhythm, the frequency for intonation) and because intonation cannot be analysed in a first and second articulation (Albano Leoni 2001). This means that a single intonational segment of prosody is meaningless when taken from its original context. This is because prosody and, by extension, intonation, can only be judged linguistically based on what comes before or after that segment (Bertinetto 1981).

For this reason, it is easier to explain the functional role of signals by referring to the immediate effect of the communicative act (Rendall et al. 2009). Burnham and colleagues (2002), for example, found in a speech reported on pre-verbal infants and animals the presence of four shared features: tone, intonation, rhythm, and vowel hyperarticulation, and saw how such prosodic features of language influenced the affective behaviour of both infants and pets, which are known to be sensitive to emotional expressiveness.

Studies of this type lead us to think that, over the course of evolution, greater control of pitch contour has allowed for greater vocal versatility and expressiveness among higher primates (Morley 2013). Emotional intonation as connected to the social dimension of communication (Sander et al. 2005) could have triggered a kind of emotional contagion (Hatfield et al. 1994) given precisely by the tendency to automatically mimic and synchronize expressive behaviours in movements and vocalisations of another conspecific. This would have represented the right species-specific drive for humans who felt the need to create social-emotional bonds and share information with their conspecifics (Fitch 2010).

The appearance of a form of musical communication that begins with animal songs and later takes a more articulate form in hominids is certainly in line with the Darwinian view on protolanguage. In the Darwinian view, the continued use of protolanguage would have increased the cognitive abilities of our ancestors, thus paving the way for articulated language. Based on widely documented similarities with other animals, Darwin (1871) suggests that sexual selection was the trigger for the evolution of language but that the vocal imitative capacity played the decisive role. However, he does not solve the mystery of how the transition from singing animal to musical animal took place.

Today, the Darwinian view can certainly be implemented and still valid if we apply some small adjustments. Applying the logic of comparative reconstruction, Fitch (2009) has already pointed out that the aspects shared between species are those of a prosodic and phonological nature and therefore considers it more appropriate to use the term prosodic protolanguage rather than musical. In this way, it is possible to put vocality back at the centre and recognize that cadence and prosodic modulation are key in determining meanings. According to Darwin (1871), the originally articulated units were nothing more than sound units without semantic value but with strong socio-emotional potential. The idea that the prosodic (and musical) dimension of linguistic utterances constitutes a mechanism of signification that is still valid today in verbal language allows us to see music and language as the two ends of a continuous line marked by several stages.

Therefore, it is plausible to think that the pattern of protolanguage was established in two stages. Initially, early humans modulated the prosodic values of their vocalisations, conveying messages highly dependent on the context of use; later, a gradual fractionation of these prosodically modulated holistic units into smaller elements came into being (Jespersen 1922; Wray 1998; Fitch 2005b). Using a comparative approach in the study of vocal modulation must remember that the real turning point in this history lies in the anatomical and physiological change in the vocal structures deputed to production. In fact, the sounds that different species make are defined by the formants that are made possible by the resonance of the vocal tract. This affects many of the most important phonetic differences in human language from an acoustic point of view (Kewley-Port and Watson 1994).

What has been argued so far reflects, in my view, everything that an evolutionary hypothesis, as suggested by Pennisi and Falzone (2016), must have to be judged as such:

    a)   provides a biological explanation for human behaviour;
    b)   precise structural constraints circumscribe it;

c) addresses universal rather than particular statements;

d) it allows us to explain the gradual paths through which a given behaviour is instantiated;

e) it can specify the ways in which this type of behaviour is instantiated in a species-specific way.

Language, understood here as a natural, biological fact, is determined by the functional possibilities offered by our body. Everything from this structure is natural, including language (Pennisi and Falzone 2016). Therefore, applying this reasoning to communication in every animal species is possible. Most of the studies conducted on animal communication demonstrate the remarkable ability of nonhuman primates (and other animal species) to modify formant frequency (F0) through a kind of dynamic filter adapted to produce vowels endowed with acoustically distinct formant frequencies (Nearey 1993; Lieberman 1984; 1991). Although its structure is not as complex as humans, it allows them to intentionally convey precise social meanings, which are considered biological constraints on social behaviour in all cases.

From an evolutionary perspective, this represents a real bridge between humans and non-human animals. According to Pennisi and Falzone's (2016) perspective, this would indicate the existence of pragmatics of voice whose functional continuity is linked to a gradual and parallel structural continuity. Therefore, just as humans modulate their voice in social contexts to communicate or accentuate traits that are deemed important to elicit a given behaviour (Pisanski et al. 2016), similarly, vocalisations emitted during an aroused state influence the reaction of conspecifics (Fitch et al. 2002) or members of other species that have intercepted the signal (Nesse 1990).

Recognition of acoustic parameters of vocal modulation and increasing survival opportunities (de Boer et al. 2015; Kitchen et al. 2010) suggest that prosodic modulation is a biologically ingrained mechanism and thus widely shared by humans and nonhuman animals with vocal capability. Although most nonhuman species use some pragmatic functions associated with voice, vocal articulation, such as prosodic modulation of formants, is nothing more than a pragmatic marker (Pennisi and Falzone 2016). Such studies not only support the hypothesis that the elementary units from which language is structured were already present in the common ancestors of humans and non-human primates but also contribute to the thesis that vocal modulation, widely shared by animal species, may have underpinned the evolution of language. Human verbal abilities should therefore be interpreted as biological adaptations due to natural selection.

Animal communication systems have remained intact over time. They have retained the sole purpose of transmitting biological information crucial for survival. No animal, apart from man, has been able to make scientific or technological revolutions. Yet, apart from the many other capabilities possessed by sapiens, language continues to be the focus of difference from other animals. In the next chapter, I will discuss the concept of motherese to understand how this musical language, accompanied by pronounced mimicry and rich in onomatopoeia, repeated words, and simple phrases, may have contributed to laying the foundations for the acquisition of actual language.

Chapter 2

MUSIC FIRST, WORDS LATER

2.1 Parental Care: A Brief Overview

One of the most popular evolutionary theories in recent years to explain the origin of some biological mechanisms at the root of sociality lies in the parent-offspring bond. This might seem obvious: a mother takes care of her baby because she develops a sense of protection towards them, helps them in case of difficulty, feeds them, and establishes an emotional and social bond with them. From a biological point of view, all this is to be understood as a positively selected behaviour because the future reproductive success of the offspring is directly related to its survival. Some of the biological processes involved in making social bonds and prosocial behaviours related to caring for children are the same ones that make bonds between people unrelated to each other or between different species. Clearly, in more complex species, these mechanisms have undergone modifications. As a result, they are no longer limited to the context of parental care. Starting from this scenario, we can reasonably hypothesise that maternal vocal behaviour has represented the first musical experience to which the ears of human and non-human infants have been subjected.

The predisposition of mothers to produce vocal sequences suggests that these songs not only have a strong impact on the cognitive activity of the young but seem to confirm that maternal singing has adaptive characteristics that allow the very increase in offspring survival (Aboitiz and Schröter 2005; Bouissac 2005; Monnot et al. 2005; Saint-Georges et al. 2013; Parlato-Oliveira et al. 2021). The processes that preside over the hearing, like those that must induce language, are determined long before birth. At this stage, the use of vocality once again proves decisive: just as the chirp can pass through an eggshell to the point of hitting the future bird and imprinting in it the songs of its species (Marion and Tzschentke 2010; Colombelli-Négrel et al. 2012), in the same way, the human maternal voice can reach the baby through the auditory diaphragm (Kisilevsky et al. 2003; Marx and Nagy 2015).

This vocal immersion as early as the prenatal stage is clear evidence of how great the need for communication is in social species. At this stage, the role of the mother is decisive because, besides creating an attunement with the young, she offers communicative modalities with rhythmic and prosodic variations that also have the role of amplifying emotions (Stern 1985). Yet, as shown by the studies of Hrdy (2000), maternal care is not so obvious: it is not uncommon that in non-human primates' females make choices about the possibility of survival of offspring and themselves, as well as infanticide is not unusual.

Like any self-respecting biological process, parental care has its costs and benefits. Clearly, the costs of parental care must be weighed against the benefits (Allport 1997). Among all the animals on Earth, human beings take care of their offspring for the longest time. Human beings continue to maintain relationships with their offspring even after reaching adulthood; in this case, we are the only primate to do so (Rodseth et al. 1991). The care of offspring is probably the high point of the reproduction process, and each species handles this moment differently.

For instance, some species have favoured quantity (see fish, frogs, and insects) and have chosen to produce large offspring even though the probability of survival of all offspring is markedly low. Some species (see mammals and birds) have opted for quality, i.e., smaller offspring but with a higher probability of survival (see Alonso-Alvarez and Velando 2012; Altmann and Samuels 1992). It should be noted that the costs of parental care are usually more difficult to identify than the benefits. In the bromeliad crab (*Metopaulias depressus*), for example, prolonged care of the offspring results in delayed moulting and growth of the mother. Because fertility in females increases with body size, intense parental care causes a reduction in future maternal fertility (Diesel and Schuh 1993).

The performance of a task such as parental care involves the application of a different behavioural pattern for each animal species, but it is the environment that plays a decisive role in their implementation. Parental care usually occurs when animals have found the right environment to adapt, procreate, and live for a long time (Rosenblatt and Snowdon 1996). Like any self-respecting biological mechanism, they were modelled on the scenarios of an adaptive need that later became a social need. According to Trivers (1972), it is possible to hypothesize that parental care has followed a sort of multi-stage evolution and that during evolution in some taxa such as teleost fishes, they have followed a pathway such as total absence of parental care, exclusively male care, bi-parental care, exclusively female care. This multi-stage development probably arose in response to ecological problems.

It seems that parental care has represented, during evolution, a sort of an added element, useful to colonize new environments even if these may be less favourable to the development of early stages of the offspring. Some of the main things that can affect or help the development of parental care are bad environmental conditions compared to the original environment and the risk of being eaten or parasitized (see Sheldon and Verhulst 1996; Champagne and Meaney 2006).

Parental care has a clear biological meaning. It is defined as the set of behaviours that promote the development and growth of offspring and increase their likelihood of survival and, ultimately, reproductive success (Trivers 1972). Parental investment is nothing more than a choice dictated by sexual selection. In general, the female will make a choice considering two possible directions: she will choose a mate, a super male, capable of giving her strong and vigorous offspring, or she will choose a male capable of giving her domestic happiness, that is, available to take care of the offspring (Dawkins 1976).

Once the reproductive strategy has been established, taking care of the offspring begins, which is diversified within the animal kingdom. In mammals, it is characterized by exclusively maternal parental care, only 10% of which involves both parents, while in no species are these cares the exclusive responsibility of the father. On the contrary, care is bi-parental, while exclusively maternal or exclusively paternal care cases are rare. Finally, among fish, although most species do not care for their offspring, about 20% implement parental care, which is characterized by its extreme variability (see Clutton-Brock 1991; Gonzalez-Voyer and Kolm 2010).

Even though parental care is distributed in the way described above, the last year's ethological studies have found not only that evolution has lengthened the periods dedicated to caring in species such as bats, cetaceans, elephants, and many families of birds but also that the paternal figure, especially in monogamous species, is precious. Although these cases are quite rare (this can this only be documented in 10% of the species), in mammals, the fertility rate, i.e., the average number of offspring per female, seems to increase when males provide food and contribute to the rearing of offspring (West and Capellini 2016).

Male participation in parental care causes an increase in the reproductive rate in females because there is a reduction in lactation time. For the male, engaging in parental care is certainly costly. An increased risk of predation and frequency of infection and parasitosis are just some of the factors contributing to his weakening. At this stage, the time devoted to one's nutrition is greatly reduced, resulting in a general weakening of the body. However, his food support during lactation, which is the most energetically expensive period of reproduction, is such an advantage that running the risk of getting sick or being preyed upon seems worth it for the good of the species (see Kvarnemo 2006). According to West and Capellini (2016), the male's certainty that he is indeed the father of those pups contributes greatly to the emergence of paternal care. Because of this, paternal care is common in species that only have one partner, and in some cases, fathers of the same species work together to care for their young.

Although these forms are rare, paternal care can take place exclusively. This is the case in the gobies (*Gobiidae Cuvier*), a family of bony fish, where the male provides all the care without receiving any help from the female (Blumer 1979). Another example comes from the waterfowl family, particularly the phalarope (*Phalaropus fulicarius*). The male of these waterfowl looks after the eggs alone for about 20 to 40 days, depending on the species, taking care of both the incubation and the breeding of the offspring, while the female only produces the eggs (Whitfield 1995). Among mammals, however, apart from a few cases of bi-parental cooperation as in marmoset monkeys (*Callithrix jacchus*) and cotton-top tamarins (*Saguinus oedipus oedipus*), being fathers does not seem to be a wise choice. Caregiving by fathers has such high ecological and physiological costs that it seems more reasonable to ask why fathers do it than why they don't.

The study conducted on male clownfish (*Amphiprion ocellaris*) would seem to provide an answer. This species is, in fact, endowed with such a strong paternal instinct that if a male without offspring were entrusted with eggs that were not his own, he would care for them and protect them as if they belonged to him, freeing them from fungi, removing debris, and spraying them with oxygen-rich water. Responsible for these gestures of unconditional love would be a particular molecule, the isotocin: this molecule pushes the male to create a bond with the eggs and take care of them. Obviously, if the molecule is blocked, the male loses all interest in the offspring (DeAngelis et al. 2017).

The relationships that a mother, father, or other caregivers maintain with pups can be distinguished into four different types: 'nesters' are defined as those animals that leave their offspring in a protected den or nest, with continuous surveillance or visits at regular intervals by the mother; 'hiders' are those species in which the mother-pup contact is intermittent and the young on their own choose the place where to hide; 'carrier' species maintain continuous physical contact with the young during the early stages of development; finally, we have 'followers', i.e., very precocious animals, in which the young move without problems and remain constantly close to the mother (Thompson et al. 2010).

Specifically, birds and mammals are the species that spend the most time caring for their young, and arguably, possessing even a mild form of vocal communication may have affected making caregiving an evolutionarily stable strategy (cf. Alonzo 2010; cf. Royle et al. 2012; cf. Boucaud et al. 2016). In general, pups, like infants, produce sounds and engage in behaviours that attract the attention of their mothers and older group members. In such a case, the aptitude for cooperation would have allowed the emergence of what ethology calls cooperative breeding, that is, sharing parental care with other group members. In many non-human primates and mammals in general, cooperative breeding is accompanied by vocalisations and behaviours that induce greater pro-sociality, contributing to improved performance in the area of social cognition (Gibson 2010; see Anastasi and Giallongo 2015).

Vocal, visual, and tactile signals characterise the cooperative breeding of many animal species, specifically the parental care of many non-human primates. The infant vocalisations they produce contain a wealth of information that likely varies with the socio-ecological context and characteristics of different primate species (Maestrepieri and Call 1996).

In this possible evolutionary scenario, mother-child vocal interactions and, in general, parental care based on significant forms of collaboration among group members may have contributed to the origination of the prosodic nature of the first protolinguistic modulations from which language subsequently emerged. The need to communicate intentionally with one another has undoubtedly been a fundamental prerequisite in this possible evolutionary scenario. This inclination was later translated into the possibility of developing cognitive and structural skills that can promote the evolution of language itself.

2.2 Prehistoric Mothers: The Biological Role of Maternal Singing

Mothers have always used singing as a form of entertainment for their babies. The musicality inherent in vocal modulation is distinguished by the exaggeration of intonational contours, the redundancy of modulatory peaks, and the amplification of rhythmic temporality (Mehler et al. 1988). The rhythmicity and modulation of sounds produce prosodic patterns that favour the development of metric competence, i.e., a true connection between the child and their caregiver (Fernald and Simon 1984). the voice adds an emotional tone to communication and, because it can turn on the pleasure and reward circuits, helps form networks that make it easier to talk back and forth in a conversation and, most importantly, builds the parts of the brain that are needed for attachment (Schore 2000; Cozolino 2008).

The motherese language that can be observed in both mothers and caregivers is characterised by its tendency to accentuate prosody, thanks to which not only makes the sound more musical and repetitive but also helps with learning the semantic and syntactic aspects of the language while also strengthening the bond between mother and child (Goldstein and Schwade 2008).

Falk (2009) has extensively discussed this special evolutionary link, and in an attempt to reconstruct the origin of its development, he identifies the assumption of the upright posture in hominids as the beginning of the process of separation between hominids and ancestral anthropomorphic apes.

Specifically, the narrowing of the birth canal would have resulted in the birth of smaller and more immature human fetuses. The physical immaturity derived from this narrowing would have prevented the newborns from being able to make use of the ability to cling to their mothers without being supported by them. This ability, instead, is maintained in the anthropomorphic apes. At this point, being unable to carry the young during the food search, the prehistoric mothers were forced to put them down, triggering a reaction of protest in the young, who would not have liked the fact of being deprived of contact with the maternal body. Driven by the need to calm their infants, mothers would have looked for a way to stay in contact even at a distance. They probably did so using primitive vocalisations.

Falk (2009), probably exaggerating the ethological observations conducted in the field on the mother-child relationship among chimpanzees (*Pan troglodytes*), argues that family relationships in non-human primates would have been silent, as expressed by gestures, physical contact, and clinging. According to anthropologists, cubs receive mainly tactile information from their mothers and grow up protected by attachment systems produced through physical contact. However, this silent love would be reserved only for pups. When mothers need to talk to their own kind, they make screeches, screams, and grunts that vary based on the situation and what needs to be said.

As documented by Goodall (1986), in the chimpanzee community, infants and youngsters benefit from a close relationship with their mothers regarding food, warmth, protection, and learning opportunities. A young chimpanzee, for instance, may attain a certain rank depending on the mother's social status (Goodall 1986; Boesch and Boesch-Achermann, 2000). During the first 30 days of life, pups are in constant ventro-ventral contact with their mother. Chimpanzees are unable to survive without maternal support. Although they possess a tenacious reflex to cling for the first two months of life, they do not have sufficient strength to support themselves for more than a few seconds. In the following months, they acquire the ability to cling to their mother's back and continue to maintain contact with her throughout the first year of life. When they reach the age of two, which corresponds to the reduction of nursing and the beginning of independent feeding, the cubs begin to move and sit independently (Bard 1995; Stanton et al. 2014).

All of this seems to reflect a way of communicating entirely based on facial and gestural expressions (Falk 2004; 2009), even though they whimper on those rare occasions when the babies are separated from their mother's body.

On the other hand, human children are unable to cling to their mothers' bodies and are often left on the ground while searching for food. They need other modes of reassurance. The comfort sounds used by mothers to soothe their young as having the expressive-prosodic modality would have stimulated vocalisation, and this would demonstrate the centrality of "linguistic stimulation" to the development of specifically human cognition (cf. Pennisi and Falzone 2016). From early on, human mothers incite their newborns' vocalisations and resort to a higher tone of voice with a musical pattern.

According to Falk (2009), the linguistic sounds produced in this phase by small sapiens should not be understood as sounds with informative content since they serve exclusively as a means of remaining in contact with the person who takes care of them even when the latter is engaged in other activities. The impression that one gets is that the similarity between sapiens and non-human primates is played, according to the anthropologist, more on the body shape than on any mental processes involved in communication. This would suggest an evolution of language development in two stages: first, a system of communication-based on a lexicon rich in signs and manual and facial expressions would have evolved, like that of current higher primates, requiring the ability to communicate combined with fine motor control of the hands and face. Then articulate verbal language would have emerged due to anatomical change that would only have taken place in our evolutionary lineage and caused the larynx to be lowered, expanding the range of sounds produced by the vocal apparatus (Marshall 1989; Fitch and Reby 2001; Nishimura 2018).

Falk's comparative approach based on the communicative rigidity of non-human primates is not confirmed by the most recent ethological investigations on using vocality in parental care. The vocalisations of mothers, despite what has been claimed in the past, have allowed the acquisition of the species-specific vocal repertoire. Studies of macaques, gorillas, and gibbons, for example, demonstrate the practice of infant-directed communication by mothers (Luef and Liebal 2012) and document the use of species-specific vocalisations among cubs that we normally refer to as babbling. In the case of baboons, we see the production of both repetitive vocalisations with several similarities to the adult repertoire and sounds with no social relevance. Through this vocal practice, cubs will come to fix their vocal repertoire, which will reach its peak once they reach physical maturity (Fischer et al. 2000). These data have allowed us to rethink vocality's function in cognitive terms.

Language production requires several steps such as conceptual preparation, access to the lemma, and phonological information. To this, we must add that the human brain is about three times larger than that of an anthropomorphic ape and that internally it is organized in a much more complex way. Mithen (2005) poses an interesting question: what was the use of a much larger brain for a Neanderthal when his predecessors with a much smaller mass were already able to make tools? The researcher's answer is very simple and perhaps for some disorientation: it was used to sing. The biological value of music would consist in the ability to instil emotional states, infect states of mind, and push cohesion between subjects.

It goes without saying that if we assume that the apparatus of sound production has been modified several times during the evolution of the human species to allow language production, this function has been superimposed on the previous ones of emotional vocalisation. For this reason, our language is to be understood as a very intricate mixture of phylogenetically very ancient emotional vocalisation components and phylogenetically very recent linguistic components. It is not a coincidence that many prosodic and paralinguistic features, like changes in fundamental frequency (F0), intensity, and certain temporal and rhythmic patterns, play a key role in marking emotional–states and also serve linguistic purposes (Meyer et al. 2018).

While our species has inherited the skills necessary for language manifestation through involved morphological structures that allow them to emit a wide phonetic range to meet communicative needs (biological constraints), the aptitude for cooperation may have made its appearance in response to sharing parental care with other group members (ecological constraints) expressed vocally (cf. Anastasi and Giallongo 2015). In the face of this evolutionary examination, language and music are to be understood as faculties that characterise every individual of the human species from birth. This implies that when we speak of a language, we mean that man is born with the potential to utter articulated sounds, produce utterances, and perform linguistic acts. This happens by his living body is equipped with a set of biological and physiological requirements that allow him to do so (cf. Virno 2002). I believe that the same process also applies to music if understood as the faculty of producing or recognizing a series of interconnected sounds. From this point of view, language and music are generic skills.

Obviously, while the ability to speak needs to be embodied in a specific historical language to manifest itself and therefore needs a specific sociocultural context of reference, it is not equally certain that this applies to music. We know that to speak, an infant needs to be immediately exposed to a specific language, to a linguistic context of other speakers. This does not seem to be equally true for music. Even if an individual has never been exposed to music since infancy, their musical faculties will not be compromised but will recover in adulthood. This not only makes music a faculty detached from the sociocultural context as opposed to language but also facilitates its taking root.

At this point, to imagine a silent prehistoric world made only of gestures, besides being a not very credible thesis, feeds the false myth that human communication derives from the gestural communication of non-human primates. The vocal component of communication, according to this view, would have been installed only later and with a clear separation from other primates. In truth, as we shall see, the prosodic modulation of expressions produced not only by the first prehistoric mothers but also by non-human primates have brought selective advantages in the function of the emotional and cognitive effects elicited by this, both in mother-child interactions and in those between pups and caregivers (cf. Fitch 2004). The idea that some sort of mutism exists among non-human primates is now widely disproved. Vocal communication has a privileged role in non-human primates, and this is not only confirmed by the existence of singing primates but also by the fact that there are species whose sound combinations play a crucial role from a social point of view, a role that is absolutely denied in Falk's thesis.

The evolution of the maternal role and parental care in general probably had strong implications for group dynamics and social structure, both in nonhuman primates, and probably unhinging many of the theoretical frameworks on which sociobiology is based (Wilson 1975), the development of cooperative and affiliative attitudes in pairs outside of sexual selection is actually very common among primates. One example is the phenomenon of allomothering (Fairbanks 1990), in which the females of some primates form real groups of help and assistance in parental care, sharing them with the offspring of other mothers, not genetically related. These special affiliative relationships (Palombit 2009) and creating niches of opportunity (Arthur 2009) in which individuals make choices from a community perspective have also triggered our attitude to cooperation in response to sharing parental care with other groups members expressed vocally. Parental care was thus accompanied by changes that led to greater pro-sociality, contributing to improved performance in the social cognition area.

Based on this, one could hypothesize that the emergence of language, from an evolutionary point of view, could be conceived as a highly collaborative scenario. In this, maternal singing, with its clear biological nature, has made a strong contribution since it not only strengthens the attachment bond but also allows for creating both a cognitive and emotional container, useful for language learning. Placing the child to listen to a song or melody may have acted, according to Cross (2001) on the flexibility of our ancestors' brains and thus on cognitive maturation. This would provide a polysemic view of music because, in addition to assuming the potential role of the propeller of protolanguage, it can convey different meanings depending on the context in which it is heard.

Motherese provides us with much information about the vital function of music, that is, the characteristics that make it a primary element of vital regulation, and its uniqueness lies in the fact that it seems to do so before and better than spoken language. That is why, although it is a language, the importance for infants of the use of motherese lies not in words but in their musicality.

2.3 Motherese: A Comparative Perspective

As illustrated above, the first mother-infant vocal interactions, created for comfort, represent the first step in the sequence of events that led our ancestors to formulate the first proto-conversations (Trevarthen 1999). As previously stated, motherese is a slower and more repetitive language with a higher pitch and a simpler vocabulary. It is, therefore, a rather musical language, which gives a certain intensity and modulation to the tone of voice of adults. Its melody, just as if it were a lullaby or a nursery rhyme, conveys emotional meaning and allows an initial approach to the actual language (Grieser and Kuhl 1988; Trehub et al. 1993a; Falk 2004; Pennisi and Falzone 2016).

According to the reconstruction made by Matsuzawa (2006), it is possible to trace the evolution of mother-infant interactions through four stages probably related to functional changes in the socio-ecological environment occupied by the species. The first stage would have begun about 65 million years ago following the divergence of the mammalian class and is characterized by milk supply during the adaptation period. The second stage is associated with the emergence of primates, differentiated from their common ancestor 50 million years ago, into species with an arboreal lifestyle. The young belonging to this order exhibit a unique behaviour among mammals, the clinging, which is the propensity to climb and attach to the maternal body due to the particular morpho-anatomical conformation of the limbs and hands made to catch and grasp. With the subsequent separation of the diurnal monkeys and the greater body size of the nocturnal prosimians, a new type of behaviour emerges the maternal embrace. Mothers hugging their young maintain physical contact in the first year of life (cf. Hayashi and Matsuzawa 2017). The fourth stage is traced back to the branching of hominids, which occurred five million years ago and included all anthropomorphic apes. In this group, new forms of face-to-face communication are developed, such as the smile and the mutual gaze, which is the direct reciprocal look without negative connotations. With the appearance of the australopithecines (five million years ago) and the genus *Homo* (about two million years ago), the adoption of the upright posture and the bipedal gait, the mother-child relationship undergoes a definitive change (cf. Parncutt 2019; cf. Wittman et al. 2007; cf. Berecz et al. 2020).

From a comparative perspective, we can immediately note some commonalities and differences. Extremely unstable supine chimpanzee infants move their contralateral upper and lower limbs simultaneously as if to achieve some postural balance. In doing so, they emit moans and whimpers. Being unable to tip over until two to three months, they have constant interaction with the mother, which implies continuous physical contact: the baby climbs on the mother's body and stands on her back during the movements. Physical attachment is maintained until the infant gradually acquires locomotor independence (Reynolds 1965). Once it has reached adulthood, the only other way to communicate with the mother or with members of the group, for example, during movements in search of food, is to produce vocalisations with specific referential and emotional content.

Infants of *Homo sapiens* are instead stable in the supine position, allowing them greater freedom of movement of limbs that can be used to touch, grasp, and point to objects. Therefore, the infant's postural condition determines a bodily detachment from the mother and promotes new forms of interaction and face-to-face communication in the developmental stages. To attract maternal attention, the infant emits cries, vocalisations, and facial expressions, to which the mother responds. Despite these commonalities, there are differences in the expression of these behaviours, which are rooted in the organisms' different morpho-anatomical and cognitive makeup (Hayashi and Matsuzawa 2017).

As previously discussed, the infant care and rearing hypothesis seem to be the most credible explanation if one tries to illustrate the evolution of musical protolanguage by referring to its adaptive function (Fitch 2005b). For this reason, considering the presented evidence, comparing phylogenetically distant species can help us understand the development of some perceptual and sensory-motor skills closely related to the social-communicative dimension of these animals. The evidence from the primate world allows us to identify similarities and differences and better understand the factors and mechanisms responsible for the emergence of the faculty of language.

It is clear at this point that this communicative interaction is not exclusively human. According to some scientific evidence, it is possible to apply the concept of motherese also in mammals, considering those vocalisations or songs that mothers use in the primate world to attract the attention of their young. In fact, the parts of the brain used for vocalisation between mother and child are, in essence, those used for language, so it is possible to assume that spoken language has developed from the vocalisations that female hominids addressed to their children (Newman 2004).

The use of these vocal forms, also known as baby talk, demonstrates how besides attracting the attention of young children, it also stimulates them to play and relate to other adults in the group (Luef and Liebal 2012; Whitham et al. 2007). In singing primates, for instance, it is also possible to observe variations in song structure by females, especially when performing duets with their cubs. In gibbons, it has been possible to observe mother-child duets distinguished by some variations. Like in human motherese, mothers adapt their singing to a more stereotypical pattern when duetting with their offspring than when singing alone. In these duets, pups sing simultaneously with their mothers but at a different tempo and with significant acoustic variation when their maturity begins. Once they reach vocal maturity, females tend to duet less with their mothers, improve their ability to synchronize, converge acoustically with the maternal acoustic pattern and reduce stereotypy and repetition (Koda et al. 2013).

According to Masataka (2003), humans within the first year of life emit language-like sounds, and this is a process that goes through two phases: the first, between the sixth and eighth week, consists of the emission of vowel-like sounds that infants begin to produce through reciprocal exchanges with their caregivers. In this case, the quality of adult vocal responses affects the infant's developing vocalisations. The second phase occurs with lallation at around eight months. The same mechanism is said to occur in Japanese macaques (*Macaca fuscata*), which by emitting calls (COOS), can maintain contact not only with the young but also with the remaining members of the group without any physical contact. Usually, after issuing the call, the macaque remains silent for a short interval, and if no response is received, it repeats the call to try to contact the herd (Masataka 2007; cf. Pennisi and Falzone 2016; cf. Takahashi et al. 2016).

Regarding lallation, non-human primates show a similar structure in long-distance calls. There would exist, in fact, a kind of parallelism between the two components that, according to Masataka (2003), would have led to the origin of the word probably through a process in which the duet came to solos and then, with time, became a language. This is certainly a bold thesis that finds support in those hypotheses according to which language probably derives from musical notes and rhythms that evolved among our ancestors. The origin of all this could be hidden in the ability of infants to grasp the smallest differences in pitch and tempo (Trehub 2000; 2003).

Given that language is understood in this text as a tool for vocal production, from the point of view of functional possibilities, examples of motherese in nonhuman animals fuel the idea of evolutionary continuity of vocal communication. Although this primitive form of communication varies in some detail across human cultures, according to Dissanayake (2017), baby-talking is an example of multimedia performance. This definition comes from the fact that it is not only talking but also repeated vocalisations that are high-pitched and marked by short pauses. These vocalisations are also accompanied by stereotyped and repetitive facial expressions such as wide eyes, long open mouths, smiles, forward and backward head movements, and gestures. The children respond to all this by producing vocalisations, facial and body movements and, in many cases, by reciprocating the caregiver's gaze in a prolonged way. This performance involves the performance of actions in synchrony as if they were a duet and actions in alternating rhythms, better known as turn-taking (see Levinson 2016).

The phylogenetic continuity in the mechanisms affecting the visually and vocally mediated socio-communicative sphere supports the evolutionary model for which the linguistic faculty is multimodal and not exclusively gestural. Moreover, applying the Evo-Devo perspective in this type of study (Takahashi et al. 2013; Takahahi et al. 2016) allows us to confirm how social organization even in species phylogenetically distant from sapiens such as marmoset monkeys (*Callithrix jacchus*) is made possible by vocally expressed parental care. From birth, these small New World monkeys produce in a completely spontaneous way vocalisations extremely like the cooing of human infants. Normally, it is characterized by the repetition of vocal sounds and is produced when the baby is happy.

The characteristic of their vocal activity is that they have a more intense vocalic peak during the production of the call; this peak is characterized by a rhythmic and repetitive string of calls that generally appears within the first two weeks of life. Peak vocalic activity occurs just before weaning, around six to eight weeks (Elowson et al. 1998). This phase is followed by babbling, a phase in which adults begin by producing specific sounds that will be learned during parental care. Through the turn-taking system, marmoset adults address their pups by producing sounds very similar to the call (fee) produced to establish relationships within the group they belong to. This is a crucial sound for accessing adult life, dividing food, and demarcating territory (Ghazanfar et al. 2018).

In the learning phase, the young practice produces different formant frequencies. But adults aim to make sure that the range of frequencies produced is slowly eliminated so that only the fee is produced. This would be possible by the cyclic activation of the autonomic nervous system and arousal that results in the random onset of sounds in marmoset hatchlings in the first few months of life (Ghazanfar and Takahashi 2016). The same type of random activation occurs in humans. Once again, we are faced with an analogy in the forms of communication involving the spontaneous production of sounds by the young of both sapiens and marmosets. Obviously, there is a difference between the type of learning and vocal performance of the two species, and it is a quantitative difference. In marmosets, selection driven by turn-taking is selection by reduction. That is, the vocal production after babbling will tend to decrease until a single call is selected. In humans, on the other hand, babbling is a crucial part of speech development, and the sounds initially produced, while not defined, will tend to increase until the development of actual language (Takahashi et al. 2013; see Falzone 2018).

Both human and marmoset babbling, while lacking apparent reference, represent a vocal form that will obviously tend to differ in the vocal production capacity possessed by the two species. Obviously, the structures that allow the production of these sounds remain identical. The application of an ontogenetic perspective (Pistorio et al. 2006; Chow et al. 2015) thus seems consonant with showing that age-related changes in the acoustic structure of nonhuman primates are mostly given by maturational factors such as growth or increased ability to control one's vocalisations. In primate ontogeny, the prosodic modulation used by mothers to interact with their offspring results in a complex communicative activity in which prosodic variation in vocalisations, physical contact, motor activity, gestures, and facial expressions stimulates the development of social relationships among conspecifics and establishes the foundations of higher cognitive processes (Greenspan-Shanker 2004).

Noting that the processing of these mother-infant protoconversations serves as triggers for both language acquisition and species-specific calls of nonhuman animals, the motherese can be viewed from the perspective of an evolutionary adaptation shaped by a natural and sexual selection that has ensured its universality (cf. Miller 2000). Through its ability to induce subjects to automatically mimic and synchronize expressive behaviours in movements and vocalisations (Hatfield et al. 1994), Motherese has conditioned the nature of our language. The vocalisations produced by early hominids made possible using an apparatus common to all mammals structurally conditioned the morphological variants (cfr. Falzone 2019) that bound us first to a form of musical vocalisation, motherese, and then to proper language (cf. Falzone 2019).

2.4 From Sound to Speech: Prosodic Bootstrapping Hypothesis

Baby talk has a strong emotional and cognitive connotation, and not surprisingly, it facilitates the access of pre-verbal subjects to the linguistic universe. While performing rigorous analysis, the first thing that could be noticed is its melodiousness and the temporal nature of synchronizations and alternations in voice and movements that immediately lead us to think of music (cf. Dissanyake 2017). The metrical and phonetic characteristics of baby talk reveal that the pattern of versification is first and foremost influenced by the type of response on the mother's part to the child's behaviour (Miall and Dissanayake 2003). When the mother perceives that the child is involved in her interaction, she tends to slow down the pace of her own versification and emphasizes strongly accented repetitions followed by short silences between sentences. When, on the other hand, the child is distracted, and the mother attempts to regain her attention, she resorts to signalling devices, e.g., pauses in mid-sentence followed by the child's name or a long pause in mid-sentence followed by faster-paced sentences, also known as "foregrounding" (Miall and Kuiken 1994).

Observing children and infants is a useful tool for recognizing how deep the biological roots of our musicality are. As extensively described by embryology studies (Fernald and Simon 1984; Grieser and Kuhl 1988; Mehler et al. 1988; De Casper 1990; Fernald 1991), as early as the sixth month of pregnancy, the fetus listens and begins to process the linguistic sounds that surround it. In particular, the maternal voice, which can be placed halfway between a sound perceived from the outside and one perceived from the inside, allows the fetus to have a unitary perception. The voice reaches the fetus through the main organs involved, that is, from the larynx, the voice descends along the spinal column, and once it reaches the pelvis, this will act as a sounding board; here, the amniotic fluid filters sounds and transforms them into vibrations. In doing so, low-pitched sounds will remain unaffected, and high-pitched sounds will undergo a slight distortion (Querleu et al. 1988; Busnel et al. 1992; De Casper et al. 1994).

Putting oneself to listen to what is happening outside makes the fetus sensitive to prosody and thus to the intonation of sentences and the rhythmic pattern of speech. While not understanding the meaning of words, the rhythm, accent, and musicality inherent in the voice predispose the infant to recognize the mother's voice (Mehler et al. 1978; De Casper et al. 1994; Huotilainen 2013). These components make motherese a universal language, and because of its prosodic contour and musicality, it serves as a trigger for language development. Language acquisition and mother tongue, in addition to being closely related, are evidence of a gradual evolution in which music and language arose from parental communications and were shown to share a biological background that converges in both structural and functional form (Brown 2000; cf. Anastasi 2016).

A key step in supporting the thesis discussed thus far is to demonstrate how the prosodic aspects can facilitate the process of word segmentation within the motherese language stream. This theoretical question focuses on the research paradigm that goes by the name of prosodic bootstrapping. The melodic-rhythmic structure of motherese fully integrates with the Prosodic Bootstrapping Hypothesis (Morgan and Newport 1981; Gleitman and Wanner 1982; Peters 1983; Fernald and McRoberts 1996), which tries to explain how infants master the syntactic dimension starting from the lexical sphere and understand the meaning of words starting from the syntactic pattern. Prosodic modulation would allow them to subdivide the sentence into its constituent syntagmas and recognize the logical-syntactic category of the terms. What emerges from studies is that infants, after only two days of life, are able to recognize syllabic units, while at four months, they begin to differentiate consonant sounds. The structural peculiarity of the syllable is precisely its musical and prosodic nature that represents a real call for auditory attention.

Experimental studies have shown that syllabic perception reaches its maximum level when it is administered within natural configurations in multisyllabic sequences or phrasal chunks. In such a case, the human voice is represented by its main acoustic properties: co-articulation between syllables, a complete variation of accents, and the appearance of an intonational contour or background (cf. Pennisi and Falzone 2016). Such features ensure phonetic perception, recognition, and syntactic recognition (cf. Moon et al. 2013; Graniere-Deferre et al. 2011). According to the bootstrapping hypothesis, children can learn phonology, morpho-syntax, and language semantics by initially leaning on only one of these aspects, which will later be leveraged to process the other aspects of language (Karmiloff and Karmiloff-Smith 2002).

The fact that infants prefer high-frequency prosodic information and motherese rhythm, according to Eimas (1996), may be related to a physiological ability present in the infant at fetal age, which allows him to separate the voice from other sounds in the environment and direct attention to speech. In this way, the child, at the moment of birth, would already be equipped with those tools necessary for linguistic representation. In the face of what has been said, Wray's (2002) perspective on phonetic segmentation as a language matrix appears most convincing for our reconstruction of the facts. The development of compositional language would arise from the segmentation of primate protolinguistic signals, which are initially non-compositional, just as happens with children when they resort to the segmentation of phonetic units during language acquisition. Children segment a signal that is already syntactically articulated and semantically compositional (Mithen 2005).

Through segmentation, humans began to fragment holistic expressions into distinct units, each endowed with its own referential meaning and combinable with units from other expressions to create an infinite series of new locutions. Wray (2002) suggests that segmentation may have emerged from recognising random associations between the phonetic segments of holistic expressions and the objects to which they were related. Once identified, these associations would have been used referentially to create new locutions of a compositional nature.

The idea, therefore, is that from early childhood, a procedure of prosodic segmentation of speech is formed, uniquely linked to the specific mother tongue to which one is exposed. In the segmentation of speech, while the adult tries to identify the boundaries between words that, for the most part, they already know, the child, at least in the initial developmental phase, has to segment the material which they do not know (Brandi and Balvadori 2004). According to Gleitman and Wanner (1982), children extract, and store accented syllables as initial representations for words, reducing the problem of identifying the boundaries between words in a sentence to the simpler problem of identifying the width of accented syllables. Children very often omit a whole series of syllables that correspond to unaccented syllables when they enter the first-word production stage, especially those that are not at word endings (Allen and Hawkins 1978).

Studies of adult English speakers show that the strategy used in sentence segmentation is metrical: listeners segment speech into words based on the presence of an initial strong accent. In practice, prosody in English is characterized by alternating a strong syllable, representing the beginning of a word, followed by a weak syllable (Cutler 1990; Jusczyk et al. 1993). Native English speakers use as a strategy the division of the heard sequence into a first part, which ends with the recognition of the second strong syllable. Consequently, word recognition requires only the recombination of the heard material between the beginning of the sound string and the segmentation point. Thus, in the second part, there will be no more obstacles to recognising the hidden word since the initial syllable is weak and the sequence is simply non-divisible. This prosodic segmentation procedure is also found in other languages. Clearly, the unit of segmentation may change, but the procedure remains the same (Cutler and Norris 1988; cf. White 2018).

In short, prosodic modulation allows us to retrieve the logical-syntactic category of the terms present within a sentence and assigns the syntagm its meaning. By doing so, the segmentation of syntagmas and their relationship will be oriented within a sentence (cf. Hunyadi 2006). However, this mechanism that is fundamental during language acquisition tends to clash with the research hypothesis of Millotte and collaborators (2006), which explores the role of functional words and prosody in facilitating the recognition of the syntactic category to which contiguous terms belong to the same grammatical unit belong. The study consisted of depriving sentences submitted to subjects of functional particles, replacing them with invented terms that possessed the same prosodic information. From the data collected, it was possible to see that the subjects, beyond the lack of specific semantic content, could identify the syntactic role of the target terms correctly. We conclude that even the sounds of nonsense terms, if combined in a sentence, can be charged with an emotional meaning that makes the sentence's meaning usable.

From the evolutionary point of view, data of this magnitude supports the Darwinian hypothesis that the originally articulated units were nothing more than sound units without semantic value but with strong, social-emotional potential. Therefore, the prosodic (and musical) dimension of linguistic utterances could be understood as co-original to the syntactic structures that regulate the articulation, since they found that the mechanism of signification is still in force in verbal language. Clearly, although the child can recognize many of the acoustic cues that come to their ear, to use most of these cues for segmentation purposes, a great deal of exposure to language will be required (Echols and Marti 2004).

Regarding production, we should not forget that the ability to articulate linguistic sounds is made possible by basic articulatory movements, such as opening and closing the jaw. The opening and closing movements combined with phonation produces an almost syllabic execution similar to lallation vocally. From this, it is possible to deduce that phonetic segments emerge ontogenetically from a process of vocal imitation in which bodily movement is also fundamental, not only vocal movement (Studdert-Kennedy 2000). Face, vocal apparatus, hands, and arms are involved in the mother-infant communicative exchange. They are so involved as to ensure synchrony of communicative exchanges and complementarity of sensations and emotions. However, it's important to remember that the early ability to understand human expression is also made possible by brain structures that are naturally devoted to emotions and how they change (Trehub et al. 1993; see also Falzone 2020). Of course, in the specific case of prosody, it is learned. It represents the sapiens' first form of auditory-vocal learning. Once the child understands the function of melodic modulation of sounds, vocality will become a behavioural strategy useful for satisfying one's needs. At this stage, however, phonetic articulation is still grappling with the development of the vocal tract, which is not yet capable of allowing fine modulation of consonantal sounds (Vorperian and Kent 2007). The prosodic performativity that is instead antecedent from the point of view of physiological maturation will make possible the learning of a primitive and musical linguistic form such as motherese.

2.5 The Adaptive Function of Speech

Motherese, as we have seen, contains a musical component that manifests itself through intonation, rhythm, and intensity. In these reciprocal melodic intonations would reside the bases that have led to the progressive development of the linguistic capacity in our species. Considered as a preverbal phase and therefore as a preparation for the real language, according to Grieser and Kuhl (1988), it is possible to identify three possible functions: linguistic, attentional, and social/affective. By linguistic function, the authors refer to the fact that in the motherese, the intonational contours emphasize the final elements to prepare the child for some properties of language. Attentional function refers to the fact that the high peaks and intonational contours typical of motherese solicit the child's attention toward the speaker. Finally, the social-affective function is given by transmitting positive emotions from the mother to the child.

Beyond the linguistic function, the role of the motherese is certainly complex because it invests in the affective and relational sphere of the child and creates communicative routines that are the basis of the interaction with the other. Mithen (2005) also points out that one of the main tasks of the prosodic component is to give rise to the alternation of turns of speech. Clearly, motherese also plays an adaptive role since it is functional in developing language and communication in both sapiens and non-human animals. It is universal and would demonstrate the centrality of linguistic stimulation to the development of specifically human cognition (cf. Anastasi 2016).

For instance, Chinese and American mothers use the same language pattern with their children, even though they are not both tonal languages (cf. Grieser and Kuhl 1988; Fernald et al. 1989; Trehub et al. 1993). The unit of segmentation may thus change across languages, but the prosodic segmentation procedure remains the same (cf. Cutler et al. 1986; Sebastian-Gallés et al. 1992; Zwitserlood et al. 1993; Pennisi and Falzone 2016).

It is not strange, then, that children worldwide listen to lullabies and show musical aptitude. From the earliest hours of life, they can pick up on the smallest differences in pitch and tempo (Trehub 2003), can discriminate between the mother's voice and another woman's, and show real preferences for certain types of singing (see Flohr and Trevarthen 2007). The proto-musical attitude of infants involves both the perceptual component and the production of sounds with their possible harmony. This, from a linguistic and evolutionary perspective, leads to the hypothesis that our ancestors did not utter their first words until they expanded their repertoire of vocalisations to understand which expressions could be used to indicate people, events, or objects (cf. Falk 2009).

The role of motherse in evolution certainly faces much criticism, especially when considered as part of the debate about the origins of language. However, I do not think it is simply an assumption to believe that the first words spoken by hominids, besides being much less refined than modern words, were initially born as signals with multiple meanings, exactly as it happens in non-human primates (see Hauser 1996).

As stated, the prosodic modulation of the voice, in addition to expressing emotional content, has the clear function of initially favouring the mother-child coordination and then making possible the vocal interaction with the other group members. As we have seen, this mechanism is not exclusive to human beings. Within animal communication systems, it has been possible to verify not only the presence of the motherese but also the reciprocity of signals between conspecifics of the group. These elements in a comparative perspective allow us to discuss the adaptive component of prosody and to analyse the role that music may have played in the origin of language (cf. Bryant 2013; Filippi 2016).

The various modes of recall that exist in nature take on connotations that we might call musical, for example, in the case of the songs or choruses emitted by singing primates. These vocalisations clearly have behavioural and functional effects, which suggest that we can approach the study of vocal signals by either investigating the ability of primates to acquire vocal skills as a result of evolutionary pressures or by identifying homologies that we share with other animals (Hauser et al. 2002; Gamba and Giacoma 2005).

Figure 2.1 Spectrogram of an indri song

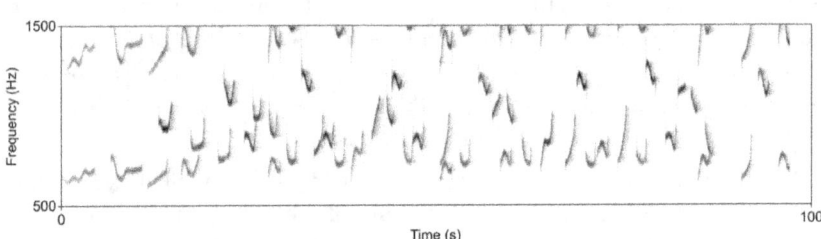

Spectrogram of a complete advertisement song emitted by an indri pair in the forest of Maromizaha, Madagascar. Recording: courtesy of Marco Gamba.

While similarities among phylogenetically distant species have allowed us to speak of evolutionary convergence, the homologies highlighted indicate the possibility of a common evolutionary legacy. The ability to modulate the prosodic characteristics of a signal is a clear example of homology found in vocal production. Most mammals show that they have a small repertoire of calls (grunts, chants, alarm calls, and so on), each of which has acoustic characteristics that develop until adulthood. Mammals can, for example, choose to vocalize or remain silent or modify their calls, albeit in a limited fashion (cf. Magrath et al. 2006; Rosier and Langkilde 2011).

Vocal production that became flexible once it evolved and originated from the vocalisations of nonhuman primates has clearly affected social species. For this reason, we can define it as a kind of social communication constituted by combining two or more categories of sounds that can be combined so that they do not belong to any sound class. Certainly, elements such as the phrasing of syllables or the segmentation of dialogue are quite complicated to identify in non-human animals (Kanwal et al. 1994), but it is also true that both our species and other animals often make use of calls with different levels of loudness, which makes it difficult to identify distinct classes of calls (Hauser 1992).

For vocal signals to be properly received, modulation of the acoustic characteristics is critical. Although modulations are not subject to the voluntary control of the signaller, any emotional conditions can change the tone and thus affect the fundamental frequency range (F0) of that signal (Rendall 2003). The use of formants and fundamental frequency (F0) play an essential role in human communication, as they allow us to distinguish the different sounds that characterise language and provide information regarding their spatial spread (Ghanzanfar and Rendall 2008). In nonhuman mammals, for example, the structure of vocalisations differs based on factors such as species, individual identity, and social context.

In light of what has been said, we could hypothesize that some animal species, as well as humans, to adapt effectively to the environment, have had to acquire the ability to decode vocal messages for their emotional content. Thus, specific expressive patterns would have developed that we can trace in pre-verbal vocal affective displays, which have been maintained and adapted to specific forms of communication such as speech and music (cf. Syal and Finlay 2011; cf. Seyfarth and Cheney 2003).

The ability to communicate as an advantageous function allows for the performance and coordination of activities related to the maintenance of the species. The vocal behaviour of non-human primates shows that the production of songs and calls helps maintain contact with group members during movements and localize their position (Werner 1984). Through audience checking (Schel at al. 2013), for example, chimpanzees agree on group movements and tend to use repeated vocalisations that allow them to influence the rest of the group. Doing so allows the behaviours of conspecifics to be monitored, and continued emission of the signal increases the likelihood that a proposal to move the group will be evaluated.

Vocalisations are, therefore, a privileged means by which to coordinate interactions between individuals in the group and develop sociality. Signals such as alarm calls, courtship calls, or territorial defence calls, in addition to having a strong adaptive value, possess a prosodic contour that seems plausible to speak of an evolutionary priority of music over language. In such a scenario, the hypothesis of Brown (2000) on the existence of a musical language in which the perception and production of vocalisations would be based initially on the lexical tone through which the meaning was conveyed is well suited.

According to this model, it is possible to combine individual units that are part of vocalisation but whose meaning is still linked to emotional expression and therefore lacks any syntactic structure. The meaning will be assigned through melody based on modulation variation of tempo, peak, accent, volume, and length. At this level of perception and production of sound units, the fundamental properties become the differentiation between units realised based on peak (auditory wave effect), rhythm (relation between pulsations), and amplitude (prominence effects). Thus, musilanguage is based on discreteness, combinatorial capacity, and intonation (Brown 2000; cf. Brandi 2003).

The vocalisations, initially constituted by a referential and emotional system, would then have embarked on their journey towards the formation of the two stages that generated musilanguage: the first, constituted using discrete tones and accents essential for referential communication; the second, involved in the development of signifying sequences, generated by combinatorial rules designed to bring together the units of different sequences (Brown 2000).

The interaction of gestures and vocal components in early communication systems, as well as the role of the mother as a manager of social learning and the emotional interaction between mother and child, would thus be children of a long evolutionary history. In this history, I believe it is possible to hypothesize two crucial moments: a first, the preparatory phase, in which evolution worked on the motor, neural, and articulatory preadaptations functional to language development (Lieberman 2007; 2016), and a second, transitional phase, represented by musilanguage from which music and language bifurcate. Musilanguage, it should be clarified, is neither solely linguistic nor solely musical but rather consists of common features from which music and language would later develop into distinctive specializations (Brown 2000).

The bifurcation, probably the result of social pressure and cerebral reorganization of early hominids, seems to have been decisive for the origin of spoken communication. Instead of a way of communicating strongly, shaped by emotions and equipped with an eminently musical vocality, evolution preferred a propositional language based on a faster neural processing speed than previous communication systems (cf. Mithen 2005). This does not mean that music and language are distant in terms of processing or that even music, or singing if you prefer, was a kind of parasite from which language managed to free itself.

If we consider the fundamental properties of vocal productions such as details of tempo, rhythm, musical intervals, and types of syllables and compare them, as Richman (2000) does, with the vocalisations of gelada baboons (*Theropithecus gelada*) we will see that the real difference is in the internal variability of vocal production. Gelada baboons use rhythm and melody in their vocal exchanges and do so in the same way humans use these components in speech and song. Through the structuring of rhythm and melody, gelada baboons distinguish the emotional content and meaning of a specific call. In these vocal exchanges, in addition to highlighting important coincidences between the communicative forms of human and non-human primates, Richman (1987) identifies four different levels of description: phonological, whole sound, rhythmic, and syntactic, which are essential for the correct use of rhythm and melody within vocalisations.

In the vocalisations of these primates, we do not find repetitions of the same vocal sequence, but we can find the repetition of three syllables at most. According to Richman (2000), formulaic repetition is a fundamental property to explain the origin of language as it denotes the ability to group sequences of sounds in such a way as to arrive at a composition that has a precise meaning. Having constant repetitions within a call allows conspecifics to learn and recognize auditory sequences and thus create interactions based on rhythmic synchrony. The holistic nature of this form of communication shows how vocalisations are associated with a complete message and not individual words; they are signals that have no internal structure and therefore are not combined with other vocalisations to create a more complex message (Wray 1998).

The holistic-music model allows us to look at language from a functionalist perspective that amplifies our understanding of it and to hypothesize that the repetitiveness of the rhythmic-melodic sequences that distinguish the language and song of human and nonhuman primates may have fixed musilanguage at an evolutionary level, such that it triggered a functional organization of the brain (cf. Blood et al. 1999; cf. Patel 2008; cf. Trimble and Hesdorffer 2017).

In the view of vocal continuity between human and nonhuman primates, cognitive components should not be ignored. In particular, the ventral pathway would have had an overlapping role in humans and primates in decoding complex sounds, such as language, whereas the dorsal pathway is credited with the task of spatial analysis of sound. According to Rauschecker (2012), the dorsal pathway has a primary role in the production and categorization of phonemes, to postulate the existence of a hierarchical model of language that originates in the primary auditory cortex and then propagates in non-auditory regions, such as the frontal cortex and motor regions, premotor and prefrontal (Rauschecker and Scott 2009). These pathways, then, would not have arisen solely for the language but would have had an adaptive pre-function in nonhuman primates transmitting vocal signals between conspecifics, only later co-opted for language development.

Figure 2.2 Ventral and dorsal streams

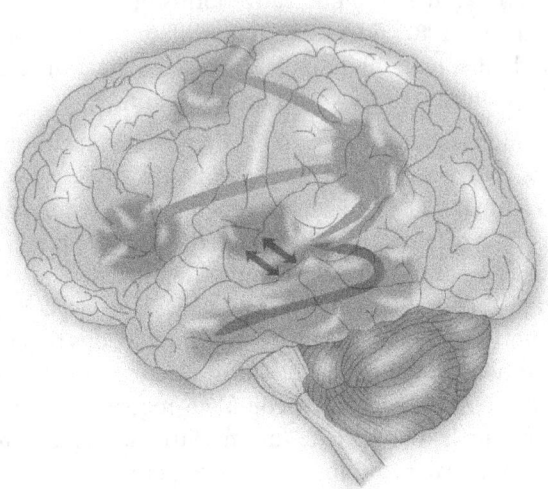

■ Dorsal stream for sensorimotor integration (mostly dominant)

■ Ventral stream for speech comprehension (bilateral)

> The ventral stream is involved in auditory object recognition, including the perception of vocalizations and speech. The dorsal stream is involved in mapping sound to articulation.

The combination of tone, rhythm, and melody inherent in the earliest vocalisations of our ancestors not only ensured the emergence of a true code of communication that distinguished the mother-child relationship but represented a springboard for what Brown (2000) would later define as musilanguage. As proof of this reconstruction of the facts, we can only point to the split that happened between the musical protolanguage of hominids and the language-cognition interface as the point when our language became unique to our species.

Chapter 3

THE ROOTS OF MUSICAL COMMUNICATION

The scenario described so far inevitably opens the door to a big question: can we speak of "musical platonism" (Payne 1996) or of a primitive musical form to which the vocal species have turned in their specific development (cf. Martinelli 2001)? The data present in literature today shows us a possible truth. Although it is not easy to date the appearance of musical activity in both humans and animals, the fact that music can provoke some of the same emotions as verbal communication, even if in a non-specific way, is evidence of its ability to have, in a sense, insinuated itself into primitive brain structures (Levitin 2006). From the moment we try to describe the universality of music (Dane 1976; Lomax 1977; Brown and Jordania 2013; Cochrane 2015; Berger 2021) using the soundscape present in nature as a unifying element, we must first identify the common sound and musical traits across species and then analyse them as Mâche (1992) suggests from a musicological perspective. Music is a great way for everyone to talk to each other. The fact that it might work for other animals forces us to talk about communication and how sound traits are organised in the species used in this chapter as examples.

The transfer of information from one subject to another is known as communication. It is a critical part of a species' success. No matter how it is accomplished, the important thing is to communicate! If human communication has been fundamental for developing the vocal and linguistic system, in non-human animals, even those without a vocal mechanism, communication has taken on different facets but is still functional and adaptive. For a long time, thinking of communication as a way of transmitting a signal that is functional to the species confirmed that this could only occur within perfect models of social organization. It is no coincidence that classical ethology has long used the communication model of bees and ants to indicate how an insect's eusociality was a perfect example of what it means to collaborate for the common good of the species (von Frish 1967; Hölldobler and Wilson 1990). The specific communication codes of animal species allow the group to maintain relationships between individuals and to recognize roles within a hierarchy. Only in this way is communication to be understood as a profitable means for the survival of a species. Although it may seem speculative, the definition of communication provided here applies to every level of knowledge, whether human, animal or artificial.

The basic principle governing any form of communication is that every action carries a message or information. And since it is not possible to assume a non-behaviour, it is not possible not to communicate either (Watzlawick et al. 1967). What, then, does it mean to communicate? Classical theories define communication as exchanging messages between a sender and a receiver. According to the axioms of communication, this presupposes that there is, first of all, the intentionality to communicate with an individual capable of understanding the content of that particular message. At the basis of communication, there is the transmission of information through a signal produced by a sender that, once perceived, triggers an action in the receiver (Wilson 1975). It is good to clarify that communication between two individuals does not necessarily involve an advantage for both in the animal world. It is likely that in some cases, to benefit from the communication will be only one of the two individuals involved. Clearly, if we want to understand the evolution of communication systems, it is essential to focus on the origin of the signal and the changes that have occurred over time, especially those related to the mechanisms that regulate the production and understanding of information. Ethological studies have shown that communication in the animal kingdom occurs according to the sensory organs through which stimuli are received. For this reason, communication is divided into chemical, visual, tactile, and auditory.

Chemical communication is probably the most ancestral. It usually occurs through the production of chemicals such as pheromones: these are spread through special glands and have the possibility to travel by air and can reach long distances. We find this form of communication both in insects such as bees and moths and in large mammals such as Asian elephants (*Elaphus maximus*) that resort to the use of the vomeronasal organ, located in the olfactory epithelium, to recognize the chemical signals contained in the urine of the female if she is receptive to mating (Rasmussen 1998).

Visual communication occurs through body movement, the particular colouration of plumage or the recognition of facial expressions, as in the case of some non-human primates. This type of communication is particularly functional during courtship. Usually, it requires the involvement of some parts of the animal's body, such as crests, wattles, and shaking of the head, or it is possible to see the realisation of real rituals as in the case of the penguin dance performed by the Great Crested Grebe (*Podiceps cristatus*) (Rogers 1990).

Tactile communication is the basis of some strong social relationships, as in the case of parental care. Just think of a cat licking her young or the antennal language used by ants during recruitment or trophallaxis (Hölldobler 1984; Hölldobler and Wilson 1990).

Finally, we have auditory communication. This occurs through the production of sounds and is characterized by the way in which they are emitted. Typically, this type of communication involves the use of specialized morphological structures in the production of sounds: the syrinx in songbirds, hummingbirds, and parrots (Greenewalt 1968); vocal muscles in bony fish (Bass et al. 2008); and the laryngeal sac and vocal tract anatomy in non-human primates (Hewitt et al. 2002; Fitch and Reby 2001).

Interest in animal communication probably reached its first peak between the 1960s and 1970s when, with the birth of zoosemiotics by Sebeok (1965), it was decided to provide a proper description of animal codes and those parts of communication considered to be shared with the human species. However, the enthusiasm for the communicative performance of non-human animals soon stalled because of the stubborn attempts of many researchers (see Hayes 1951; Gardner and Gardner 1969) to undertake studies on interspecific communication between humans and chimpanzees. The result that zoosemiotics has been able to comment on is reducible to a list in which it mentions what animal abilities are and what animals are not able to do compared to humans.

The period following Sebeok's publication (1968) was a deafening silence on the part of the hard core of semiotics that seemed to ignore the Chomskyan cognitive (Chomsky 1959) turn that had taken place in the cognitive sciences in the same years. Thanks to what will become a kind of manifesto of cognitive science, the idea that animals, and organisms in general, are simply the result of several parts assembled is dropped. They are finally accorded cognitive capacities. Let it be clear that with this, Chomsky does not open his perspective to the recognition of animal communication but rather bases his theory on the fact that language is a decisive and innate component of the human species. The grammatical, recursive and syntactic structure of human language thus becomes the leading element of human cognition (Chomsky 1975; cf. Aarsleff 1970). In this scenario, Sebeok's (1968) zoosemiotic perspective gives way to a semiotics that focuses entirely exclusively on human language, denying the possibility of being able to address minds other than humans (Gensini 2019).

This failed approach to the communication codes of the animal kingdom positions zoosemiotics below what Eco (1975) called threshold semiotics because it "considers the communicative behaviour of non-human and therefore non-cultural communities." (Eco 1975, 21). Eco's position was clearly based on the idea that semiotic phenomena coexist with cultural ones. Therefore, considering culture as something referable and tangible only in the human species, approaching the concept of culture to animal species is not feasible.

Leaving aside some of its critical issues, the advent of the cognitive turn has allowed animal communication scholars to broaden their scope by calling into question not only the biological aspects but also the cognitive processes involved in a species' communicative behaviour (see Griffin 1976; 1992). This step will prove to be fundamental to understanding that not only the communicative behaviour of humans and animals has a specific biological basis, but also the cultural aspects cannot be exempted from the biological investigation as the result of genetic predisposition and experiential learning (see Pennisi and Falzone 2010). The panorama of communication research can now boast of a cognitive approach that can only recognize a zoosemiotic relevance to the entire animal communication system.

From this scenario emerges the desire to rethink not only the animals in their entirety, but it begins to include biology in the theories of knowledge and language (Edelman 1992). The abandonment of a model of communication based on mechanism and behaviourism opened the way to new evolutionary interpretations of animal communication. It allowed us to consider not only the aspects operated by selective pressure but also to recognize an "aesthetic use of sound communication among animals" (Martinelli 2011, 23). At this point, all that remains is to transfer the concept of music from a zoological, ethological, and biological perspective.

3.1 Musical Communication in Non-Human Animals

From a scientific point of view, combining music and ethology might seem a risk, but it is not unusual to ask oneself in front of the vocal courtship performances of birds, deer, and mice in any documentary: do animals sing? An answer to this question is due today to a discipline that is certainly young but with well-defined contents: zoomusicology. When Mâche (1992), its founding father, affirmed that extending a phenomenon such as music to animal species implies having to question both the definition of music and the very idea that we have of animals, he probably did not imagine that he was opening the door to the interdisciplinary nature of music. Since ancient times, the science of music has been the object of investigating the study of the human voice and the sound produced by musical instruments. Since the attention has shifted to the ethological side, the musical vocalisations produced by non-human animals have become a part of the communicative system which zoosemiotics cannot disregard. Music as a real communication system must be investigated as a form of language. This statement could appear dangerous in some ways. However, the renewed interest in the evolution of language has allowed many scholars to resume studies on language to reach a univocal evolutionary theory. On this last point, we are certainly far from finding an agreement, and this is because language is an enormously complex capacity, which includes a multitude of components (see Christiansen and Kirby 2003).

Considering the current theories of language, I believe that bringing the topic of vocality back into the current debate is essential to investigate what concerns linguistic articulation and cognitive ability. These elements are also at the basis of a capacity such as music, which does not belong only to human beings but can be traced in its most elementary form, even in phylogenetically distant species. Therefore, vocal communication assumes a privileged role and music as a combination of sounds will be described herein strictly in biological and cognitive terms. Without detracting from historical and cultural variability, I intend to give music a universal connotation because it is part of the panorama of human capabilities with its biological derivation. In this sense, adopting the bio-naturalistic paradigm allows me to report on how musical communication or musicality, in general, are not exclusively human traits.

Retracing the roots of sound communication necessarily means making a journey within the animal kingdom and among the species phylogenetically closest to us from which it is possible to obtain answers. All of this allows us to trace an evolutionary path of human musical abilities starting from the idea that music has its roots in animal songs. For two reasons, offering a panorama of the singing manifestations of which non-human animals are capable can be useful. On the one hand, it grants the possibility of understanding how the musicality inherent in producing signals can convey meaning. On the other hand, it allows us to discuss how vocalic production, which is possible in several animal species, and the ability to generate real songs could represent the natural precursor of language.

From the singing of birds to the chirping of crickets, passing through the duet of gibbons and the singing of penguins, the animal kingdom presents a universe of sounds. From the point of view of the theory of evolution, let us try to understand what kind of musical capabilities we are really talking about and why, in the light of the data that will be presented, the human being is really in good company.

3.1.1 Birdsongs

Bird song research has been highly influenced by Darwinian theory, which holds that a skill such as singing, regardless of what performs it, is a functional mechanism for sexual selection. Singing is a complex form of communication, and everything about it has autonomous and specific peculiarities. It is generally described as a male musical performance that fulfils two primary functions: attracting a partner and fighting against one's rivals (Kroodsma and Byers 2015). Given its function in courtship, it is nothing more than the vocal equivalent of the peacock's tail (cf. Miller 2000), so one might call it an honest signal and a carrier of good genetic quality: only an experienced male can boast the ability of a vocal, melodic, rich, and varied performance. If we limit ourselves to interpreting the songs of birds following the theory of sexual selection, what emerges is that the choice made by the female is purely aesthetic. The sense of beauty, however, puts us in front of a thorny question. As Wallace (1889) well notes, the choice made by the female represents a selective force, but Darwin (1859) does not explain the connection between the reproductive choice of the partner and aesthetic appreciation.

The mechanism of aesthetic choice and sexual preference can be explained today by resorting to two defined research perspectives: The first can be framed both in aesthetic terms as understood by Miller (2000) and in a more ethological point of view, i.e., understanding the choice by perceptual and sensory mechanisms (see Endler and Basolo 1998). The second model, on the other hand, is adaptive. Therefore, the choice is explained using the fitness indicator theory (cf. Mithen 2003). In both cases, these models carry the handicap of reducing the aesthetic preference to a mere sexual drive. This certainly makes the idea that the reproductive choice is solely responsible for selecting a trait such as singing, ornaments, or feather colouration. In truth, the choice is variable but not arbitrary. Although, in the Darwinian view, birds are considered among the most aesthetically gifted birds, the effects of sexual selection on musicality are not unambiguous across species (see Bartalesi 2012; Honing 2020).

For thousands of years, we have admired the beauty of birdsong, and the aesthetic perspective of studies of animal communication has illustrated that among the various functions of signals (signals of alarm, territorial conflict, care for offspring), courtship signals seem to be the most complex as well as aesthetically pleasing to hear (Bradbury and Vehrencamp 2011). However, the scientific understanding possessed of this phenomenon today limits us to giving a mechanical interpretation of the song and the ecological function that comes with it. If we assume that the primary function of most communication systems is to communicate information, then it makes sense to ask what makes birdsong so biologically effective.

In birdsong, which by its definition shows itself as a complex prolonged vocal performance that is often tonal and melodic (Thorpe 1961), the variation of numerous extremely high-pitched and fast rhythmic-melodic micro-cells with a prevalence of *glissandos* and modulations make the song meaningful and distinctive (Beason 2004). In most cases singing in songbirds seems to be a male prerogative. However, some studies have found that even females of some species, which usually do not sing, are induced to do so under particular conditions of hormonal balance (Frankl-Vilches and Gahr 2017).

It is precisely on females singing that it is good to make a brief elaboration. According to Darwinian theory, natural selection has provided females with inconspicuous plumage and a much-reduced vocal capacity. If we want to give an extreme vision, they seem almost reduced to silence. The reason is soon said: the plumage's showiness and the song's melodiousness would make the female and her nest an easy target for predators. Yet recent studies show that not only the females of many species are able to sing but are also protagonists of real duets with the male during the courtship phase (Odom et al. 2014). Although still poorly studied, the singing of females likely has a social function that deserves investigation. Females of shining blue wren (*Malurus splendens*), a small Australian passerine, for example, sing to their eggs in the nest throughout the nesting period, which seems to already contribute in the embryonic stage to the young learning the begging call that is specific to each nest. In this way, the mother ensures that the young respond only to her call. Within this song it is possible to distinguish both the vocal signature produced by the mothers during nesting and the one used by the mother to urge the father to search for food (Colombelli-Negrel et al. 2012).

Historically, bird song has been considered a sex-specific signalling trait; males sing to attract females, and females, like perfect art critics, make a choice. This precluded attributing a functional role to their song when the first evidence emerged. While in humans, this capacity is equally distributed between men and women, due to the different evolution that singing has had in our species, in birds, vocal learning would have evolved in both sexes, especially in species present in equatorial zones, to be then lost by females once they migrate to temperate zones (Morton 1975).

The study of female song has had the merit of opening new scenarios on the selective pressures that have allowed the appearance of different songs in the two sexes, thus calling into question the Darwinian hypothesis that bird song is a sexually selected trait.

In the last 50 years, ethologists have studied birdsong, obtaining a rich amount of comparative data relevant to biology and musical evolution. These studies, as well as providing excellent insights on the melodic structure, represent a valid neurobiological model to refer to for understanding the analogies with the human being. From the acoustic point of view, it is known that each species emits a call that is species-specific and whose range of formant frequencies is useful to generate a kind of semantic encoding. An interesting aspect of signification in communication among birds is that it is entrusted to rhythm and intonation. The latter seems to be fundamental in some species of birds to get the better of their competitors. Hall (2006) has shown that the perfectly tuned exchange of notes and warbles between male and female Australian magpie-larks (*Grallina cyanoleuca*) is a tool these birds use to intimidate other species. Magpie-larks defend their territory in pairs, alternately singing two types of notes, pewee, and wit. Hence most disputes with other species (or other pairs of the same species) occur solely through pair warbles.

Beyond this, however, it is worth noting that recognition of individuals through their vocal signature (or semantic communication) in which a given call is associated with a precise meaning, such as signalling danger, is present even in animals without vocal learning (Nowicki and Searcy 2014). In general, animal signals, whether they are alarms or to indicate the presence of food, appear to be indivisible packages. Their meanings can boast that they are not fixed but can be modulated, for example, when calls are emitted rapidly, slowly, or in loud or mild modes (Marler 1992). This indivisibility may suggest that there is no phonological syntax (Ujhelyi 1996); in fact, the structure of songbirds' songs has revealed their ability to create different repertoires. Repertoires are generated using the basic set of minimal acoustic units, i.e., the equivalent in birds of phonemes and syllables. Classic examples include the repertoire of the song of the marsh sparrow (*Melospiza georgiana*) studied by Marler and colleagues in 1986 and that of the winter wren (*Troglodytes troglodytes*) by Kroodsma and Momose (1991).

What emerges from the study of these specimens is that each male has a repertoire of three to five songs lasting about ten seconds in these species. The composition of these melodies is based on alternating the six main notes. Each song usually contains the repetition of a verse organized, however, with different frequencies. This highlights the recombination capacity of songbirds and invites us not to underestimate the hypothesis that the vocal behaviour of birds may be useful in understanding the origins of music.

Musical realisation by songbirds is reminiscent of the behaviour of humans during the speech phase; in the most complex songs, birds generate enormous vocal repertoires and use the same basic processes of recombination or syntactic phonology that we use to create words. There is, of course, a crucial contrast with human language. The singing sequences are not distinct as sense-referenced but rich in non-symbolic affective content. Singing appears, therefore, as a distinctive genre or sign denoting the population's identity, membership, and social status (Catchpole and Slater 1995).

Although the minimal definition of music sees the latter as a set of intervals, notes, and timbres combined with either the repetition of phrases or their suppression to form a melody, in comparing humans and other animals, it must be determined whether any animal sounds conform to these taxonomic criteria and are potentially studious (cf. Anastasi 2016).

In the case of birdsong, the analogy to human language is striking. As we will see, birds and humans are examples of convergent evolution in their way of learning to communicate. In this case, we are dealing with a molecular convergence since the anatomical and behavioural convergences between birds and humans are believed to be due to the convergent expression of genes that form and regulate vocal learning circuits (Hara et al. 2012; Wang et al. 2015; Pfenning et al. 2014).

This does not mean that two species so phylogenetically distant have shared a common musical ancestor, rather, it is a matter of establishing how, between birdsong, music, and language, there can be a formal similarity given by the evolutionary pathway of vocal signals. How does the theory of birdsong evolution find common ground with the evolution of verbal language? According to some scholars, songbirds' songs show similarities with human language with respect to syntax. The study carried out on the Japanese sparrow (*Lonchura striata domestica*) shows the presence of a complex syntactic architecture within the song of this species that could seem like human grammar. In fact, in this song, it is not only possible to identify a sequence of sound units separated by silence (Berwick et al. 2011) but Japanese sparrows recognize the syllabic sequences to which they are accustomed and react to unfamiliar ones by singing noisily. According to Okanoya (2004), it is possible to group the notes of Japan sparrows' songs into sets of two or three elements called chunks that this species is able to recombine.

Such an ability could indicate parallelism of extreme relevance from an evolutionary point of view, as it shows that it is possible to discern a similar trait between two species such as sapiens and birds that, in the face of the same evolutionary pressures, would have developed the ability to syntactically manipulate the units that constitute their language (cf. Okanoya 2002; Berwick et al. 2011). Such a hypothesis projects us in the direction provided by Darwin (1859), according to whom the evolutionary prelude to propositional syntax is to be identified in articulations analogous to the songs made by other animal species in contexts having to do with the conquest/defence of a sexual partner or defence of territory.

In general, in studies on the animal communication system, there are still some shadows related to the lack of components such as pragmatics, semantics, and communicative intentionality, without underestimating, then, that the substantial difference between the two species, at least in terms of grammatical structure, remains the principle of recursivity and therefore the Chomskyan idea that the sentence consists of a deep structure (which determines the semantic interpretation of the sentence) and a surface structure (which determines the phonetic interpretation) (Chomsky 1957).

However, this view of the facts, however, carries with it the enormous disadvantage of not finding a motivation of an evolutionary nature. It is not possible to understand which selective pressures would have pushed our ancestors to acquire the syntactic and recombinatory components useful for their melodic expression. Therefore, I believe that, although human language can be defined as qualitatively different from any form of animal communication, in terms of recursiveness and referentiality, the appearance of a musical protolanguage places the development of human vocalisation in a context that is much more akin to the functional criteria of natural selection (cf. Tinbergen 1951) rather than those of a purely syntactic nature.

3.1.2 Singing in the trees

An extremely relevant phenomenon from the evolution of communication comes from several species of non-human primates whose ability to produce real songs can be understood as the origin of musical language, which we discussed in the previous chapter. Before further analysing the ways through which music would have taken part in the development of language, however, it is good to provide some details about the production of songs by some non-human primate species, which according to Haimoff's (1983) classification, affects about 10% of genera and species. This small circle of individuals is now known as singing primates. It boasts among its main protagonists the lemurs of Madagascar (*Indri indri*) and the gibbons of Southeast Asia (*Hylobatidae*). Sexual selection (Cowlishaw 1996) is said to have triggered and shaped the evolution of primate songs, but contrary to the usual logic, males and females of the group produce dimorphic songs. The evolution of the vocal repertoire of these primate species has also been influenced by social organization, membership, and territorial defence (McComb and Semple 2005). The emission of songs and, in particular, their intrinsic characteristics have the peculiarity of varying by the context and, at the same time, evoke different behavioural responses in the receivers (Clarke et al. 2006; Torti et al. 2013). Precisely following this scenario, it is possible to hypothesize that music evolved as a result of the need for signals to propagate over long distances and thus reach group members, for example, while moving or searching for food (cf. Mitani and Stuht 1998; Oliveira and Ades 2004; Torti et al. 2013). In this evolution that occurred in several stages, communication would first manifest in the form of songs and vocalisations of high intensity and later would take the form of proto-musical signals (Fitch 2006; Anastasi 2016; Gamba et al. 2018). Since communication is an essential part of the everyday life of a vocal species, we seek to understand who singing primates are and why they are important to the argument made here.

Among the most illustrious examples of their acoustic sophistication and their versatility in animal communication, we have gibbons (*Hylobatidae*). Typically, gibbon song lasts 10 to 30 minutes, usually articulated in the early morning hours, but it is not unusual to hear them sing during the rest of the day. The songs of gibbons can be defined as stereotyped as well as sex-specific and species-specific (Geissmann 1993). The vocal characterizations of these songs make possible the identification of the different species belonging to the family Hylobatidae. An element not to be underestimated is the ability of these primates to perform real duets that show an extreme level of accuracy. Male gibbons, for example, during their execution, tend to modulate the composition of the phrases that make up the song gradually. They go from executing simple "phrases" to more complex ones. On the other hand, the females emit a strong and stereotyped call, which generally is accompanied by a form of locomotion when this reaches its climax. Finally, the male may contribute to the duet by using a vocal sequence called a "tail", which allows him to accompany the female's call (Geissman 1993). The manifestation of song-splitting would be more limited between male and female gibbons, given the diversity of notes produced.

In contrast, diversity in the acoustic structure of notes, particularly in duration and some spectral features, is more evident. It should also be added that gibbon song under both alarm and normal conditions is acoustically the same, but notes differ in composition (Clarke et al. 2006). The duet performed by these primates, better known as song-splitting, is probably the most complex musical song of a land vertebrate other than that produced by humans. What makes it special is that it could provide a conceptual framework to reconstruct the process that led from song-based communication to spoken language (Masataka 2007).

According to Geissmann (2002), the elaboration of the phrases that make up song-splitting is evidence of a real phylogenetic pathway of the song: from a song initially common to both sexes, it is possible that a separation into male-specific and female-specific song-splitting occurred first. Subsequently, from a process defined as duet-splitting, the bipartition between duet and non-duet species would have occurred, in which the pair's contributions are temporally divided through solo songs. Thus, solo species would be derived from duetting species, and the solo song would be related to the spatial distribution of different gibbon species. The idea of a phylogenetic pathway of the duet is opposed. However, the hypothesis is that it is the result of the imitative and learning capacity of gibbons that would have merged the songs produced by other species to create their duet-splitting (Srikosamatara 1982).

Personally, I feel confident in rejecting the latter hypothesis because, as demonstrated by Geissmann (1993), the singing ability of gibbons is innate, and it is no coincidence that they reproduce the same signals even when raised in a context of isolation. This means that their vocal repertoire and variability are independent of the individual's ontogeny-related experience. Also, even though we can examine the existence of a sort of creativity in the composition of these songs, we cannot exclude that such vocal behaviour is innate as species-specific. The repertoires of primate songs thus seem limited to a pattern consisting of various variations.

The fact that the singing of gibbons, although possessing inter-individual characteristics, is stereotyped opens an interesting scenario on its own selection. If sexual selection is usually used to explain the evolution of the song, the study conducted by Snowdon (2004) opens the door to the possibility that, at least in the case of gibbons, individual variations in vocal behaviour have a weak impact on their reproductive decision. In contrast to what happens in birds, the singing of the male gibbon seems to have no influence on the choice made by the female. The spectacular vocal displays so useful to songbirds in choosing a partner would seem, at this point, to be completely irrelevant among singing primates.

The song of the lemurs of Madagascar, also known as Indri (*Indri indri*), has become, in the last few decades, a particular case of study because of its intensity and complexity, reasons that make it unique among prosimians. Indri's song is a complex vocal mannerism that can be emitted in at least two different contexts: cohesion among the individuals of a group and territorial advertisement. Again, we are in the presence of a dimorphic song whose differences play out in terms of notes and acoustic structure (Pollock 1975; Sorrentino et al. 2013; Zanoli et al. 2020).

Recording techniques used in the field today have allowed Indri scholars to observe different types of singing based on their frequency, coming to identify as many as eight different types of vocalisation (Giacoma et al. 2010) in addition to the actual singing that represents the most intense and complex vocalisation emitted by members of the entire group (Pollock 1986). Interesting differences have been demonstrated by Giacoma's (2010) team between male and female singing. Generally, females have greater note frequency modulation than males and use more notes than males (7:5) in each sung sequence. Males, on the other hand, can boast the ability to maintain emissions for a longer time, and this is probably due to a subtle morphological difference in the Indri vocal sac that would be decisive not only in the intensity of the call but also in its duration (Hewitt et al. 2002).

Just as it happens among gibbons, Indri's singing is not a solitary song but occurs through pair synchronization. There is a real duet between male and female in which sometimes it is possible to hear a third voice; these are the youngest members of the group that tend to fit into this coordination of the couple with their own rules. This song is made of many different notes of the harmonic type that follow a precise grammatical structure. Indri's song is never a love song. Still, it is a song that regulates relationships with neighbouring groups because it can be heard up to four kilometres away and regulate relationships within the group (Maretti et al. 2010).

The social organization of singing primates leads us to discuss the multiple uses of vocality, and thus the relationship between vocal signalling and social cohesion and between certain vocal signals and specific social interactions. The role of vocality in the social dimension has been documented in detail in many non-human primate species accustomed to living within social groups (Krams et al. 2012). In this setting, singing becomes a means of communication by which to articulate the needs and social mechanisms of the group. In a highly social species where communication not only represents a means of information exchange but often forms the foundation of the social organization itself (Tomasello 1999), possessing a form of vocal expression is binding for the purposes of social organization.

In a society such as chimpanzees (*Pan troglodytes*), visual and vocal communication maintains balance and interactions between individuals and groups. For example, a closed grin, such as the full closed grin, can be manifested in response to an unexpected stimulus and thus evoke an immediate fear response in other individuals (Goodall 1986). On the other hand, a vocalisation such as the pant-hoot, the most frequent call among adults, is used to express pleasure in the presence of food or positive feelings involving the group. In this specific case, what is being reproduced is a rhythmic, noisy sound lasting about 10 seconds that begins softly until it reaches the peak of pleasure. Four components could be identified in its performance: introduction, the build-up (or gradual growth), pleasure, and production; the pant-hoot includes about 15-30 different sounds characterized by whistling, screaming, and a kind of moaning, produced during both inhalation and exhalation (Marler and Hobbett 1975). The temporal structure of chimpanzee pant-hoots appears to facilitate choral vocalisation with other group members, which would support the hypothesis that the duration of the gradual growth phase of the pant-hoot correlates with the latency with which the partner joins in the execution of the call. Phases indicating extreme pleasure in execution appear significantly longer when the pant-hoot is produced in the chorus rather than alone. However, the choral activity appears rather stereotypical, and this vocal behaviour appears to occur more for affective than informational reasons (Fedurek et al. 2013).

Studying the vocal behaviour of nonhuman primates can be helpful in identifying any similarities that allow us to infer the presence or absence of traits with common ancestors (Fitch 2000a). Certainly, primate singing is quite different from human language. Their loud, powerful voices were created so that songs could travel through dense forests and reach the attention of their conspecifics to ensure the maintenance of their social system. In contrast, the soft voice used by humans arose for communication to take place face-to-face. Identifying the ingredients of this shared musicality is certainly not an easy task; and even less do I think I have an answer that can put everyone in agreement.

But, if it is true that evolution has given humans greater neural control over vocal production and the anatomical changes implemented on our supralaryngeal vocal tract (Fitch 2000a), at the same time, the anatomical changes that have occurred in singing primates. However, they may appear less drastic, and have a clear biological function. Because of this, studying and comparing morphological correlates is a good way to figure out how language came to be.

According to bio-musicology (Wallin 1991) one of the elements of great importance in this sense is vocal learning, which involves the ability to produce vocalisations based on listening to an auditory stimulus and, in some cases, the ability to synchronize their movements to that stimulus. Learning and synchronization are also present in some phylogenetically distant species. Therefore, their study can be the first approach to reconstructing their nature and interaction (Tyack 2008). The modalities of investigation used by bio-musicology represent the starting point on which to base a second analysis, that is, that of the species-specific traits of musicality. This would make it possible to support, in the next few paragraphs, the idea that animals' singing and musical skills are the result of a vocal continuity of music, not an instrumental one.

3.2 Learning or Imitation?

Vocal learning can generally be defined as learning new vocalisations through imitating of conspecifics or individuals of different species. The data provided by ethology and cognitive sciences specifically show that it is now unthinkable to discuss vocal learning as a cognitive ability belonging only to humans. Certainly, vocal learning does not occur in all animals at the same level: regarding vocalisation, humans are the most productive due to their recursive capacity. However, it is not common to find specimens of the animal kingdom that are just as prolific and capable. Among birds, for example, parrots, hummingbirds, and some corvids are capable of producing hundreds to thousands of sounds (Petkov and Jarvis 2012), likewise some species of cetaceans and bats, elephants, and non-human primates.

The parallels between the ontogeny of vocal learning in some species and ours seem to be due to the sharing of similar cognitive, neurobiological, and perhaps genetic mechanisms. These would have changed through a separate process of convergent evolution, but they would have kept a common starting point that is thought to be shared with other species that have changed this way, even ones that aren't mammals. Generally, vocal learning is limited to conspecifics, and the ability to imitate signals or songs belonging to different species is very rare (Jarvis 2006). Since learning in many vertebrates and invertebrates is regulated by the information contained in the genetic heritage of the animal, it is plausible to define learning as a case of deep interaction between the process of cultural transmission on the one hand and the innate predisposition on the other hand. This does not imply that instinct is opposed to learning but acts as a trigger; it is not by chance that Gould and Marler (1987) spoke of it in terms of learning instincts.

Figure 3.1 Syrinx

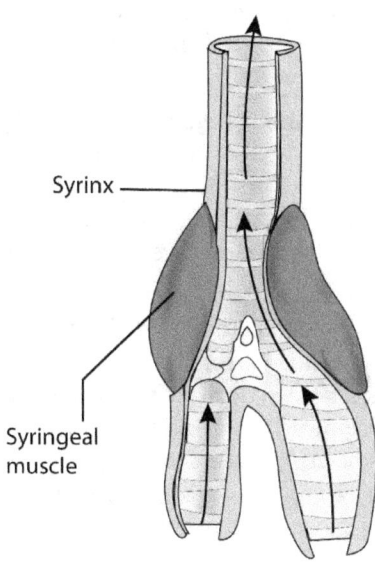

Syrinx is located at the base of the windpipe (trachea), where the trachea divides into the bronchi. The syrinx serves two main functions, i.e., control of air flow and labial tension. The syrinx is used to produce extremely loud and complex vocalizations.

Recent advances in understanding the neurobiology of bird songs suggest the existence of shared mechanisms underlying vocal learning in birds and humans (Jarvis 2004). This hypothesis is motivated by the fact that the human species and songbirds are among those taxa in which the innate ability to produce vocalisations is modified in the individual as a result of experience. Learned vocal communication is therefore determined by social experience. For vocal signals to undergo any modifications, there must be audio-motor feedback that allows the individual to evaluate the sound emitted and/or heard to achieve the desired vocal "output" (Farries 2004). A substantial difference between birds and other vertebrates lies in their vocal organ: the syrinx. This is an organ dedicated solely to producing sounds that change according to the type of bird. The syrinx is a complex structure located at the trachea's lower end at the tracheal bifurcation level. Two pairs of crescent-shaped membranes partially or totally close off the two branches that reach the lungs. When the bird contracts the lungs, air passing through these membranes causes them to vibrate, producing a melodious sound (Greenewalt 1968).

Several common properties characterize all animals with vocal learning:

a) The presence of auditory feedback to maintain the correct pronunciation of learned vocalisations;

b) a critical period for vocal learning is termed the sensitive period, in which there is the cultural transmission of the vocal repertoire from one generation to the next (Thorpe 1963).

In songbirds and humans, learning begins with an initial phase of listening to and memorizing the song or sound, followed by a sense-motor phase of experimentation (Bolhuis et al. 2010). Early attempts to learn singing are termed sub-singing (Thorpe 1963) and are comparable to infant babbling or lallation, in which well-defined pairs of vowels and consonants are repeated.

In this first learning phase, we are faced with a type of plastic singing in which vocal errors are corrected until a faithful reproduction of the original song is obtained; the latter will then be personalized to endow it with its own vocal signature. In some cases, it is possible to see such recombination of the sounds heard that the singing appears unrecognizable (Bolhuis et al. 2010). Once perfected, the song will be crystallized and, in species such as the mandarin diamond (*Taeniopygia guttata*), will be maintained almost constant throughout its life. Other species, on the other hand, will modify their song over time.

Two important circuits provide the functional requirements for song learning in the forebrain: one specialized to support the actual learning process, the so-called anterior forebrain pathway, and the other, the motor pathway, responsible for controlling the production of learned sounds (Nottebohm 1993). Recent studies have shown that the ability to learn is made possible in songbirds by the presence of specific neuronal structures specialized in the perception and production of the corresponding sounds, both in avian songs and in human language. In the avian brain, acoustic stimuli reach the superior vocal centre (HVC) that controls the muscular movements of the vocal organ the motor centre and through an aggregate of neurons located in the basal nuclei known as Area X or the song learning centre (Reiner et al. 2004). Area X is now considered the equivalent of the cortico-basal circuits of the human telencephalon that are essential for learning but not for performance. In the avian brain, there is a molecular interaction between the motor pathway dedicated to vocal performance and the corticobasal circuitry useful for learning and modifying the already learned song (Kubikova et al. 2007).

Figure 3.2 Diagram of the song system

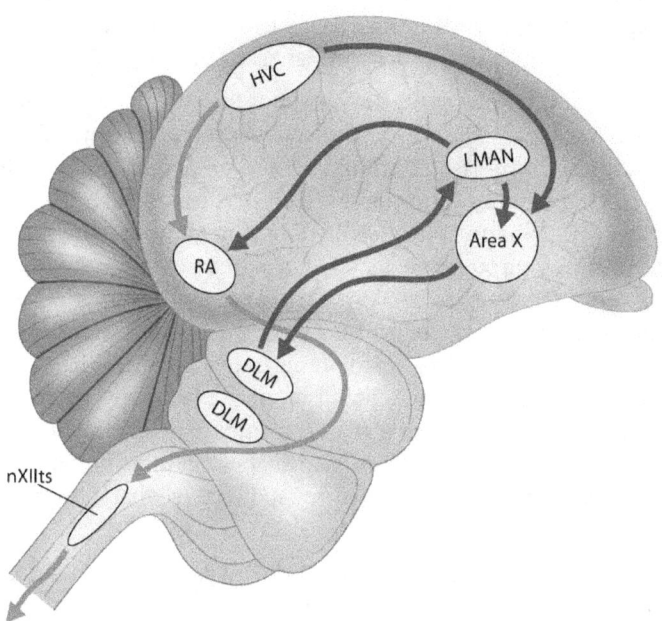

Lines show the anterior forebrain pathway necessary for song learning and adult song maintenance. HCV is a nucleus in the brain of the songbirds (order passeriformes) necessary for learning and the production of bird songs. Area X of the medial striatum is a songbird basal ganglia nucleus that is required for vocal learning. Only HVC and Area X receive new neurons in adulthood within the song system. LMAN, lateral magnocellular nucleus of the anterior nidopallium; RA, robust nucleus of the arcopallium; DLM, dorsal lateral nucleus of the medial thalamus; nXIIts, tracheosyringeal part of the hypoglossal nucleus.

Studies conducted by Prather and colleagues (2008) suggest that the function of neurons located in the upper vocal centre, also known as HVCX cells, in species such as *Melospiza georgiana* respond to only one type of song in the repertoire. Therefore, these cells are activated according to a very precise temporal pattern after the onset of the main song. These neurons thus respond to a specific pattern for a given song, both when the bird listens and performs. This would demonstrate that song performance is not the direct consequence of auditory feedback but of a phenomenon known as *corollary discharge* (Tchernichovski and Wallman 2008), according to which the mutual interconnection of two parts organize a circuit, i.e., both when the bird listens (auditory input) and when it sings (motor output). HVCX neurons would thus reflect the essential mechanism in songbirds for learning vocal communication. The similarity that emerges from this type of study certainly excludes the possible common musical ancestor hypothesis but confirms the thesis of evolutionary convergence between the two species generated by an evolutionary similarity of learning vocal signals (cf. Anastasi 2017).

The question at this point is whether all birds are constrained to learning to sing or if there are species in which this faculty is innate. In general, what can be said is that birdsong is both an innate and an acquired ability. Just like language, singing requires an experiential form during which the individual exercises this vocal ability. It is a faculty that is genetically transmitted from parents to offspring through the genetic makeup, but vocal skills, to develop, require auditory feedback from a master singer. Social experience plays a crucial role in the mechanism of learning to sing. Therefore, birds learn how to sing by listening and imitating. If this imprinting is lacking and the young specimens do not listen to the singing of an adult of the species, what is obtained will be abnormal singing, distorted and made of few notes. For this reason, it can be argued that imitation and innate singing are probably children of separate processes but constrained by auditory feedback (Gardner et al. 2005).

The study by Lachlan and collaborators (2018) on swamp sparrows (*Melospiza georgiana*) adds a key element to what has been said so far. These specimens adopt a strategy known as conformist biases, normally among those prerogatives recognized only by humans. The birds learn, copy, and pass on the song they have learned from one generation to the next, thus creating a song tradition that is stable over time. To create yet another analogy with the human language, we have the fact that even among the songs of songbirds, it is possible to hear inflexions that can be defined as dialectal forms of singing. Their degree of difference depends on factors such as acoustic interference problems, ecological barriers, different foliage types in the forests, and the period in which song learning occurs (see Baker and Cunningham 1985).

Surely, the maximum example of imitative ability among birds is represented by Prince Albert's lyre bird (*Menura alberti*) and the superb lyrebird (*Menura novaehollandiae*). We might describe these species as sound thieves. In fact, about 80% of their song is made up of stanzas from the songs of other birds, and their imitation borders on such perfection as to confound the imitated species (Dalziell and Magrath 2012). The medley of sounds produced can include verses from other animals, human noises, machines of all kinds, gunfire, and musical instruments. Therefore, these specimens take advantage of everything that the sound environment surrounds and offers them. Theirs is not only an example of one of the most complex songs in the bird kingdom, but it also demonstrates how such ability has assumed a key role in the courtship phase.

What has been said so far is even more surprising if we think that non-human primates, despite being equipped with a vocal apparatus that allows them to produce a wide range of sounds, cannot do better. Shared mechanisms underlying vocal learning in birds and humans (see Jarvis 2004) and the origin of vocal nuclei or pre-existing auditory circuitry for birds and humans (Feenders et al. 2008) could account for this real difference. According to the theory of Petkov and Jarvis (2012), all animals could be endowed with vocal learning, but the limiting factor would be their ability to sustain the cognitive processes involved. But, if it is true that animals with vocal learning show advanced cognitive abilities such as memory, attention, and learning, it is also true that examining the evolutionary convergence between species' morphological aspects can affect vocalic production or very simply prevent it. Cognition, learning, and vocality are interrelated, so it is important to remember that vocal signals are species-specific behaviours because they are the direct consequence of the biological constraints that condition their use and function (Minelli 2007).

Recent ethological and neurobiological studies have addressed the long-standing issue of vocal learning among non-human primates trying to explore possibilities and functions. An interesting study conducted by Russell and collaborators (2013) investigated the ability of chimpanzees (*Pan troglodytes*) to learn so-called AG sounds (attention-getting), i.e., vocal signals used to attract the attention of participating subjects within an artificial context. The specimens were able to learn these signals and implement a type of communicative strategy by using one of the four AG sounds proposed during training and applying them to attract the attention of the experimenters. Studies of this type are the full demonstration of how the use of vocalisations that do not belong to their vocal repertoire is made possible by certain flexibility of use and then by a fair degree of control of the orofacial muscles, an essential condition for the voluntary and intentional production of sounds.

Another noteworthy element is that AG sounds have been the object of transgenerational transmission among the group members and have characterized mother-child communication. In fact, pups have learned these vocalisations from their mother and have applied them within their vocal repertoire (Tagliatela et al. 2012), demonstrating the presence in this species of a vocal learning capacity, previously thought to be precluded to non-human primates. To date, it is possible to identify three types of vocal learning (cf. Egnor and Hauser 2004; cf. Janik and Slater 2000):

a) vocal comprehension learning.
b) vocal usage learning.
c) vocal production learning

Vocal comprehension learning involves learning appropriate responses to vocalisations produced by other group members. Vocal usage learning involves learning which calls should be used in certain contexts. Finally, vocal production learning is learning how to make songs and/or calls (Yamaguchi and Izumi 2008).

For vocal comprehension learning, studies carried out on baboons (*Papio ursinus*) (Cheney et al. 1996; Fisher et al. 2000), in addition to demonstrating the presence of a particularly sophisticated communicative system based on vocalisations which vary according to the situation in which they are produced, have shown how learning occurs in puppies through interaction with the mother. Initially, they emit repetitive vocalisations that have several points of contact with the repertoire of adults. Sometimes it is also possible that there are variants even if without any social relevance. Calls such as *contact barks*, produced when contact with group members is lost, and *alarm barks*, produced instead to signal predators, are learned by the cubs after careful observation of adults. Baboons first learn to have control over *contact barks*: they respond to these types of calls only if their family members or group members with whom they have interactions make them, and later, they learn to discriminate between types of alarms (Fisher et al. 2000). Another not insignificant requirement is their ability to recognize not only the identity of the emitter but also the object of their attention (Engh et al. 2006).

Among New World monkeys, squirrel monkeys (*Saimiri sciureus*) have demonstrated vocal usage learning and vocal production learning abilities. Recent studies have argued that learning *chuck calls* play a central role, and cubs gradually learn to recognize members within the group acoustically. Tests conducted to test the role of learning in *chuck call* recognition have shown that individuals of different developmental ages respond preferentially to *chuck calls* from peers in genetically unrelated familiar social groups compared to those from unfamiliar individuals outside the social group (Fisher and Hammerschmidt 2020).

Determining vocal learning within nonhuman primates may certainly be the key to reconstructing the stages that marked the evolution of language. The studies have shown the presence of an individually learned and flexibly used communicative repertoire, regardless of whether vocalisations have been described in the last 50 years as stereotyped, genetically determined, or highly effective (cf. Ploog 2002; Jürgens 2002).

At this point, it is fair to ask how this vocal control evolved and what enables the replication of sounds in birds and nonhuman primates. We immediately notice that while many species of birds and parrots can replicate sounds, the species much closer to us do not seem capable of vocal imitation, despite possessing a vocal apparatus much more like ours. A possible explanation comes from the hypothesis of phonological segmentation (Studdert-Kennedy 2000; Nguyen and Delvaux 2016), according to which the basis of vocal imitation would be facial imitation; this implies that the movements of lips and jaw would have modified the vocal tract and therefore the spectral structure of vocalisations. In addition to this, there is a system of mirror neurons selected for verbal production (see Corballis 2010; Levy 2012). Wanting at this point to establish a parallelism between ontogenetic and phylogenetic development, scholars believe that the parts that constitute the vocal tract (lips, tongue, veil, and larynx) emerged as independently controlled organs along with the evolution of vocal imitation. Allowing the emergence of discrete phonetic units would have been the differentiation of the discrete organs of the vocal tract.

Why do species phylogenetically close to us, such as chimpanzees, not possess the ability for vocal imitation, whereas parrots, whose vocal tract is completely different from ours, possess this ability? The solution to this question would lie in the lack in non-human primates of a real mechanism of vocal imitation, that is, of a device that allows them to control their phonatory organ (Lieberman 2003). Parrots, on the other hand, can learn to use and control their organs to replicate the sounds they hear, but they are also able to use organs that are different from human ones. For example, since they do not have lips to produce the bilabial occlusive, they produce the /p/ through a sort of esophagal speech using the syrinx (Pepperberg 2007). The study on the motility of the tongue in monk parakeets (*Myiopsitta monachus*) showed the ability of these animals to change the frequency and amplitude of sounds through lingual movements that would be the basis of their ability to imitate human speech (Beckers et al. 2004).

Vocal learning thus refers to the ability of species to add new vocalisations within their repertoire (Petkov and Jarvis 2012), typically through vocal imitation. The imitation and modification of various natural sounds or the voices of other animals could be the basis for developing the earliest elementary forms of language. As hypothesized by Darwin (1871), the direct imitation of numerous animal sounds and the emergence of a rudimentary song would have produced the strengthening and refinement of the vocal apparatus of our predecessors. Subsequently, the resulting increase in cognitive abilities would have paved the way for articulated language.

What has emerged so far shows that the mechanism of vocal learning plays a key role in auditory feedback. The resulting vocal output is nothing more than adaptation to the specific vocalisation of the group. Although studies of vocal communication in non-human primates show a highly-conserved structure of vocalisations, it is possible to see modifications by virtue of the auditory experience while remaining within species-specific constraints. The auditory perception systems in all animals are species-specific for decoding sounds emitted by their reference vocal system. Thus, it is not only the peripheral and central structures of production that constrain our ability to produce language but also the primary system of language, perception (hearing) would be biologically constrained to the perception of highly specific stimuli (cf. Zoloth et al. 1979; cf. Kuhl 1998; cf. Falzone 2012b; cf. Anastasi 2018). Indeed, auditory perception is associated with intraspecific communication. Thus it plays a key role for species with a high degree of sociality, such as primates, namely, discriminating the biological meaning of communicative sounds (Petersen et al. 1978).

These abilities followed a long evolutionary path before becoming available to our ancestors. Just think of the production of language that requires changes both at the peripheral level (anatomy) and the neural level (vocal control and imitation). Even if we argue that the evolution of language is independent of communicative mechanisms (Lieberman 1984), we cannot deny that it depends on the mechanisms of production and perception of sound.

3.3 Species-Specific Traits of Musicality

The concept of species-specificity used in this text deliberately recalls the definition adopted by Lorenz (1978), who proposed the adoption of the term not only in the ethological but also in the biological field. According to Lorenz, members of a given species are forced to enact behaviours in each environmental condition: nest building, mating rituals, and struggle for group dominance. In addition, recent declinations of this definition within evolutionary developmental biology have allowed us to consider even the most complex cognitive functions, such as language, anatomically determined and constrained capacities. This was made possible by the evolution of central (brain) and peripheral (vocal tracts) correlates that have linked us to our predecessors, even though we differ in our possibilities (Minelli 2007; Falzone 2014).

Considering the presence within the animal kingdom of several species that possess a vocal repertoire made of songs and calls that can be defined as species-specific, it is safe to assess that the biological roots of musicality are to be found precisely in vocal communication. Specifically, animals accustomed to using sounds, songs, and vocalisations within their ecological and social contexts provide important insights. The individual or group performances present in the animal kingdom could be understood here as an expression of musicality precisely because it develops naturally and is therefore tied to the cognitive capacities and biological traits that make its manifestation possible (cf. Honing 2018). The search for the biological underpinnings of musicality inevitably leads biomusicology scholars to attempt to map its roots by leveraging precisely comparative data (Fitch 2006, 2018). The study of components such as rhythm and synchronization has, in my opinion, proven to be among the most compelling for reconstructing human musical capabilities and beyond.

Typically, studies based on the comparative approach assume that if two related (or phylogenetically close) species share a particular trait, then it is very likely that their common ancestor had that trait. Applying this same modality to musical components makes it possible to date the origins of a specific musical trait (see Fitch 2015). At the bio-ethological level, the issue of synchrony is not new. Although in different facets and not necessarily musical, we have several examples of entrainment: fireflies (*Luciola*) that synchronize their light at intervals of about three seconds (Buck 1988), and the migratory movement of birds or schools of fish. While the examples given so far could be understood as species-specific behaviours, coordination to musical rhythm is quite different. Many musical cognitive components show deep roots in brain functions shared by other species (Fitch 2006). For example, the perception of the combination of sounds of a certain pitch with rough sounds originates in the mechanics of the peripheral auditory system of vertebrates. Thus, all primates probably perceive such roughness (Fishman et al. 2000), but only humans are able to understand the eventual pleasantness of these sounds (Vassilakis 2005).

The study of musically relevant abilities in other species has opened a new scenario since the ability of perception and synchronization (BPS), that is, the ability to perceive a rhythm in music and to synchronize the movement of one's body with it (Nettl 2000), until recently thought to be exclusive to humans, has also been manifested in other animal species. Probably the case of Snowball, the yellow-crested cockatoo (*Cacatua sulphurea*) is the most emblematic example in this sense. However, there are also some examples among pinnipeds, less vocally flexible (see Cook et al. 2013). Famous for the video in which he is filmed moving to the rhythm of "Everybody" by the Backstreet Boys, Snowball seems to demonstrate that species equipped with vocal learning are also those capable of moving following a certain rhythm (Schachner et al.

2009). This not only allows for the hypothesis of vocal learning as a precondition for rhythmic perception (Patel 2006) but also that it represents an evolutionary convergence made possible by the close connection between the auditory circuits of the cerebral cortex (Doupe et al. 2005; Patel et al. 2005) and the neural substrates of vocal learning (basal ganglia and motor areas), (Chen et al. 2006). Snowball's choreography not only showed that this animal had a good sense of rhythm but also led to the idea that spontaneous dance is not just for humans.

To avoid any misunderstanding, however, it should be made clear that the ability to synchronise is not a strictly musical adaptation because animals in nature do not have actual music. The fact then, that even some vocal species such as diamonds (*Taeniopygia guttata*), although endowed with the capacity of vocal learning, have shown not to pay any attention to rhythmic regularity (ten Cate et al. 2016). Contrarily, species certainly little known for their vocal and rhythmic ability, such as sea lions (Schusterman 2008), have challenged the hypothesis of Patel (2006) and opened new possible scenarios.

The study of musicality, as well as the ability to perceive, appreciate, and produce music, are certainly to be sought in the musical skills possessed by other species, but in doing so, it is good to consider not only the species with vocal capabilities. The ability to synchronize to a certain rhythm is detectable only in parrots and not in all avian species. For example, it could be a suggestion that synchronization and entrainment are more widespread in the animal kingdom than we think.

Proper consideration of the relationship between music and evolution can only emerge from understanding musical identity within an evolutionary framework and as part of a socio-cultural and linguistic context. If we understand musicality as an element at the basis of motor behaviour, and at the same time evaluate the infant's first vocalisations in the communicative exchange he has with his mother, we will realise that they are woven on musicality (cf. Trevarthen 1999). Musicality could be understood as a cognitive capacity (cf. Cross 2000) resulting from the need to want to interact with one's conspecifics. This can occur although one possesses great vocal skills. Like language, music is not a private matter but a social matter, and its nature is to share. Putting ourselves in this perspective, we attribute to musicality a biological time and a cultural time; there is no need to consider as natural what can be genetically transmitted and what culture all that remains.

The perception of rhythm should then be intended as a combination of factors, including the ability to represent one's own biorhythms and the ability to synchronize with the rhythm of perceived sounds. Animals capable of perceiving rhythm and synchronizing to it are essentially social animals. Therefore, rhythm is a central aspect of vocal communications (think singing primates), and other behaviours subordinate to rhythm, such as the synchronization of movements of frogs and crickets (Kotz et al. 2018; Gamba et al. 2016). This leads us to think that the perception of rhythm as an essential part of musicality has a strong adaptive value not only because it is an element to draw on during courtship (see the synchronous movement of claws in the courtship of the fiddler crab), but especially because it plays a role in the formation and intensification of social bonds.

At this point, it is more than ever useful to give a representation of which categories help us to define human and animal musical activity. The theoretical proposal of Martinelli (2011) identifies three possible categories: structures, practices, and experiences, which in fact, bring together the worlds of zoology and anthropology. The structures are nothing more than the purely musical traits we can summarise in the quality of sounds and their organisation. Practices concern the activities and behaviours related to musical structures, like the emission and reception of sound messages.

Lastly, experiences concern the subjectivity with which the natural phenomenon is experienced. The aspects linked to the practice of music certainly allow us to see more closely the commonalities between the species defined as musical. The environment in which a human being produces music differs from the bioacoustic environment of an animal that has to produce a song that can be heard for miles around. Beyond the differences we can find in musical production between species, the organism's relationship to the environment is fundamental to musical action. Therefore, given my idea of the existence of a common musical basis in all vocal species, music must be understood as the result of a gradual and natural selection process during which the combination of the organism and biological structures has made possible its accommodation, first within vocal communication and then in verbal language. Therefore, the musical question is an animal question, despite those who think that making music or singing is biologically useless.

Chapter 4

BIOLOGICAL FOUNDATIONS OF MUSIC AND LANGUAGE

4.1 Music, Language, and Performativity

Cross's (2014) hypothesis that music should be understood as a communicative and interactive process and not as a mere representation of sounds finds its concrete realisation in studying the neural and hormonal basis of musicality (Chanda and Levitin 2013; Mehr et al. 2019). The data available in literature today suggest that the correct way to describe the interactional-social nature of musicality is by conceiving music as an embodied language rooted in the brain and culturally adapted structures (Clarke et al. 2015). In this chapter, I will attempt to demonstrate that it is possible to talk about music as an embodied language and how music can fit within a model of joint action that enables the performative act to be realised through the involvement of body, interaction, and sociality (Pacherie 2012; Bolt and Loehr 2017; Dell'Anna et al. 2021).

Like language, music straddles between what Dennett (2017) has called genetic and contextual imperatives. As I have repeatedly stated in this book, music has a biological component that it shares with animals endowed with vocalic capabilities and a cultural component given by its ability to create interaction between members of a group. This distinction implies using two divergent approaches to the cognition and biology of music while simultaneously keeping alive the idea that music, regardless of how it is understood, should be studied by applying a biologically oriented approach that values its functional aspects. In this way, the study of species-specific vocal communication systems becomes decisive in identifying the evolutionary and morphological basis that enables our species' vocal and musical performativity.

But what is performativity? The definition of performativity has been the subject of debate in the cognitive sciences, especially since the embodiment paradigm has put the concept of the body back at the centre of the discussion on cognition. While the focus on the role of the body within embodied theories has allowed us to look closely at the role of the sensorimotor system in complex cognitive processes, it has also reignited the debate on the role of bodily, environmental, and relational components that can contribute to the definition of human cognition (O'Regan 2001, 2002; Noë 2004, 2009; Falzone 2018).

Much has been written about embodiment theory in recent decades. Some studies have described the environment as a component of cognition; others have focused on action as a means of constructing cognitive processes; others have focused on sensory perception (Caruana and Borghi 2013; 2016). In this melting pot of notions, the synthesis better known as 4E Cognition - embedded, extended, enacted, and embodied cognition - has proved to be very useful in comparing the different declinations of the role of the body within cognition (Rowlands 2010; Menary 2010; Newen et al. 2018).

The concept of embodiment has also been useful in understanding the principles on which musical interaction is based (Schiavio et al. 2014, 2017; Leman 2017; Lesaffre et al. 2017; van der Schyff and Schiavio 2017). The starting intuition is quite simple: rather than considering a listener as a mind that receives input (sound) and produces output (perceived emotions or bodily movements), the embodied mode considers the listener as being enclosed in a circuit of interaction with their own mind or musical environment. This circuit would be bound by the body itself and thus embodied. For this reason, it is assumed that human musical action and perception are reciprocal processes that fuel the sensorimotor circuit. Thus, action and prediction are co-determined by the constraints of the musical environment and biological ones (Leman 2017; Leman and Maes 2015).

The main idea of the embodied music cognition paradigm is that musical interaction is established through bodily articulations and imitations of physical information sensed from the musical environment. According to Leman (2007), the human body can be seen as a biologically designed mediator, capable of transferring action-oriented physical energy to a mental level where it forms values, experiences, and intentions, among others, the fundamental components of musical meaning. This means that the sense-motor experience provides the essential mechanism underlying the expressive interaction between musician and instrument; this sense-motor experience is rooted in a neuropsychological process, which, shaped by the evolution of the central nervous system, allows us to distinguish the external world from the internal one. However, it should not be forgotten that the social mode through which joint-action occurs (Schilbach et al. 2013; Hari et al. 2015) is a default feature of the sapiens brain and all animal species.

To support the idea of cognitively embodied music, Leman and Maes (2015) offer two possibilities. The first is to show that embodiment plays a central role in the connection between cognitive and emotional functions; this is crucial regarding the use of instruments and functions that provide meaning to music. The second is to demonstrate that embodiment is more than just the effect of music on the action. Both approaches are not mutually exclusive but are complementary and necessary for the thesis of embodied music cognition.

According to this theoretical perspective, the mechanisms underlying the musical meaning formation are rooted in sensorimotor principles, meaning that musical perception's influence on human action works reciprocally. In this context, Leman and Maes (2015) refer to the concepts of selective attention and signal identification to explain how body movements, performed to music, can direct attention to specific musical signals. These mechanisms can guide the perception of structural features of music (melody, rhythm, pitch, etc.) in a specific direction as well as convey affective properties related to expressiveness and intentionality. Hence, how can an action be defined as musically embodied?

I think the idea of the body and what it can do is more in line with the concept of performativity from an evolutionary perspective rather than corporatised mental processes. This may seem to be too generic of a view of the subject. Still, when one embraces an evolutionary perspective, the body becomes the highest expression of what biological evolution has made possible. This is not to say that the body is not the medium through which music can take on an expressive form. Music is a holistic and multimodal form of language; therefore, it can convey information related to the sense of hearing, implicit visual information (imagining movement), somatosensory information (perceiving movement), and emotional information. For this to happen, the body is crucial, but the idea of embodied music should not exclude the possibility that there may be a model that envisages an interdependence between movement, emotion, and perception as part of a specific embodied module (cf. Barsalou 1999; 2010).

In this regard, I am much more comfortable with the grounded cognition hypothesis since this model of perception-action processing, in addition to being connected to language, also allows for the conceptualisation and narrative sharing of musical experience and aesthetics (Barsalou 2010). From this point of view, the studies of grounded cognition (Barsalou, 1999) have tried to show how language is closely linked to cognitive skills like perception or the ability to interact with the world around us through action. They do this because they think that action and motor interaction have been called for by language as it has evolved. According to grounded cognition, they play a decisive role in the processes of constructing our representations. In linguistics, this approach has tried to demonstrate how the body, simulation, and cognition are constitutive parts of the linguistic function (Lakoff and Johnson 1999). Investigating the role of the body in the study of language implies studying the biological foundations of language, and this, consequently, opens up new scenarios, especially from the point of view of the tendency to limit the study of the body to the study of the brain. Clearly, the way in which language rules develop in a biological body is to be considered a central and not an accessory fact of the linguistic function (Pennisi 2021). The concept of "grounded" is therefore preferable to "embodied" since the latter might lead to the mistaken belief that only body states are to be considered necessary for cognition (Barsalou 2008). For this reason, he suggests that cognitive processes are "grounded" in multiple ways, including simulations and situated action along with body states.

From the moment one decides to consider language as a biological form of embodied species-specific intelligence, one must not only consider the body structures based on evolution, but one must first understand how a given biological constitution makes a given function possible (cf. Pennisi 2021; Buccino et al. 2016). This is intended to argue that all intelligent behaviour of human and nonhuman animals arises from specific capacities of their bodies (Pennisi 2021). Therefore cognition cannot be understood as the product of something. It makes more sense as Shapiro (2004) tries to show that the different structuring of bodies creates different bits of intelligence. A small functional mechanical difference is enough to bring about profound cognitive and mental adaptations (Carroll 2006).

In the case of language, the hearing-voice combination has enabled our brain to receive and process vocal feedback, which in turn has meaning. Several authors (Lahav et al. 2007; Viinikainen et al. 2012; Aggius - Vella et al. 2017), for example, have argued that we tend to mentally imitate the action that produces the sound and imagine tracing and drawing its contours as it unfolds. To carry out an evolutionary analysis of language, it is first necessary to rediscover the dimension of the organism as a mind-body whole that moves and performs its biological functions in the environment. Therefore, just as a mind cannot exist without a brain, the latter cannot exist without a body. The mind-body complex only exists within a social and environmental context in which it develops dynamically, contingently, and functionally for its survival (Pennisi 2016; 2021; Pennisi and Falzone 2016). For this reason, I believe that the embodied perspective can only be partially useful to the hypothesis supported in these pages.

From an evolutionary perspective, what a body can do is not to be understood as a special condition within which to locate the human being but rather as a binding condition for the survival of a species. Performativity is clearly a cognitive mechanism of the species, but to be functional, it needs the body through which it is carried out to develop certain structures. The current vision of embodied cognition, including that, applied to music, seems to have espoused an excessively cerebrocentric view and therefore makes the mistake of not considering the impact that the slow and gradual evolution of the body has had on the sometimes more rapid functioning of the neurocerebral systems (Pennisi 2016; 2021).

It is clear now impossible to imagine a cognitive science that does not deal with the structures of the body in which cognitive processes take place (Rowlands 2010; Shapiro 2011), but it is equally true that many of the hypotheses in literature tend to provide a weakened view of those body structures that deal with perceptual and emotional functions. To get out of this theoretical bind, there is no better solution than to suggest a cognitive theory of performativity to be implemented through the study of phylogeny and ontogeny of language. It is, therefore, a question of considering the close correlation between language's biological constraints and linguistic cognition's maturation processes. In such a scenario, ideas about language and how it may have evolved are certainly varied. Therefore, thinking that music may have been a matrix force in the evolutionary processes that led to language development can only fuel the current debate on the biological bases shared by both.

For this reason, the performativity I am referring to in these pages has nothing to do with the enactment of a performance of artistic nature. My idea is to rethink language as a performative act made possible by a biological, and therefore natural, body. Briefly taking my inspiration from Austin's study (1955), we cannot fail to mention his distinction between performative and constative[1] utterances, in which language not only has a descriptive function but is also action. Performance designates an area of human action in which attention is paid to the way in which communicative acts are performed (Briggs and Bauman 1992), but it is equally true that the use of biological data has made it possible to place linguistic capacity within an interpretative framework that considers the study of material (or morphological) structures on which complex functions are instantiated (Minelli 2007).

The key to the musicality of our language thus lies in that peculiar education of the organs of phonation as defined by Valentin in 1855, i.e., in the prosodic variation that involves each phoneme and whose modulation allows the implementation of prosodic features such as accent, tone, joint, and rhythm (Nespor and Vogel 2007). The modulation of the voice, the acted word (as understood by Austin), and the rhythm that marks dialogue and silence come to life thanks to those performative components, bound by the bodily structures to which language is ontogenetically and phylogenetically linked.

---

[1] Austin (1955) divided words into two categories: constatives (words that describe a situation) and performatives (words that incite action).

4.2 Vocal Performativity: Morphological Aspects and Biological Constraints

As already discussed by Darwin in 1871, the improvement of phonatory organs played a key role in the origin of language: it is not by chance that an immediate consequence of such morphological perfecting was the inception of early vocalisations in non-human primates. This phenomenon allowed us to hypothesize that the ability to modulate sounds (motherese) emerged first, almost as a sort of primitive song; it was later followed by an increasingly complex vocal imitation, eventually marking the inception of articulate language. The development of a non-referential communicative system such as motherese has certainly affected the nature of our language; nevertheless, morphological variants (which bonded us to motherese first, and proper language later) were necessary for linguistic expressiveness to become functional. A more sophisticated way of communicating makes it possible to send emotional information, and emotional prosody may have played a key role in this (Morley 2013; 2014). Discussing the species-specificity of articulate language became possible after applying the EvoDevo perspective to vocal communication. This introduced the concept of biological constraint, seen as morphological and structural conditioning which, in turn, drove the *Sapiens* to resort to verbal language to decodify and represent the knowledge of their own world (cf. Hagoort et al. 2004). It appears adequate, at this point, to clarify the usage of 'constraint': while it involves various research areas within the macro-investigation of evolutionary processes, the term has often been used quite generically (Antonovics and Van Tienderen 1991). For a clear grasp of its meaning and possible applicability across the evolutionary process, reference literature can be helpful (Gould 1980, 1989; Maynard Smith et al. 1985; Bürger 1986; Stearns 1986; Wagner 1988; Arnold 1992; Sarà 1993). In any case, I believe that Gould's perspective (1989) explains clearly and definitively the connection between a structure and its functional possibilities.

Gould defines constraints as the elements that determine the direction of a given change or prevent selection from carrying out changes. This means that the evolutionary change of a given structure depends on the influence exerted by natural selection on genetic variability. Gould's analysis is hinged on the etymological component of the term, which has both positive and negative effects: what is positive is that such constraints force or phenotypical channel changes according to phylogenetic contingencies; oppositely, constraints are often interpreted as hindering or restricting natural selection.

The relationship between constraints and natural selection is far from clear (cf. Dullemeijer 1991); therefore, when approaching this phenomenon, the best solution is to consider the evolutionary mechanism based on the role played by biological constraints. In line with Gould and Lewontin's hypothesis (1979) on the types of action exerted by natural selection, it can be inferred that the latter also operates constantly because of the constraints imposed by the organic structure. Thus, evolution would result from interactions between selective push and structural resistances (Pievani 2005). Given the findings discussed so far and borrowing from Balari and Lorenzo's perspective (2015), it can now be argued that language is clearly the result of biological development. This development defined the organs in charge of hearing and verbal articulation through neural growth, ensuring the neural control of tasks linked with the articulation and the processing of vocal sounds.

The requisition of a structure to repurpose it for a function that is different from the original one is, therefore, not an exception. Thus, it is possible to refute a direct connection between language and the adaptability of the supralaryngeal vocal tract (from now on SVT). Many studies (Aiello 1996; Stedman et al. 2004; Fitch 2005a; Rotilio 2006) offered various alternative hypotheses to prove this lack of connection, demonstrating how peripheral structures (although comparable with non-human animals) show clear adaptive advantages that are not directly linked with the linguistic function. The main issue of the origin of language theories lies in providing an exhaustive clarification of how the evolution of such a complex cognitive ability happened in such a short evolutionary time. I believe that one of the possible explanations for this problem is that the cognitive abilities currently seen as crucial for the execution of articulated language are phylogenetically very old. For this reason, it makes sense to assume that this faculty originated in non-human primates far earlier than its inception in modern *Sapiens* (cf. Zuberbühler 2005).

The selection of SVT responsible for the vocal performance has also enabled the modulation of sounds, which, other than representing a potential social advantage (cf. Cheney and Seyfarth 2018), may have played a crucial role in the inception of articulate language. Vocal modulation, which was already present in non-human primates, not only shows their ability to combine sounds depending on social context but also provides a firm foundation to describe the evolutionary path of human vocality. Within this reconstruction, the modulation of formant frequencies (particularly the F0 fundamental formant) has a prominent role because it allows to distinguish the various sounds that characterise language or vocalisations, providing information about territorial diffusion. Additionally, this phenomenon occurs in human and animal communication (Fitch 2000a; Ghanzanfar and Rendall 2008).

A further element emphasized by Lieberman and Blumstein (1988) is that most differences related to human and animal vocality depend on the dimension of the larynx and the length of the SVT. Acoustic characteristics become vital when recognizing and communicating between individuals of the same species. The fundamental elements needed to recognize the communicative potentialities of a speaker are the length of the SVT, strictly related to body size (Fitch 1997; 2000a), and the formant frequencies (Taylor and Reby 2010).

Of course, there are species-specific differences in each species' vocal performance. Both non-human animals and sapiens can perform what their biological limits allow them to in relation to their environment. An example would be the ability of vocal control and modulation. As sopranos are able to modulate their voice through a drastic decrease or increase of the key frequency – they can increase their F0 and pair the first formant to achieve a frequency higher than 1200 Hz (Joliveau et al. 2004; Kreiman and Sidtis 2011) – in the same way, the white-handed gibbons (*Hylobates lar*), during their song, can modulate the fundamental frequency from F0 at the moment of opening their mouth and push it to F1 when the laryngeal sound is amplified and enriched by the harmonies (Koda et al. 2012). Their sound propagation ability rests on both the efficiency of their larynx and the brevity of their vocal cords: the thicker and longer the vocal plicae, the lower the vibration frequency. According to Némai and Keleman (1933), gibbons possess a double string of vocal ligaments attached to the bifurcated vocal processes of the arytenoid cartilages bilaterally (cf. Koda et al. 2012), which might contribute to keeping an increased tension of vocal folds.

The ability to modulate F0 and the base formant (not only in non-human primates but also in other species of mammals and birds) is the demonstration of a slow and gradual evolution of those structures that have been instantiated in the bodies of human and non-human primates (Pisansky et al. 2016). Let us point out that an increasing amount of evidence (Karpf 2006) suggests how the *Sapiens* species can willingly modulate its voice in social contexts such as job interviews, political debates, or when attempting to deceive somebody (Anolli and Ciceri 1997). In the same way, according to Lameira and colleagues (2016), orangutans would be able to modulate the tone and volume of vocalisations produced while imitating human sounds.

Applying a physiological and biological approach to the study of the voice, the data that emerge show that despite the use of vocalisations, songs and grunts are common across the animal kingdom; nevertheless, human beings are the only species in which vocal expression achieves the communicative efficiency and elegance of words (Fant 1960; Marler 1975; Mitani and Stuht 1998; Ghazanfar and Hauser 1999; Fischer 2003; Swadesh 2017).

Although the *Sapiens'* articulating ability derives from non-human primates, its vocality-related structures are specific, emphasizing the functional finesse of our species. Simonyan and Horwitz (2011) observed that in a human body, the innervation of the laryngeal nucleus is directed to the motor cortex. Although marginally involved in controlling innate vocalisations, the latter becomes crucial to oversee learnt and voluntary vocal behaviours, such as speech and song (Simonvan et al. 2009). Regardless of the evidence provided by this data, some linguistic theories (Chomsky 1975; Hauser et al. 2014; Berwick and Chomsky 2016), to this day, show a completely different stance, refusing the possibility that linguistic performativity is made possible by biological components, in favour of a theory that rests on the universality of language.

Yet, within the discussion on species-specificity, it is possible to identify some dichotomies like communication. In fact, from a structural point of view, according to some theories, SVT is to be considered a mark of the uniqueness of human language (Lieberman 1984) because of its curved conformation with two barrels, with the horizontal barrel of the same size as the vertical one (1:1) allows the production of formant frequencies in a constant manner and with a very wide frequency range. (Fant 1960; Taylor and Reby 2010; Gamba 2014). In terms of functional possibilities, instead, the morphological specialization responsible for the correct performance of articulate language must be considered (cf. Van Eijden and Turkawski 2001).

Supporting the idea of morphological continuity of the structures involved in articulate language implies considering that human articulatory abilities derive from a mutation in the previous anatomical structure, as well as being a special adaptation of the respiratory acts linked to phonation (cf. Lo Piparo 2001). For this reason, the biological necessities intertwined with communication include the morpho-functional components responsible for articulation and the process of adapting and re-functionalizing the involved structures. However, knowing the given function of a given structure is not sufficient to understand the evolutionary dynamics of functional and structural adaptations. At this point, understanding the history of evolutionary change can shed light on the subject (Pennisi and Falzone 2010).

4.3 Music as Adaptation

So far, the evolutionary, cognitive, and performative relationship between music and language has prompted me to search for as many clues as possible on which to base my thesis. Many of these clues come from the comparative analysis between music and verbal language, from which I believe an incontrovertible fact has emerged: using prosodic modulation is decisive for transferring pragmatic, syntactic, and emotional information. Regardless of the adopted investigative approach, possessing a communicative system undeniably constitutes a strong evolutionary advantage. Through a closer examination of the linguistic evolution concept, we can see how the diffusion of languages is much faster when they are not constrained by the social rules, expansion, parental degree, or economic control of a dominating population (Cavalli Sforza 2004).

In the same way, the evidence available in literature shows that music has existed in our species since the dawn of time. Archaeological findings prove that traces of musical activity can be found wherever human remains are present (Levitin 2006), and this opens up a much-debated issue in the current study of language evolution, namely the possible adaptive value of music for the human species.

According to Pinker's interpretation (Pinker 1997), music would be nothing more than an *auditory cheesecake*, a trait selected for the sole purpose of delighting our lives, which is also guilty of exerting a parasitic action on language. Music would not be a primarily functional activity for our survival, being therefore useless from a biological point of view. Yet, Huron (2001) highlighted the necessity of understanding the advantages of individuals with musical behaviour compared to subjects who lack it.

As Pinker argued, if the music were a non-adaptive component, it would have died out; any activity with low adaptive value has little survival chance because behaviour that yields no advantages is meaningless. Pinker's criticisms mainly rest on a mistaken interpretation of the concept of adaptation (a mistake made by many music researchers, according to his words). The definition of adaptation does not refer to a trait that is healthy, frivolous, or reassuring; rather, it involves all the requisites capable of increasing one's offspring (Pinker 1997). To acknowledge the biological value of music, its involvement in reproduction or survival dynamics should be proved. If I imagine the possible evolutionary paths leading to the origin of music and explain its inception in adaptive terms, I cannot exclude at least three theoretical paradigms: a) sexual selection (Darwin 1871; Miller 2000); b) kin selection (Fitch 2004; 2007; 2009); c) group selection (Mithen 2005; Cross 2007).

In 1871, Darwin suggested that the features of sexual selection contributed to the evolution of the species' cognitive abilities. He acknowledged the musicality of some species as an essential component of evolutionary fitness, creating a sort of romantic explanation. According to his theory, it was plausible that music had existed since ancient times, as well as encouraging a sort of 'kindest emotions reawakening' thanks to its combination of rhythm and tone. For this reason, our ancestors would have used a musical protolanguage to establish social bonds before moving to the verbal one. Although leaning towards Darwin's hypothesis on sexual selection, the current evolutionary theory allows a wider perspective on the scenario. Acquiring musical abilities can be interpreted as an evolutionary adaptation shaped by natural and sexual selection. In turn, selection guaranteed the universality of this capability also through its strengthening effect on the group and interpersonal relationships (Miller 2000). This leads us to discuss the evolutionary meaning of music and how it may have held a sexual attraction value (in the same way as a peacock's tail). Across the animal world, any element that can be an attractive sign of sexual nature (long tails, unique plumage, melodic singing, the building of nests) plays a clear communicative role other than being biologically relevant.

It is not completely clear what forced our ancestors to develop the syntactical and recombinatory parts that are necessary for melodic expression. However, it is possible to argue that bird songs, music, and language all evolved from the same place because they all have similar mechanisms and behaviours (Jarvis 2004). Initially interpreted as a sort of survival and courting paradigm, Darwin's theory on music is the first valid hypothesis on how morphological structures involved in both the mechanism and execution of singing differ, depending on the gender (cf. Snowdon 2004; Geissman and Nijman 2006; Giacoma et al. 2010; Garcia and Favaro 2017). Despite having little knowledge of the vocal structures involved in vocalisation, Darwin's hypothesis rests on observing species such as birds, gibbons, and howler monkeys, establishing that the half-human ancestor of the modern *Homo sapiens* may have been a sort of primate/hominid with singing abilities.

If it is true that primates' vocalisations played a key role in the inception of musical protolanguage, it follows that the morphogenetic comparison and the potential type of selective pressures (which occurred during the evolutionary history of human and non-human primates) constitute essential starting elements. Sexual selection, which Darwin saw as a mechanism to explain the reproductive success of a species, acts as a litmus paper marking the aesthetic, morphological, and behavioural features as actual fitness indicators. Moreover, these features probably regulate a species's survival faster than natural selection (cf. Pilastro 2007).

As with birdsongs observed by Darwin, language could thus represent a form of courting made by millions of words. The voice tone modulated according to age, gender, sexual maturity, and hormonal level may sound attractive to the listener (Miller 2000). While Darwin did not explicitly state that the singing selection might have been the prompting element for the evolution of human vocal and musical abilities, in the last pages of his work, there is a clear link between human music and sexual selection. It should be pointed out that he spoke of 'musical development abilities' and not of actual, proper vocal abilities.

Notwithstanding this fact, the Darwinian paradigm does not prevent us from arguing the existence of a musical protolanguage, which evolved primarily within the mother-offspring communication; neither excludes the influence of natural selection on the evolution of morphological structures used across communication (cf. Menninghaus 2013). Be that as it may, modern evolutionary biology has led us to explore other potential solutions. The paradigm of Rougharden (2012), for example, has demolished some of the

Darwinian pillars on which sexual selection is founded. The biologist saw social selection as the pivotal element upon which some natural choices are made. In other words, females are not necessarily attracted by the most eye-catching traits (until today interpreted as good gene carriers) but also consider males' active abilities, such as offspring care or the role within the social hierarchy.

In light of the contemporary biological debate, Darwin's stance on sexual selection and its potential link with musical protolanguage can be questioned based on two elements. First, musical protolanguage has equal development across males and females (the latter occasionally shows superior linguistic competencies to males). Secondly, both genders develop the same linguistic ability to conquer the best partner (Fitch 2004; 2009; 2017), even if recent ethological studies proved the existence of songs in female birds as well (Slater and Mann 2004; Garamszegi et al. 2007; Odom et al. 2014).

Fitch's view (2004) offers an alternative to this theory, according to which music was originally employed in a childhood assistance context (e.g., lullabies). The acquisition of a binding social value could simply be a collateral effect of this central function, while its occasional use in courting may be an incorrect clue to pursue. Fitch's theoretical stance leads us to a selection model based on almost immediate advantages, made possible by behaviours carried out within the closest kinship (e.g., parental care).

The model in question, known as kin selection, was originally suggested by Hamilton (1964; 1965) to provide a genetic motivation for social bonds between animals and their kinship. According to this theory, when two groups aim for the same resources, prompting a competition scenario, the individuals of a group activity with an unfavourable (or altruist) behaviour take advantage of their blood relatives and preserve their survival. In doing so, they increase their personal fitness and their genetic makeup, that is, their inclusive fitness. But how is this model useful for explaining the inception of musical protolanguage?

The answer may lie in those communication systems that evolved within a parental system: the so-called mother languages that proved crucial for the evolution of complex communication systems such as verbal language. The ease of transmission of these languages would rest on a principle of honest communication, where the speaker and the listener show a certain involvement because of mutual genetic interest (Fitch 2004). An honest communication (Dawkins and Guilford 1991), producing an accurate but not necessarily perfect signal containing relevant information for the listener (gender, species, dimensions, etc.), represents an advantage in terms of inclusive fitness. From a kin selection point of view, a subject that emits a signal while having the adequate cognitive ability to deceive the listener and obtain a reproductive advantage would not do so based on a sort of altruist sacrifice (cf.

Trivers 1971; 1974; 1985), which the individual carries out to advantage a family member.

This scenario inevitably involves the hypothesis of signal reliability supported by Zahavi (1977), according to which inter- and intra-specific animal communication would always be based on producing a reliable signal. This phenomenon occurs because transmitting the signal implies an energy cost or a morphological or behavioural investment that proves its validity (cf. Falzone 2012). The metabolic costs sustained to produce an honest signal are not an exception. According to studies that measured energy costs during linguistic and non-linguistic production (cf. Horn et al. 1995; McCarty 1996; Lachmann et al. 2001), the execution of an honest communication would have a surprising low metabolic cost. However, these studies do not allow us to discuss the reliability of the signal.

Additionally, their investigation is different from the hypotheses on the evolution of language, which demonstrate how the production of formant frequencies (in both human beings and other vertebrates) requires an effort or a cost borne by the morphological structures responsible for its execution. The production of articulated sounds is all but economical: let us think of lowering our larynx, crucial indeed for the phonation process but also responsible for the transit of food and air through the same tract. There is a potential choking risk if the epiglottis does not seal the respiratory tract properly (cf. Negus 1949; 1927). Therefore, speaking is a costly activity that implies a high oxygen consumption while decreasing the CO_2 expulsion frequency. The result is overall body fatigue, the consequence of the accumulation of elements involved in metabolic synthesis (Moon and Lindblom 2003).

At this point, if the production of an honest signal represents the default communication condition, how can the production of a deceptive signal be explained in adaptive terms? When an animal pretends (unconsciously) to be larger than it really is, it does so by producing antennal frequencies (e.g., the red deer muscularly lowering its larynx to obtain a greater resonance and a consequent increase in the severity of the signal), which gives it a clear advantage in terms of reproduction. This is because, in most cases, the length of the SVT is related to body size. Therefore, the same formants that will be produced are a clue to the body size of the animal producing the vocalisation (Fitch 1997; Fitch and Giedd, 1999; Hauser and Fitch 2003). Considering this argument, transmitting information about one's own body size would not entail any cost because it is the result of the anatomy of the vocal apparatus possessed by the animal.

Deceit is the result of natural selection, which sometimes emphasises formant frequencies through the elongation of the vocal tract beyond its anatomic boundaries (Fitch and Reby 2001; Fitch 1999). The root of the deceit would thus lie in the structural adaptation, while the signal remains true. From a kin selection perspective, all signals produced by non-human primates to communicate about the presence of food and predators may be explained as a helping instrument for individuals of the same species. The phenomenon's importance does not rest, for example, on counting how many different alarm calls a given species can produce, but rather on the adaptive meaning hidden in processing that signal. Various hypotheses discussed the advantages for the subject who emits the alarm, concluding that while related individuals benefit from the alarm signal by fleeing and increasing their receptiveness, the emitting subject increases his/her own inclusive fitness (cf. Dundford 1977; Fitch 2004; Meuthen et al. 2014).

Kin selection may have been useful to establish the specificity of signals (cf. Sevfarth et al. 1980), i.e., to distinguish aerial predators from terrestrial ones. These calls and songs during the species' life seem quite common. According to Fitch (2004), they may represent the crucial starting point for the explanation of how language has evolved, as they constitute parental and honest communication. Such a rudimentary communication may seem almost intentional if explained through the kin selection perspective. Long-distance songs produced by gibbons are a good example of this phenomenon. As this species is where groups change frequently, members from different groups scattered across the territory may be related. Therefore, one of the evolutionary drives capable of selecting long-distance song emissions may lie in encouraging the reproduction of one's own genes, helping individuals with a similar genetic patrimony, that is, parents and offspring (Clarke et al. 2006). If I want to employ the communicative ability of non-human primates as an element to explain vocal continuity, I should argue that the shift from prosodic protolanguage to propositional language lies precisely in the melodic structure of these signals. Such shifting became possible after a communication impulse occurred across genetically related individuals (Fitch 2004; 2005). Other than encouraging the perpetuation of common genes, it would have been functional for their survival, generating selective advantages because of the emotional effects developed during interactions with their offspring (Falk 2004).

Besides the genetic and reproductive advantages, having a form of communication may also be indispensable to sustain any social organisation (Bickerton 2002; Dunbar 2003). Once the necessary cognitive possibilities to share information, emotions, or behaviours (cf. Tomasello 1999; 2008; Ulbaek 1998) emerge, the inception of a communication form is unavoidable. Because animals living in groups interact continuously, it becomes evident that the most significant aspects of communication that guarantee the species' survival (signals for food, alarms, or defence of the territory). Available data allow us to approach language after identifying those modes shared with other animals.

Specifically, the combinatory ability of some sounds uttered by bonobos and baboons plays a significant role in social terms (Engh et al. 2006). The social aspect of communication, while often underestimated by authors such as Falk (2009), clearly proves that the emission of some signals allows to establish special relationships: I am talking about relationships that are not based on the sexual aspect (Barber 2004), but rather on an emotional and cognitive involvement (Fox et al. 2001).

The production of songs and calls in the vocal behaviour of non-human primates plays an important role in keeping contact with the group members during movement, other than localizing their position (Gamba et al. 2012): from this, it may be inferred not only the privileged position of vocal communication during the development of social relationships but also the existence of cultural and social constraints (cf. Zuidema 2013; Morley 2013; Merker et al. 2015), which confirm the adaptive role of vocal communication. Let us not forget the further functional role of music, its capability to crystallize coordination and group bonds through the production of songs and music (Blacking 1995). The debate on the potential social roots of our language also leads us to consider the possibility that if a species is more social, its communication will equally be richer and more elaborate.

Ethological data provide valid examples: let us think about the communicative modes in eusocial insects or the communicative relationship occurring across dominant and gregarious members of singing primates (e.g., gibbons, indri). It is interesting to consider that the vast majority of the communicative repertoire of animals, both social and solitary, is not limited to food/partner search but is often aimed at other animal species (Zahavi and Zahavi 1975). Non-human primates can selectively answer calls, showing a representational process (Cheney and Seyfarth 1990; Hauser 1998; Gifford et al. 2005; Andics and Faragó 2019) resting on the available acoustic information; this allows them a form of vocal expression, which is socially binding in terms of organization. The theory for non-human primates is devoid of the referential communication system (Premack 1986) and may appear radical.

I believe, that even though animal vocalisations do not possess the referential power of human words (both in objective and emotional terms), their system is advanced enough to be classified as the precursor of articulated language. When we speak of language, we refer to communication-based on a lexicalized structure, made up of semantics and syntax, and in which pragmatic skills seem superfluous in terms of encoding meaning (cf. Scott-Phillips 2015). Although these features are not present across most animal vocalisations, there are universal statistical patterns that do not depend on the communication system (cf. Favaro et al. 2020). It is the case of the emotional nature of signals produced by the animal species, which has occasionally been interpreted as a deterrent against deceit or conflict (cf. Power 1998).

Certainly, the purely contextual use of animal vocalizations (alarm calls, food calls, courtship calls) constrained this communication to express signals related to some kind of need. In contrast, sapiens' verbal language is not constrained to attaining a need, is never an end in itself, and does not run out once produced; rather, it leaves traces. At the same time, however, many animal calls have an emotional origin, which is an effective starting point for developing a perspective on the similarities between sounds and music: while both hold an emotional meaning, no symbolic one can be observed in human and animal songs.

The necessary requirement for a reconstruction of the music origin is a theory known as Musilanguage (Brown 2000), where music and language are viewed as mutual specializations of a precursor with a double nature, which resorts to the emotion and reference of sound to create communicative sounds. A protolanguage made of isochrone rhythms and discreet signals may have diffused precisely through group selection because, across the so-called social species, complex communication forms guarantee the upkeeping of relationships within groups. A socio-biological approach can be helpful in explaining this theory. When eusocial species (swarms, flocks) move in a coordinated way, the phenomenon can be easily explained by virtue of behavioural norms within the group. However, the role of vocality is crucial to achieving this social organization. Through moving calls, for example, meerkats (*Suricata suricatta*) can decide to change their food source. Generally carried out by two or three group members, such vocal coordination affects the actions of all other individuals, making them switch to a different food source and move faster within the territory (Bousquet et al. 2010).

The hypothesis of a co-determination between song/vocal signals and social structures implies, in my view, a co-determination of the cognitive structures. Therefore, songs may have developed to vehiculate concrete meanings before the inception of verbal language itself, becoming a protolanguage on which language itself would have flourished at least from a melodic/prosodic point of view (cf. Anastasi 2014). Considering everything discussed so far, it can be stated that human vocality represents, within the construction of social relationships, a strong cognitive restraint that allows a sort of communication bond. Such a bond would have co-evolved with the corporeal one and re-functionalized for complex cognitive tasks (Falzone and Anastasi 2018). Although the hypotheses above are indeed fascinating, it is also possible that they result being mere speculative paradigms. As language is not prone to fossilization, a plausible and exhaustive explanation of its evolution remains a difficult endeavour. For this reason, the Darwinian theory of musical protolanguage still appears to be the most congenial in terms of functional reconstruction and experimental research.

4.4 Music as Exaptation

Resting on the idea that primates' vocalisations can represent a protolinguistic form, it is suitable to clarify the morphological instruments of both human and non-human primates and the selective pressures to which they were subject. Length of the SVT and larynx dimensions define most of the differences between human and non-human vocality (cf. Fitch and Reby 2001). Therefore, when investigating the vocalisation systems, it is necessary to consider the constraining relationship between the anatomical structure and its function (Falzone et al. 2014). The hypothesis of how anatomical precursors are also functional across species can be found in the primates, which, although phylogenetically distant from us, possess an SVT that allows them to vocalize and elaborate complex songs. The articulated language, a result of coordinating the peripheral anatomical structures, plays a crucial role in producing language sounds (motherese included). Once a parallel between ontogenetic and phylogenetic development is established, I can evaluate the hypothesis that argues how components of our peripheral structures were initially born as completely independent organs. After an exaptation process (Gould and Vrba 1982), they were predisposed to executing vocalisations and songs in non-human primates first, for musical protolanguage later, and eventually proper language in the *Sapiens* (Anastasi 2016).

The anatomy of human SVT, with a permanently low position of the larynx, represents a typical case of exaptation: in fact, it allowed an anatomical trait (which was initially selected for a neutral or non-adaptive function) to be reused (cf. Pievani 2005). In this case, reusing these structures gave way to the inception of language. Although the species-specificity of a larynx in a low position makes *Sapiens* the only beings able to produce articulated language (Lieberman and Blumstein 1988), it is also true that ethological studies paved the way for the debate about anatomical homologies between human verbal language and animal communication. Thus, comparative analysis of other living species plays a crucial role in the correct reconstruction of the evolution of language; in fact, it helps understand how and why human vocal communication took a different path from the primates' one during its evolutionary history (Fitch 2000b). Studying the primates' vocal behaviour is relevant to identifying analogies that allow us to infer the presence (or absence) of specific traits shared with our common ancestors. An ethological comparison shows that most differences related to the human and non-human voice are determined by the laryngeal size and the length of SVT. In non-human mammals, for example, the structure of vocalisations differs depending on factors such as species, individual identity, and social context (Lieberman and Blumstein 1988). What is crucial for communication is not the anatomical structure itself but the formant production enabled by that structure (Fitch 1997; Taylor and Reby 2010).

Formant frequencies are susceptible to the slightest change in the transversal section, especially in the constriction point between the vocal cords and the beginning of the oral cavity (Lieberman 2006). Ethologically speaking, a valid example of this phenomenon is the Indri lemur (*Indri indri*): this animal can enlarge his mouth to alter the vocal tract length, producing tones and frequencies loud enough to be heard at a great distance (Gamba et al. 2011), in the same way as human singers do (Sundberg 1975). This is a valid example of how anatomical precursors are functional precursors within species.

When attempting a reconstruction of the origin of language, a critical element is the absence of an intermediate vocal form, a sort of bridge between the vocal repertoire of primates and the human language. In reinterpreting some defining elements of evolutionary history, I can give more importance to the hypotheses of structural continuity, so much, so that structural similarity with other species is considered part of the genomic toolkit (Kaufmann 2000), which preserved the genetic aspect of the specie and guaranteed the consolidation of structures during evolution.

Thanks to the process that drives the whole morphological and structural features of an organism according to its genetic substrate, natural selection allows changes and preserves the stability of a species. Hence, it becomes possible to establish the limitations, shapes, and functions of a structure (Minelli 2007). Applying an ethological perspective to language allows us to understand how even the smallest difference (be it mechanical or related to genetically modified traits), other than having a functional role in performance and behaviours linked to the species' fitness, can also determine deep cognitive adaptations (cf. Carroll 2005). Human articulated language, the result of adaptation and re-functionalization of organs originally designated for respiration and deglutition, requires us to consider the link between structural continuity and functional realisation. Based on my hypothesis, the species-specificity of the human vocal structure was positively selected with the same devices and functions of non-human phonatory structures. The re-adaptation of *Sapiens*' vocal structure lies outside the initial tasks assigned by the selection, constraining the *Sapiens* to produce sounds in more or less complex sequences and with typical formant frequencies (cf. Pennisi and Falzone 2016).

The vocal production in various animal species and the ability to generate real songs could, represent the natural precursor to language. Language, music, and the complex vocal sequences of some animal songs are nothing more than forms of communication that have reached a considerable degree of structural and functional complexity during their evolution. This, in addition to highlighting unique and shared mechanisms, makes it possible to identify these structures' cognitive and evolutionary components. In this quick review of mine, the need to use a non-anthropocentric approach emerges since I believe it is the only one capable of describing what is relevant in the study of vocal and linguistic communication.

4.5 Music as a Natural Precursor of Language

The alternation of linguistic theories allowed us to explain music's inception in linguistic terms, spotting analogies and differences with verbal language. Once again, the ethological comparison has been useful to emphasize how the prosodic language and its related vocal control are, for all purposes, the foundation of songs. Although it is easy to hypothesize that early hominids had scarce voice control due to obvious morphological limits (cf. Lieberman and McCarthy 2007), it is also true that they were able to develop a wide variety of sounds giving birth to primitive singing. While attempting to chronologically mark the moment in which singing emerged and acquired a central role in the *Sapiens*' culture remains a complex task, I have stated that songs can be seen as a precursor of language itself in a prelinguistic context (Anastasi 2016).

During the reconstruction of this broad linguistic puzzle, I identified traits that show similarities with other species (for example, the SVT morphology, allowing us to interpret songs as a natural precursor of language), as well as species-specific traits that pointed to differences across the human phylogenesis (for example prosody, syntax, and grammar). If, on the one hand, the analogies between phylogenetically distant species (cf. Fitch 2000b) enable me to talk about evolutionary convergence, then, on the other hand, the homologies in the acoustic ritualisation (cf. Fitch 2015) hint at the possibility of a common evolutionary legacy. Considering the gap between the *Sapiens* and other non-human animals, most linguists have not considered the possibility that language may have evolved from some common animal ancestor. Once the list of human species-specific traits was refined, it became possible to conduct a comparative study and interpret the differences with other animals as degree differences (Diamond 1992), prompting a reinterpretation of possible evolutionary events.

A typical example can be found in neonates' babbling: the free production of sounds, governed by an innate constraint that determines which sound follows which. Clearly, potential morphological restrictions affect the uttering of vocal sounds (cf. Deacon 2010). The spontaneous production of sounds and the acquisition of linguistic abilities shown by little *Sapiens* during their first months/years of life (cf. Kuhl 2004; Swingley 2009) seems to be, once more, a speciality not exclusive to human beings. Pygmy marmosets (*Cebuella pygmaea*), world's smallest monkeys, represent an exceptional analogous case. Other than communicating with their conspecifics through guttural sounds at a loud level (Elowson et al. 1998), they spontaneously produce a rhythmic and repetitive call within two weeks of life. It is a vocal activity that can be paralleled to the human pre-babbling, which is the early manifestation of an emerging linguistic ability. Soon after the inception of the babbling phase in baby marmosets, adults select some vocal sounds (phee), which become specific during communication. This paves the way for a turn-taking system (Takahashi et al. 2013; 2015), like what occurs between *Sapiens* parents and their offspring, developing a parental relationship within the group to which they belong. The subsequent learning phase entails the offspring losing the vocal peak used to communicate during the first weeks, focusing exclusively on producing the phee. This mechanism of random communication activation engenders an undeniable analogy regarding spontaneous sound production, occurring both in young marmosets and *Sapiens*.

Though it may appear a vocal form devoid of any reference, the difference lies in the vocal production ability of the two species: babbling plays a crucial role in the development of words of *Sapiens* neonates across pygmy marmosets. The vocal production instead decreases after the babbling phase. Except for the difference in the vocal production levels, the structures involved in such products are identical; therefore, I can identify a species-specific communication determined by a common evolutionary base (cf. Falzone 2018). My hypothesis on the continuity with the animal communication systems, at least in terms of structures involved in its execution, implies that the linguistic species-specificity must indeed be interpreted as an adaptive response to unique ecological conditions, but it holds a phylogenetical continuity with other species (Anastasi 2017).

The evolutionary phylogenesis of our musical ancestor is to be sought precisely in those response mechanisms involved in the proto-forms of communication. For this reason, the comparative analysis of language and musical systems lays the foundations to examine two apparently contrasting perspectives in a parallel way. Interdisciplinary studies on the pragmatic and performative nature of linguistic communication (Austin 1962; Davis 1991), ethological research on the role of vocalisations for the survival of the species (Zuberbühler 2009) and the pragmatic nature of the musical performance (Sawyer 2009) contributed to emphasize the primary functional role of musical and vocal communication. Approaching the idea of evolutionary convergence between animal songs, music, and language, as well as a parallel exploration of the mechanical and behavioural parallels they share, may be feasible when considering language features as a result of music.

The elements and theories I discussed in this chapter allowed me to define the concept of vocality across human and non-human species highlighting that, although phylogenetically distant, point to an evolutionary convergence set in motion by selective pressure. The ability to make music, or at least to use forms of musical communication such as songs, is attested in various animal species. The selective pressures that have determined them are part of that very continuum of bio-cognitive elements from which propositional language originated.

CONCLUSION

Through the various yet complementary perspectives encountered within this book, I analysed the elements that relate to music through theoretical assumptions and modes of expression that distinguish it. In the view presented here, I have considered the inevitable appeal that music brings with it. The current scientific literature has made us aware of the ability of music to solicit emotional responses and to become an integral part of our experience. We know that it is possible to wonder about its meanings and give them different keys to interpret them. But how did all this begin?

In this book, I discussed the biological foundations of language, intending to highlight how the vocal structures involved in the modulation of sounds were originally created as the biological basis of music. I believe that music is closely related to language and represents, in all probability, a part of language itself. The human musical ability resulting from a combination of components, probably the result of social and environmental challenges faced by our species during its evolution, has been fundamental to identifying the link between animal communication and the musically organized communication of human beings. The undeniable similarities with the communication of non-human primates, determined by the voice's biomechanics, represent in this hypothesis the prelinguistic substrate of communication. Adding to this is the ubiquity of music and its being a social glue that represents itself as proof that it is tethered by a biological and cultural bond (Anastasi 2014; 2016). If only a certain muscular and bony conformation, coupled with a control system based on continuously learning feedback, allows producing articulate voice (biological constraint), it goes without saying that the cultural constraint is demonstrable through its adaptive role. Thus, one does not exclude the other.

Through a critical analysis of the key aspects that have affected the evolution of language both at the phylogenetic and ontogenetic levels, I tried to highlight the factors that drove the first hominids to use protomusical communication. In this study, therefore, I brought out the possibility of exploring music by resorting to several levels of investigation: morphological-structural, prosodic, syntactic, semiotic, and cognitive, supporting the thesis, which states that the first form of singing attributable to the hominids may have been a vocal variation based on pre-existing vocal calls in the world of non-human animals. In doing so, it was possible to give a different view of the role of communication in the ethnological world, often understood as a means for the sole transmission of information related to food and reproduction (cf. Read and Weary 1990; cf. Clay et al. 2012; cf. Luef et al. 2016).

Writing a book is always a wonderful journey, and on this occasion, I have returned to Darwin (1871) and his idea of music as an adaptive component. I was able to see that Darwinian theory, considering the data we know today, came to terms with the lack of applicability of the idea that our ancestors and animals used musical notes and rhythm to attract the opposite sex. As noted by Fitch (2006; 2009) the error made by Darwin lies in having taken as an example species in which the male is singing at the height of his sexual maturity. In fact, we know that in nature, there are several species in which the female is endowed with the ability to sing and does not do so only for reasons related to reproduction. From an evolutionary perspective, this mechanism tends to fail if we apply this reasoning to sapiens. The ability to sing is comparable both in men and in women, and it should be noted that in sapiens, we do not wait for sexual maturity to demonstrate the ability to sing; on the contrary, we can boast of a certain precociousness since we already demonstrate it a few months after birth (Falk 2004).

Yet it is plausible to argue that musical ability is determined by natural selection. In this sense, a proof that I think we should consider comes from the pathologies related to music, such as congenital amusia (Ayotte et al. 2002; Sacks 2008; Peretz 2016). Recent studies have shown that individuals with congenital amusia have difficulty picking up on the pitch changes typical of emotional prosody while performing spoken language (Thompson et al. 2012), and this leads back to the prosodic modulation ability that distinguishes human and non-human primate communication. Evidence of this kind shows us that Darwin's intuition was not totally wrong.

The prosodic aspects of protolanguage and their intonational modulation have therefore crossed the evolution of language and have arrived in our current language, both to allow us to continue to express our emotional state through verbal language and to allow the production of musical activities (lullabies, musical performances of a ritual nature, symbolic manifestations of a musical type). This, in addition to confirming the role of music as a means of social communication, leads us to believe that music is not something that simply tickles our minds or cheers our daily lives (cf. Pinker 1997). We are linguistic and musical beings, and as such, it is plausible to believe that singing has been distinguished as a universal component used by different animal species to create and maintain parental and social bonds (Anastasi 2013).

In the chain of events that have marked the evolution of language, I identified which traits were analogous to other species, i.e., vocal tract morphology, that allow us to interpret singing as a natural precursor to language and species-specific traits that marked its differences within human phylogeny (Fitch 2010; cf. Anastasi 2016). Based on this, the need to consider the biological and cognitive constraints that would have allowed the appearance of musical protolanguage converges. On the one hand, the analogies between species that are phylogenetically very far from each other, have allowed us to talk about evolutionary convergences; on the other hand, the homologies highlighted have indicated the possibility of a common evolutionary heritage.

Evolution responded to the temporary absence of an articulate language with a pre-verbal component, namely, motherese. Described by Falk (2004) as a primitive language made up of melodic and rhythmic expressions devoid of symbolic meaning but endowed with emotional impact, I only partially agree. His idea of the existence of a primitive language made of melodic and rhythmic expressions devoid of symbolic meaning but endowed with emotional impact clashes with what has been argued here about the communication of non-human primates. The existence of a silent world in which primates communicate only with gestures denies, in my opinion, an important element of our evolutionary history, that is, the natural history of our vocality. Sticking to the idea that the vocal structures of non-human primates (especially those phylogenetically closer to us) prevent them from performing melodious songs does not mean they cannot communicate. Many species, both distant and phylogenetically close to sapiens, use the voice to communicate, which is the evolutionary guarantee of the articulate voice.

Leaning on such an interpretation, besides making the understanding of the musical predisposition of our species more appropriate, also implies not having to take refuge in the definition of music as a mere cultural product. As Cross (2001) points out, what we call music today is not necessarily what it was 50,000 years ago. Therefore, considering its biological and cultural connotations, we might consider that the predisposition to be musical is not just a tendency to be a competent listener. Music is an extraordinary element of knowledge between different cultures that stands out among all human activities for its antiquity and ubiquity.

Regarding the link between music and language, science still has a lot to discuss, but in this immense mosaic of theoretical ideas, I think it is wrong to deny the plausibility of musical protolanguage. The existence of ancient natural-historical languages such as Mandarin Chinese or the languages of Sub-Saharan Africa (better known as tonal languages) is to be considered as just one of many pieces of evidence for which musicality allows to convey a meaning. In drawing a difference between tonal and non-tonal languages, it was noted how in the former, the pitch of the sounds can modify the meaning of a word, while in the latter, tonality is necessary to give the right nuance to a sentence and therefore understand whether it is affirmative or interrogative (Wang et al. 2006). In a sense, it seems that the modulation of sounds is responsible for highlighting what a language is and how it can be differentiated from all other human and animal languages, while evolution is responsible for presenting music as a living body, which respects the laws of natural selection and as such is the object of biological events.

Considering what is described in this book and without detracting from the historical and cultural variability of music, the bio-naturalistic approach has been indispensable in tracing the evolutionary lines of music. In particular, biomusicology has proven necessary to explain what made us musical animals. When addressing a question such as the origin of musicality, one cannot help but dwell on the evidence and the relationship between music and language. The studies that I have reported and commented on in this book have told us something about music, and they have done so starting from the idea that the musical protolanguage was a form of communication born from the first mother-child interactions. The idea then that music had an important role in the development of cognition has allowed me to highlight how music and language use specialized structures to which they are bound and that have their own specific evolutionary history. In this way, it was possible to discard any idea of the uniqueness of the human species and lean toward the criterion of species-specificity and evolutionary continuity between human and animal species.

In all its forms, music has certainly produced a profound change in the scores that mark the accord between the individual and the environment. In my opinion, it is an evolutionary and biological foundation. In support of this hypothesis, the evidence reported in this book was:

a) The biological criterion of diffusion within species. The biological constraints on which the activity of singing in animals and protolanguage in early hominids rested before the refunctionalization of these for purely linguistic purposes are evidence of how natural selection identified language as a powerful adaptive resource and favoured its path through intermediate forms of communication.

b) The use of the ethological perspective has shown us how different animal species possess a capacity for vocalic production that varies according to the structural peculiarities of the species: each animal species possesses its own phonatory equipment that is applied to different ecological and social contexts.

c) Motherese and the similarities in communication between human and non-human primates have revealed how prosodic modulation is a biologically ingrained mechanism. Small humans (and non-humans) are an excellent "laboratory" for recognizing how much is biological in our musicality and how much is derived from the culture we belong to.

Conclusion

The turning point of our species-specific language is to be found in that sort of apparently meaningless *grammelot*[1] (Fo 1977) whose ability to transmit and convey a message, without the need to be combined, has made possible, in this order: for the appearance of the first vocalisations, the birth of musical protolanguage, and, finally, the birth of language.

---

[1] It is a scenic language that is not based on the articulation in words but reproduces some properties of the phonetic system of a given language (intonation, rhythm, sounds, cadences, etc.) and recomposes them in a continuous flow. The arbitrary sequence of sounds can be reminiscent of a child's babbling.

BIBLIOGRAPHY

Aarsleff, Hans. "The history of linguistics and Professor Chomsky." *Language* 36, no. 3 (1970): 570-585.

Aboitiz, Francisco, and Carolina G. Schröter. "Prelinguistic evolution and motherese: A hypothesis on the neural substrates." *Behavioral and Brain Sciences* 27, no. 4 (2004): 503-504.

Aggius-Vella, Elena, Claudio Campus, Sara Finocchietti, and Monica Gori. "Audio spatial representation around the body." *Frontiers in Psychology* 8, (2017): 1932.

Aiello, Leslie C. "Terrestriality, Bipedalism and the Origin of Language." In *Evolution of Social Behaviour Patterns in Primates and Man: A Joint Discussion Meeting of the Royal Society and the British Academy*, edited by Walter Runciman, John Maynard-Smith, and Robin I. Dunbar, 269-289. London: Oxford University Press, 1996.

Aiello, Rita. "Music and language: Parallels and contrasts." In *Musical Perceptions*, edited by Rita Aiello and John Sloboda, 40-63. Oxford: Oxford University Press, 1994.

Albano Leoni, Federico. "Il ruolo dell'udito nella comunicazione linguistica. Il caso della prosodia." *Italian Journal of Linguistics* 13, (2001): 45-68.

Albano Leoni, Federico. 2009. *Dei suoni e dei sensi. Il volto fonico delle parole.* Bologna: Il Mulino.

Albouy, Philippe, Lucas Benjamin, Benjamin Morillon, and Robert J. Zatorre. "Distinct sensitivity to spectrotemporal modulation supports brain asymmetry for speech and melody." *Science* 367, no. 6481 (2020): 1043-1047.

Allen, George D., and Sarah Hawkins. "The development of phonological rhythm." In *Syllables and segments*, edited by Alan Bell and Joan B. Hooper, 173-185. Amsterdam: North-Holland, 1978.

Allport, Susan. 1997. *A Natural History of Parenting: A Naturalist Looks at Parenting in the Animal World and Ours.* New York: Harmony Books.

Alonso-Alvarez, Carlos, and Alberto Velando. "Benefits and costs of parental care. The evolution of parental care". In *The Evolution of Parental Care*, edited by Nick J. Royle, Per T. Smiseth, and Mathias Kölliker, 40-61. Oxford: Oxford University Press, 2012.

Alonzo, Suzanne H. "Social and coevolutionary feedbacks between mating and parental investment." *Trends in Ecology & Evolution* 25, no. 2 (2010): 99-108.

Altenmüller, Eckart O., Marc W. Bangert, Gundhild Liebert, and Wilfried Gruhn. "Mozart in us: How the brain processes music." *Medical Problems of Performing Artists* 15, no. 3 (2000): 99-107.

Altmann, Jeanne, and Amy Samuels. "Costs of maternal care: infant-carrying in baboons." *Behavioral Ecology and Sociobiology* 29, no. 6 (1992): 391-398.

Anastasi, Alessandra, and Laura Giallongo. "Il ruolo del cooperative breeding nell'evoluzione del linguaggio." *NeaScience* 7, no. 2 (2015): 14-16.

Anastasi, Alessandra. "Biology, learning, and evolution of vocality: Biosemiotics of birdsong." *Cognitive Semiotics* 10, no. 1 (2017a): 19-39.

Anastasi, Alessandra. "Il ruolo della comunicazione nella costruzione della dimensione sociale." In *Le ragioni della natura. La sfida teorica delle scienze della vita*, edited by Alessandra Falzone, Sebastiano Nucera, and Francesco Parisi, 29-40. Messina-Roma: Corisco Edizioni, 2014.

Anastasi, Alessandra. "Il ruolo della specificità uditivo-vocale nella comunicazione linguistica." *Sistemi intelligenti. Rivista quadrimestrale di scienze cognitive e di intelligenza artificiale*, no. 2 (2018): 317-338.

Anastasi, Alessandra. "L'ordito del bello. Trame bio-etologiche dell'evoluzione del senso estetico." *Mantichora. Italian Journal of Performance Studies*, no. 3 (2013): 3-24.

Anastasi, Alessandra. "Music Protolanguage. Comparison to Motherese in Human Mother - Infant Interactions and animal." In *Proceedings of ICMPC15/ESCOM10*, edited by Richard Parncutt and Sabrina Sattmann, 35-38. Austria: University of Graz, 2018.

Anastasi, Alessandra. "Music R-Evolution. From sound to speech." *Reti, saperi, linguaggi, Italian Journal of Cognitive Sciences*, no. 2 (2014): 267-282.

Anastasi, Alessandra. "Música y emociones. Un vínculo entre filosofía y ciencia cognitiva." In *El devenir de las civilizaciones: Interacciones entre el entorno humano, natural y cultural*, edited by Sandra Olivero Guidobono, 1615-1628. Madrid: Dykinson, 2021.

Anastasi, Alessandra. "Sintassi, musica e linguaggio. Una prospettiva evoluzionistica". *Rivista Italiana di Filosofia del Linguaggio* 11, no. 2 (2017b): 80-95.

Anastasi, Alessandra. 2016. *Musicanti naturali. Prospettive biologiche sulla vocalità umana e animale.* Messina-Roma: Corisco Edizioni.

Anderson, David J., and Ralph Adolphs. "A framework for studying emotions across species." *Cell* 157, no. 1 (2014): 187-200.

Andics, Attila, and Tamás Faragó. "Voice perception across species." In *The Oxford Handbook of Voice Perception*, edited by Sascha Frühholz, and Pascal Belin, 363-392. Oxford: Oxford University Press, 2019.

Anolli, Luigi and Rita Ciceri. 1992. *La voce delle emozioni, verso una semiosi della comunicazione vocale non-verbale delle emozioni.* Milano: Franco Angeli.

Anolli, Luigi, and Rita Ciceri. "The voice of deception: Vocal strategies of naive and able liars." *Journal of Nonverbal Behavior* 21, no. 4 (1997): 259-284.

Antonovics, Janis, and Peter H. van Tienderen. "Ontoecogenophyloconstraints? The chaos of constraint terminology." *Tr. Ecol. Evol.* 6, (1991): 166-167.

Arbib, Michael A. ed. *Language, music, and the brain. A mysterious relationship.* Cambridge, MA: MIT Press, 2013.

Arbib, Michael A., and Atsushi Iriki. "Evolving the language and music ready brain." In *Language, Music, and the Brain: A Mysterious Relationship*, edited by Michael A. Arbib, 359-375. Cambridge, MA: MIT Press, 2013.

Arlet, Malgorzata, Ronan Jubin, Nobuo Masataka, and Alban Lemasson. "Grooming-at-a-distance by exchanging calls in non-human primates." *Biology Letters* 11, (2015): 20150711.

Arnold, Stevan J. "Constraints on phenotypic evolution." *The American Naturalist* 140, (1992): S85-S107.

Arthur, W. Brian. 2009. *The Nature of Technology: What it is and how it evolves.* New York: Simon and Schuster.

Asano, Rie, and Cedric Boeckx. "Syntax in language and music: What is the right level of comparison?." *Frontiers in Psychology* 6, (2015): 942.

Austin, John L. 1962. *How to do things with words.* Oxford: Oxford University Press.

Ayotte, Julie, Isabelle Peretz, and Krista Hyde. "Congenital amusia: A group study of adults afflicted with a music-specific disorder." *Brain* 125, no. 2 (2002): 238-251.

Baker, Myron C., and Michael A. Cunningham. "The biology of bird-song dialects." *Behavioral and Brain Sciences* 8, no. 1 (1985): 85-100.

Balboni, Paolo E. 2006. *Italiano lingua materna: Fondamenti di didattica.* Novara: De Agostini Scuola.

Balconi, Michela. 2008. *Neuropsicologia della comunicazione.* Milano: Springer.

Ball, Philip. 2010. *The Music Instinct. How music works and why we can't do without it.* UK: Random House.

Bannan, Nicholas, (ed.). *Music, Language, and Human Evolution.* Oxford: Oxford University Press, 2012.

Barber, Nigel. 2004. *Kindness in a Cruel World. The Evolution of Altruism.* New York: Prometheus Books.

Bard, Kim A. "Parenting in primates." In *Handbook of Parenting, Vol. 2, Biology and Ecology of Parenting*, edited by Marc H. Bornstein, 99-140. Mahwah: Lawrence Erlbaum Associates, 1995.

Barsalou, Lawrence W. "Grounded cognition." *The Annual Review of Psychology* 59, (2008): 617-645.

Barsalou, Lawrence W. "Grounded cognition: Past, present, and future." *Topics in Cognitive Science* 2, no. 4 (2010): 716-724.

Barsalou, Lawrence W. "Perceptual symbol systems." *Behavioral and Brain Sciences* 22, (1999): 577-660.

Bartalesi, Lorenzo. 2012. *Estetica Evoluzionistica. Darwin e l'origine del senso estetico.* Roma: Carocci.

Barthes, Roland. 1982. *L'Obvie et L'Obtus: Essais critiques III.* Paris: Éditions du Seuil.

Bass, Andrew H., Edwin H. Gilland, and Robert Baker. "Evolutionary Origins for social vocalization in a vertebrate hindbrain-Spinal Compartment." *Science* 321, (2008): 417-421.

Beason, Robert C. "What Can Birds Hear?. " In *Proceedings of the Vertebrate. 21° Pest Conference*, edited by Timm, Robert M., and Paul Gorenzel, 92-96. University of California. 2004.

Beckers, Gabriël J. L., Brian S. Nelson, and Roderick A. Suthers. "Vocal Tract Filtering by Lingual Articulation in a Parrot." *Current Biology* 14, no. 17 (2004): 1592-1597.

Bekoff, Marc. "Cognitive ethology: The comparative study of animal minds." In *A Companion to Cognitive Science*, edited by William Bechtel and George Graham, 371-379. Oxford: Blackwell Publishers, 1995.

Bent, Ian, and William Drabkib. 1980. *Analysis*. London: MacMillan.

Berecz, Bernadett, Mel Cyrille, Ulrika Casselbrant, Sarah Oleksak, and Henrik Norholt. "Carrying human infants - An evolutionary heritage." *Infant Behavior and Development*, 60, (2020): 101460.

Berger, Kevin. "What makes music universal." *Nautilus*, 2021. https://nautil.us/what-makes-music-universal-9716/

Bertinetto, Alessandro. 2012. *Il pensiero dei suoni. Temi di filosofia della musica*. Milano: Bruno Mondadori.

Bertinetto, Pier Marco. 1981. *Strutture prosodiche dell'italiano: accento, quantità, sillaba, giuntura, fondamenti metrici*. Vol. 6. Firenze: Accademia della Crusca.

Bertirotti, Alessandro. 2003. *L'uomo, il suono e la musica*. Firenze: Firenze University Press.

Berwick, Robert C., and Noam Chomsky. 2016. *Why Only Us: Language and Evolution*. Cambridge: MIT Press.

Berwick, Robert C., Kazuo Okanoya, Gabriel J. L. Beckers, and Johan J. Bolhuis. "Songs to syntax: the linguistics of birdsong." *Trends in Cognitive Sciences* 15, no. 3 (2011): 113-121.

Best, Catherine T. "The diversity of tone languages and the roles of pitch variation in non-tone languages: considerations for tone perception research." *Frontiers in Psychology* 10, no. 364 (2019): doi.org/10.3389/fpsyg.2019.00364.

Bhatt, Dinesh, Anil Kumar, Y. Singh, and Robert B. Payne. "Territorial songs and calls of the oriental magpie robin Copsychus saularis." *Current Science*, (2000): 722-728.

Bickerton, Derek. "Foraging versus Social Intelligence in the Evolution of protolanguage." In *The Transition to Language*, edited by Allison Wray, 207-225. Oxford: Oxford University Press, 2002.

Bidelman, Gavin M., Stefanie Hutka, and Sylvain Moreno. "Tone language speakers and musicians share enhanced perceptual and cognitive abilities for musical pitch: evidence for bidirectionality between the domains of language and music." *PloS one* 8, no. 4 (2013): e60676.

Blacking, John. 1995. *Music, culture and experience*. Chicago: University of Chicago.

Blood, Anne J., Robert J. Zatorre, Patrick Bermudez, and Alan C. Evans. "Emotional responses to pleasant and unpleasant music correlate with activity in paralimbic brain regions." *Nature Neuroscience* 2, no. 4 (1999): 382-387.

Bloomfield, Leonard. 1933. *Language*. New York: Henry Holt and Co.

Blumer, Lawrence S. "Male parental care in the bony fishes." *The Quarterly Review of Biology* 54, no. 2 (1979): 149-161.

Boë, Louis-Jean, Frédéric Berthommier, Thierry Legou, Guillaume Captier, Caralyn Kemp, Thomas R. Sawallis, Yannick Becker, Arnaud Rey, and Joël Fagot. "Evidence of a vocal proto-system in the baboon (Papio papio) suggests pre-hominin speech precursors." *PLOS One* 12, no. 1 (2017): e0169321.

Boeckx, Cedric. "Homo Combinans". In *Evolution of the Language. Proceeding of the 9th International Conference (EVOLANG9)*, edited by Thom C. Scott-Phillips, Monica Tamariz, and Erica A. Cartmill, 413-415. Singapore-London: World Scientific Publishing, 2012.

Boesch, Christophe, and Hedwige Boesch-Achermann. 2000. *The Chimpanzees of the Tai Forest: Behavioural Ecology and Evolution*. Oxford: Oxford University Press.

Bolhuis, Johan J., Kazuo Okanoya, and Constance Scharff. "Twitter evolution: Converging mechanisms in birdsong and human speech." *Nature Reviews Neuroscience* 11, no. 11 (2010): 747-59.

Bologna, Corrado. 1992. *Flatus vocis. Metafisica e antropologia della voce*. Bologna: Il Mulino.

Bolt, Nicole K., and Janeen D. Loehr. "The predictability of a partner's actions modulates the sense of joint agency." *Cognition* 161 (2017): 60-65.

Boucaud, Ingrid C., Mylene M. Mariette, Avelyne S. Villain, and Clémentine Vignal. "Vocal negotiation over parental care? Acoustic communication at the nest predicts partners' incubation share." *Biological Journal of the Linnean Society* 117, no. 2 (2016): 322-336.

Boudon, Raymond. 1968. *A quoi sert la notion de Structure?*. Paris: Gallimard.

Bouissac, Paul. "How plausible is the motherese hypothesis?." *Behavioral and Brain Sciences* 27, no. 4 (2004): 506-507.

Bousquet, Christophe A. H., David J. T. Sumpter, and Marta B. Manser. "Moving calls: a vocal mechanism underlying quorum decisions in cohesive groups." *Proceedings of the Royal Society B: Biological Sciences*. 278, no. 1711 (2010): 1482-1488.

Bowers, Jeffrey S., and Colin J. Davis. "Is speech perception modular or interactive?." *Trends in Cognitive Sciences* 8, no. 1 (2004): 3-5.

Bradbury, Jack W., and Sandra L. Vehrencamp. 2011. *Principles of animal communication. Second Edition.* Sunderland, Massachusetts: Sinauer Associates.

Brandi, Luciana, and Beatrice Balvadori. 2004. *Dal suono alla parola. Percezione e produzione del linguaggio tra neurolinguistica e psicolinguistica*. Firenze: Firenze University Press.

Brandi, Luciana. "Tra musica e linguaggio: all'origine della parola." *Quaderni del Dipartimento di Linguistica - Università di Firenze* 13, (2003): 31-53.

Brandt, Anthony, Gebrian, Molly, and Robert Slevc. "The role of musical development in early language acquisition." In *The Oxford Handbook of Music and the Brain*, edited by Thaut Michael H. and Hodges Donald A., 567-591. Oxford University Press, 2019.

Brown, Steven, and Joseph Jordania. "Universals in the world's musics." *Psychology of Music* 41, no. 2 (2013): 229-248.

Brown, Steven. "A joint prosodic origin of language and music." *Frontiers in Psychology* 8, (2017): 1894

Brown, Steven. "The "Musilanguage" Model of Music Evolution." In *The Origins of Music*, edited by Nils L. Wallin, Bjon Merker, and Steven Brown, 271-300. Cambridge: MIT Press, 2000.

Brown, Steven. "Evolutionary models of music: From sexual selection to group selection." In *Perspectives in ethology. Evolution, Culture, and Behavior*, edited by Nicholas S. Thompson, and François Tonneau, 231-281. Boston, MA: Springer. 2000.

Bryant, Gregory A. "Animal signals and emotion in music: Coordinating affect across groups." *Frontiers in Psychology* 4, (2013): 990.

Buccino, Giovanni, Ivan Colagè, Nicola Gobbi, and Giorgio Bonaccorso. "Grounding meaning in experience: A broad perspective on embodied language." *Neuroscience & Biobehavioral Reviews* 69, (2016): 69-78.

Buck, John. "Synchronous rhythmic flashing of fireflies II." *The Quarterly Review of Biology* 63, no. 3 (1988): 265-289.

Bürger, Reinhard. "Constraints for the evolution of functionally coupled characters: a nonlinear analysis of a phenotypic model." *Evolution* 40, (1986): 182-193.

Burnham, Denis, Christine Kitamura, and Uté Vollmer-Conna. "What's new, pussycat? On talking to babies and animals." *Science* 296, no. 5572 (2002): 1435.

Burns, Edward M., and Dixon W. Ward. "Categorical perception - phenomenon or epiphenomenon: Evidence from experiments in the perception of melodic musical intervals." *The Journal of the Acoustical Society of America* 63, no. 2 (1978): 456-468.

Busnel, Marie Claire, Carolyn Granier-Deferre, and Jean Pierre Lecanuet. "Fetal audition." *Annals of the New York Academy of Sciences* 662, no. 1 (1992): 118-134.

Busnel, René-Guy, and André Classe. 1976. *Whistled languages*. Berlin: Springer Verlag.

Carapezza, Marco. 2005. *Segno e simbolo in Wittgenstein*. Acireale - Roma: Bonanno.

Carreiras, Manuel, Jorge Lopez, Francisco Rivero, and David Corina. "Neural processing of a whistled language." *Nature* 433, no. 7021 (2005): 31-32.

Carroll, Sean B. 2005. *Endless Forms Most Beautiful: The New Science of Evo Devo and the Making of the Animal Kingdom*. New York: W.W. Norton & Company.

Carroll, Sean B. 2006. *The Making of the Fittest. DNA and the Ultimate Forensic Record of Evolution*. New York: WW Norton & Company.

Carruthers, Peter. "The cognitive functions of language." *Behavioural and Brain Sciences* 25, (2002): 657-726.

Caruana, Fausto, and Anna M. Borghi. "Embodied Cognition: una nuova psicologia." *Giornale italiano di psicologia* 40, no. 1 (2013): 23-48.

Caruana, Fausto, and Anna Maria Borghi. *Il cervello in azione: introduzione alle nuove scienze della mente*. Bologna: Il Mulino, 2016.

Catchpole, Clive K., and Slater Peter J. B. 1995. *Bird Song: Themes and Variations*. Cambridge: Cambridge University Press.

Cavalli-Sforza, Luigi L. 2004. *L'evoluzione della cultura*. Torino: Codice Edizioni.

Champagne, Frances A., and Michael J. Meaney. "Stress during gestation alters postpartum maternal care and the development of the offspring in a rodent model." *Biological Psychiatry* 59, no. 12 (2006): 1227-1235.

Chanda, Mona Lisa, and Daniel J. Levitin. "The neurochemistry of music." *Trends in Cognitive Sciences* 17, no. 4 (2013): 179-193.

Chen, Joyce L., Virginia B. Penhune, and Robert J. Zatorre. "Interactions between auditory and dorsal premotor cortex during synchronization to musical rhythms." *Neuroimage* 32, (2006): 1771-1781.

Cheney, Dorothy L., and Robert M. Seyfarth. "Flexible usage and social function in primate vocalizations." *Proceedings of the National Academy of Sciences of the United States of America* 115, (2018): 1974-1979.

Cheney, Dorothy L., and Robert M. Seyfarth. "Why animals don't have language." *The Tanner Lectures on Human Values* 19, (1997): 173-210.

Cheney, Dorothy L., and Robert M. Seyfarth. 1990. *How Monkeys See the World: Inside the Mind of Another Species.* Chicago: University of Chicago Press.

Cheney, Dorothy L., Robert M. Seyfarth, and Ryne Palombit. "The function and mechanism underlying baboon "contact" barks." *Animal Behaviour* 52, (1996): 507-518.

Chomsky, Noam. "A review of B. F. Skinner's verbal behavior." *Language* 35, (1959): 26-57.

Chomsky, Noam. 1957. *Syntactic structures.* Paris: The Hague Mouton.

Chomsky, Noam. 1965. *Aspects of the Theory of Syntax.* Cambridge: MIT Press.

Chomsky, Noam. 1966. *Cartesian linguistics.* New York: Harper & Row.

Chomsky, Noam. 1975. *The Logical Structure of Linguistic Theory.* New York: Plenum Press.

Chow, Cecilia P., Jude F. Mitchell, and Cory T. Miller. "Vocal turn-taking in a non-human primate is learned during ontogeny." *Proceedings of the Royal Society B* 282, (2015): 20150069.

Chow, Ivan, and Steven Brown. "A musical approach to speech melody." *Frontiers in Psychology* 9, (2018): 247.

Christiansen, Morten H., and Simon Kirby. 2003. *Language Evolution.* Oxford: Oxford University Press.

Clarke, Eric, Tia DeNora, and Jonna Vuoskoski. "Music, empathy and cultural understanding." *Physics of Life Reviews* 15, (2015): 61-88.

Clarke, Esther., Reichard Ulrich H., and Klaus Zuberbühler. "The syntax and meaning of wild gibbon songs." *PloS one* 1, no. 1 (2006): e73.

Clay, Zanna, Carolynn L. Smith, and Daniel T. Blumstein. "Food-associated vocalizations in mammals and birds: what do these calls really mean?" *Animal Behaviour* 83, no. 2, (2012): 323-330.

Clutton-Brock, Tim H. 1991. *The Evolution of Parental Care.* Princeton: Princeton University Press.

Cochrane, Tom. "The Music Between Us: Is Music a Universal Language?." *MIND* 124, no. 496 (2015): 1288-1292.

Colombelli-Négrel, Diane, Mark E. Hauber, Jeremy Robertson, Frank J. Sulloway, Herbert Hoi, Matteo Griggio, Sonia Kleindorfer. "Embryonic learning of vocal passwords in superb fairy-wrens reveals intruder cuckoo nestlings." *Current Biology* 22, (2012): 2155-2160.

Comte, August. 1830. *Cours de philosophie positive.* Paris: Rouen Frères Libraires Éditeurs.

Conard, Nicholas J., Maria Malina, and Susanne C. Münzel. "New flutes document the earliest musical tradition in southwestern Germany." *Nature* 460, no. 7256 (2009): 737-740.

Cook, Nicholas. 1994. *A guide to musical analysis.* Oxford - New York: Oxford University Press.

Cook, Peter, Andrew Rouse, Margaret Wilson, and Colleen Reichmuth. "A California Sea Lion (Zalophus californianus) can keep the beat: Motor Entrainment to Rhythmic Auditory Stimuli in a Non-Vocal Mimic." *Journal of Comparative Psychology* 127, no. 4 (2013): 412-427.

Corballis, Michael C. "Mirror neurons and the evolution of language." *Brain and Language* 112, (2010): 25-35.

Cornec, Clément, Yves Hingrat, Thierry Aubin, and Fanny Rybak. "Booming far: the long-range vocal strategy of a lekking bird." *Royal Society Open Science* 4, no. 8 (2017): 170594.

Cowlishaw, Guy. "Sexual selection and information content in gibbon song bouts." *Ethology* 102, (1996): 272-284.

Cozolino, Louis. "The social brain." *Psychotherapy in Australia* 12, no. 2 (2006): 12-17.

Cozolino, Louis. 2014. *The Neuroscience of Human Relationships: Attachment and the Developing Social Brain.* London: WW Norton & Company.

Critchley, Macdonald, and Ronald Alfred Henson, ed. *Music and the Brain: Studies in the Neurology of Music.* London: Butterworth-Heinemann, 2014.

Cross, Ian. "Music, cognition, culture and evolution." *Annals of the New York Academy of Sciences* 930, (2001): 28-42.

Cross, Ian. "Music and biocultural evolution." In *The Cultural Study of Music: A Critical Introduction*, edited by Martin Clayton, Trevor Herbert and Richard Middleton, 19-30. New York, London: Routledge, 2003.

Cross, Ian. "Music and cognitive evolution." In *Handbook of Evolutionary Psychology*, edited by Robin I. Dunbar, and Louise Barrett, 649-667. Oxford: Oxford University Press. 2007

Cross, Ian. "Music and communication in music psychology." *Psychology of Music* 42, (2014): 809-819.

Cross, Ian. "Music, cognition, culture, and evolution." *Annals of the New York Academy of Sciences* 930, no. 1 (2001): 28-42.

Cross, Ian. "Musicality and the human capacity for culture." *Musicae Scientiae* 12, no. 1 (2008): 147-167.

Cutler, Anne, and Dennis G. Norris. "The role of strong syllables in segmentation for lexical access." *Journal of Experimental Psychology: Human Perception and Performance* 14, (1988): 113-121.

Cutler, Anne, Jacques Mehler, Dennis G. Norris, and Juan Segui. "The syllable's differing role in the segmentation of French and English." *Journal of Memory and Language* 25, (1986): 385-400.

Cutler, Anne. "Exploiting prosodic probabilities in speech segmentation." In *Cognitive Models of Speech Processing: Psycholinguistic and Computational Perspectives*, edited by Gerry T.M. Altmann, 105-121. Cambridge, MA: MIT Press, 1990.

Dalziell, Anastasia H., and Robert D. Magrath. "Fooling the experts: accurate vocal mimicry in the song of the superb lyrebird, Menura novaehollandiae." *Animal Behaviour* 83, no. 6 (2012): 1401-1410.

Darwin, Charles. 1859. *On the Origins of Species by Means of Natural Selection.* London: John Murray.

Darwin, Charles. 1871. *The Descent of Man, and Selection in Relation to Sex.* London: John Murray.

Davidson, Richard J., Klaus Sherer, and Hill Goldsmith. 2003. *Handbook of Affective Sciences.* New York: Oxford University Press.

Davis, Steven. 1991. *Pragmatics: A Reader.* Oxford: Oxford University Press.

Dawkins, Marian S., and Tim Guilford. "The corruption of honest signalling." *Animal Behaviour* 41, (1991): 865-873.

Dawkins, Richard. 1976. *The Selfish Gene.* New York: Oxford University Press.

de Boer, Bart, Serge A. Wich, Madeleine E. Hardus, and Adriano R. Lameira. "Acoustic models of orangutan hand-assisted alarm calls." *The Journal of Experimental Biology* 218, no. 6 (2015): 907-914.

De Casper, Anthony J. "Histoire de foetus par un nouveauné." *Progrès en néonatologie* 10, (1990): 168-173.

De Casper, Anthony J., Jean Pierre Lecanuet, Marie Claire Busnel, Carolyn Granier-Deferre, and Roselyne Maugeais. "Fetal reactions to recurrent maternal speech." *Infant Behavior and Development* 17, no. 2 (1994): 159-164.

Deacon, Terrence W. "A role for relaxed selection in the evolution of the language capacity." *Proceedings of the National Academy of Sciences* 107, no. 2 (2010): 9000-9006.

Deacon, Terrence W. 1997. *The Symbolic Species: The Co-evolution of Language and the Brain.* New York: W.W. Norton & Company.

DeAngelis, Ross, Joseph Gogola, Logan Dodd, and Justin S. Rhodes. "Opposite effects of nonapeptide antagonists on paternal behavior in the teleost fish Amphiprion ocellaris." *Hormones and Behavior* 90, (2017): 113-119.

Dehaene-Lambertz, Ghislaine, and Sylvain Baillet. "A phonological representation in the infant brain." *NeuroReport* 9, (1998): 1885-1888.

Dehaene-Lambertz, Ghislaine. "Electrophysiological correlates of categorical phoneme perception in adults." *NeuroReport* 8, no. 4 (1997): 919-924.

Deliège Célestin. "La musicologie devant le structuralisme." *L'Arc*, no. 26 (1965): 45-52.

Dell'Anna, Alessandro, Marc Leman, and Annamaria Berti. "Musical Interaction Reveals Music as Embodied Language." *Frontiers in Neuroscience*, (2021): 818.

Dennett, Daniel. *From Bacteria to Bach and Back.* London: Penguin Books, 2017.

Deutsch, Diana. 1999. *The Psychology of Music.* New York: Academic Press.

Dewey, John. 1925. *Experience and Nature.* New York: Dover Publication.

Diamond, Jared M. 1992. *The Third Chimpanzee. The Evolution and Future of the Human Animal.* New York: Harper Collins.

Diesel, Rudolf, and Martina Schuh. "Maternal care in the bromeliad crab Metopaulias depressus (Decapoda): maintaining oxygen, pH and calcium levels optimal for the larvae." *Behavioral Ecology and Sociobiology* 32, no. 1 (1993): 11-15.

Dissanayake, Ellen. "Motherese is but one part of a ritualized, multimodal, temporally organized, affiliative interaction." *Behavioral and Brain Sciences* 27, no. 4 (2004): 512-513.

Dissanayake, Ellen. "Incunamboli estetici". *Atque - materiali tra filosofia e psicoterapia*, no. 20 (2017): 109-124.

Doolittle, Emily, and Bruno Gingras. Zoomusicology. *Current Biology* 25, (2015): R819-R820.

Doolittle, Emily. "Other species' counterpoint: An investigation of the relationship between human music and animal songs." PhD diss., Princeton University, 2007.

Doupe, Allison J., David J. Perkel, Anton Reiner, and Edward A. Stern. "Bird brains could teach basal ganglia research a new song." *Trends Neuroscience* 28, (2005): 353-363.

Duanmu, San. "Tone and non-tone languages: An alternative to language typology and parameters." *Language and Linguistics* 5, no. 4 (2004): 891-923.

Dugas-Ford, Jennifer, Joanna J. Rowell, and Clifton W. Ragsdale. "Cell-type homologies and the origins of the neocortex." *Proceedings of the National Academy of Sciences* 109, no. 42 (2012): 16974-16979.

Dullemeijer, Piet. "Evolution of biological constructions: concessions, limitations and pathways." In *Constructional morphology and evolution*, edited by Norbert Schmidt-Kittler, and Klaus Vogel, 313-329. Berlin Heidelberg: Springer Verlag, 1991.

Dunbar, Robin I. "The social brain: mind, language, and society in evolutionary perspective." *Annual review of Anthropology* 32, no. 1 (2003): 163-181.

Dunford, Christopher. "Kin selection for ground squirrel alarm calls." *The American Naturalist* 111, no. 980 (1977): 782-785.

Echols, Catharine H., and Nathan C. Marti. "The identification of words and their meanings: From perceptual biases to language-specific cues." In *Weaving a Lexicon*, edited by Geoffrey D. Hall, and Sandra R. Waxman, 41-78. Massachusetts: MIT Press, 2004.

Eco, Umberto. 1973. *Segno*. Milano: ISEDI.

Eco, Umberto. 1975. *Trattato di semiotica generale*. Milano: Bompiani.

Edelman, Gerald M. 1992. *Bright Air, Brilliant Fire: On the Matter of the Mind*. New York: Basic Books.

Egnor, Roian S. E., and Marc D. Hauser. "A paradox in the evolution of primate vocal learning." *Trends in Neurosciences* 27, (2004): 649-654.

Eimas, Peter D. "The perception and representation of speech by infants." In *Signal to syntax: bootstrapping from speech to grammar in early acquisition*, edited by James Logan Morgan, and Katherine Demuth, 37-52. NJ: Lawrence Erlabaum Associates, 1996.

Elowson, A. Margaret, Charles Snowdon, and Cristina Lazaro-Perea. "Infant babbling in a nonhuman primate: Complex vocal sequences with repeated call types." *Behaviour* 135, no. 5 (1998): 643-664.

Endler, John A., and Alexandra Basolo. "Sensory ecology, receiver biases and sexual selection." *Trends in ecology & evolution* 13, no. 10 (1998): 415-420.

Engh, Anne L., Rebekah R. Hoffmeier, Dorothy L. Cheney, and Robert M. Seyfarth, "Who, me? Can baboons infer the target of vocalizations?" *Animal Behaviour* 71, no. 2 (2006): 381-387.

Everett, Caleb, Damián E. Blasi, and Seán G. Roberts. "Climate, vocal folds, and tonal languages: Connecting the physiological and geographic dots." *Proceedings of the National Academy of Sciences* 112, no. 5 (2015): 1322-1327.

Fairbanks, Lynn A. "Reciprocal benefits of allomothering for female vervet monkeys." *Animal Behaviour* 4, (1990): 553-562.

Falk, Dean. "Prelinguistic evolution in early hominins: Whence motherese?" *Behavioral and Brain Sciences* 27, no. 4 (2004): 491-503.

Falk, Dean. 2009. *Finding our Tongues. Mothers, Infants, and the Origins of Language*. New York, Basic Books.

Falzone, Alessandra, Alessandra Anastasi, and Antonino Pennisi. "Biological constraints and evolution of language: a hypothesis on the exaptation of human vocal structures." *PESHE* 3, (2014): 66.

Falzone, Alessandra, and Alessandra Anastasi. "Prospettive embodied della cognizione sociale: un approccio comparative." In *L'impatto della mente. Percorsi di scienze cognitive sociali*, edited by Sebastiano Nucera, and Paola Pennisi, 83-102. Messina-Roma: Corisco Edizioni, 2018.

Falzone, Alessandra, and Valentina Cardella. "Per una natura linguistica della mente umana: la cognizione sociale alla prova delle specie-specificità verbale." *Rivista Italiana di Filosofia del Linguaggio*, no. 2 (2015): 164-178.

Falzone, Alessandra. "Evolution of Language. Continuity and Discontinuity through Models and Empirical Data." *Theoria et Historia Scientiarum* 16, (2019): 63-81.

Falzone, Alessandra. "Natural Performativity: How to Do Things with Body Constraints". In *The Extended Theory of Cognitive Creativity*, edited by Antonino Pennisi, and Alessandra Falzone, 217-227. Chaim, New York, London: Springer International Publishing, 2020.

Falzone, Alessandra. "Performatività ed evoluzione." *Reti, saperi, linguaggi, Italian Journal of Cognitive Sciences* 1, (2018): 149-160.

Falzone, Alessandra. "Specie-specificità, linguaggio, rappresentazione: la tecnologia uditivo-vocale nel sapiens." *RSL. Italian Journal of Cognitive Sciences* 4, no. 2 (2012b): 44-47.

Falzone, Alessandra. "Structural Constraints on Language." *Reti, Saperi, Linguaggi* 2, (2014): 13-36.

Falzone, Alessandra. "Vincoli biologici ed etologia sociale del linguaggio: i nuovi dati sulla corteccia uditiva." *Rivista Italiana di Filosofia del Linguaggio*, (2012a): 86-100.

Falzone, Alessandra. 2012. *Evoluzionismo e Comunicazione. Nuove ipotesi sulla selezione naturale nei linguaggi animali e umani*. Messina-Roma: Corisco Edizioni.

Fant, Gunnar. 1960. *Acoustic Theory of Speech Production*. The Hague, Netherlands: Mouton.

Farries, Michael A. "The avian song system in comparative perspective." *Annals of the New York Academy of Sciences* 1016, no. 1 (2004): 61-76.

Favaro, Livio, Marco Gamba, Eleonora Cresta, Elena Fumagalli, Francesca Bandoli, Cristina Pilenga, Valentina Isaja, Nicolas Mathevon, and David Reby. "Do penguins' vocal sequences conform to linguistic laws?." *Biology letters* 16, no. 2 (2020): 20190589.

Fedurek, Pawel, Anne M. Schel, and Katie E. Slocombe. "The acoustic structure of chimpanzee pant-hooting facilitates chorusing." *Behavioral Ecology and Sociobiology* 67, no. 11 (2013): 1781-1789.

Feenders, Gesa, Miriam Liedvogel, Miriam Rivas, Manuela Zapka, Haruhito Horita, Erina Hara, Kazuhiro Wada, Henrik Mouritsen, and Erich D. Jarvis. "Molecular Mapping of Movement-Associated Areas in the Avian Brain: A Motor Theory for Vocal Learning Origin." *PLoS one* 3, no. 3 (2008): e1768.

Feldman, Ruth. "Parent-infant synchrony: Biological foundations and developmental outcomes." *Current directions in psychological science* 16, no. 6 (2007): 340-345.

Fernald, Anne, and Gerald McRoberts. "Prosodic bootstrapping: A critical analysis of the argument and the evidence". In *Signal to Syntax: Bootstrapping from Speech to Grammar in Early Acquisition*, edited by James Logan Morgan, and Katherine Demuth, 365-387. NJ: Lawrence Erlabaum Associates, 1996.

Fernald, Anne, and Patricia Kuhl. "Acoustic determinants of infant preference for motherese speech." *Infant Behavior and Development* 10, no. 3 (1987): 279-293.

Fernald, Anne, and Thomas Simon. "Expanded intonation contours in mothers' speech to new-borns." *Developmental Psychology* 20, (1984): 104-113.

Fernald, Anne, Traute Taeschner, Judy Dunn, Mechthild Papousek, Bénédicte de Boysson-Bardies, and Ikuko Fukui. "A cross-language study of prosodic modifications in mothers' and fathers' speech to preverbal infants." *Journal of Child Language* 16, no. 3 (1989): 477-501.

Fernald, Anne. "Prosody in speech to children: Prelinguistic and linguistic functions." *Annals of Child Development* 8, (1991): 43-80.

Fernandez, Ahana A., and Mirjam Knörnschild. "Pup directed vocalizations of adult females and males in a vocal learning bat." *Frontiers in Ecology and Evolution* 8, no. 265 (2020): doi.org/10.3389/fevo.2020.00265

Filippi, Piera. "Emotional and interactional prosody across animal communication systems: a comparative approach to the emergence of language." *Frontiers in Psychology* 7, no. 1393 (2016): 1393.

Filippi, Piera. "Emotional voice intonation: A communication code at the origins of speech processing and word-meaning associations?." *Journal of Nonverbal Behavior* 44, no. 4 (2020): 395-417.

Fischer, Julia, and Kurt Hammerschmidt. "Towards a new taxonomy of primate vocal production learning." *Philosophical Transactions of the Royal Society B* 375, no.1789 (2020): 20190045.

Fischer, Julia, and Tabitha Price. "Meaning, intention, and inference in primate vocal communication." *Neuroscience & Biobehavioral Reviews* 82, (2017): 22-31.

Fischer, Julia, Dorothy L. Cheney, and Robert M. Seyfarth. "Development of infant baboons' responses to graded bark variants." *Proceedings of the Royal Society of London. Series B: Biological Sciences* 267, no. 1459 (2000): 2317-2321.

Fischer, Julia. "Developmental modifications in the vocal behavior of nonhuman primates." In *Primate Audition: Ethology and Neurobiology*, edited by Asif A. Ghazanfar. 109-125. Boca Raton: CRC Press, 2003.

Fishman, Yonatan I, David H. Reser, Joseph C. Arezzo, and Mitchell Steinschneider. "Complex tone processing in primary auditory cortex of the awake monkey. I. Neural ensemble correlates of roughness." *Journal Acoustical Society of America* 108, (2000): 235-246.

Fitch, Tecumseh W., and David Reby. "The descended larynx is not uniquely human." *Proceedings of the Royal Society of London. Series B: Biological Sciences* 268, no. 1477 (2001): 1669-1675.

Fitch, W. Tecumseh, and Jay Giedd. "Morphology and development of the human vocal tract: a study using magnetic resonance imaging." *Journal of the Acoustical Society of America* 106, (1999): 1511-1522.

Fitch, W. Tecumseh, Jürgen Neubauer, and Hanspeter Herzel. "Calls out of chaos: The adaptive significance of nonlinear phenomena in mammalian vocal production." *Animal Behaviour* 63, no. 3 (2002): 407-418.

Fitch, W. Tecumseh. 2010. *The Evolution of Language*. Cambridge: Cambridge University Press.

Fitch, W. Tecumseh. "Acoustic exaggeration of size in birds by tracheal elongation: comparative and theoretical analyses." *Journal of Zoology* 248, (1999): 31-49.

Fitch, W. Tecumseh. "Empirical approaches to the study of language evolution." *Psychon Bulletin & Review* 24, (2017): 3-33.

Fitch, W. Tecumseh. "Evolving meaning: The roles of kin selection, allomothering and paternal care in language evolution." In *Emergence of Communication and Language*, edited by Caroline Lyon, Chrystopher L. Nehaniv, and Angelo Cangelosi, 29-51. New York: Springer. 2007.

Fitch, W. Tecumseh. "Four principles of bio-musicology." *Philosophical Transactions of the Royal Society B* 370, (2015): 20140091.

Fitch, W. Tecumseh. "Kin selection and "Mother Tongues": A Neglected Comnponent in Language Evolution." In *Evolution of Communication Systems: A Comparative Approach*, edited by D. Kimbrough Oller, and Ulrike Griebel, 276-96. Cambridge, MA: MIT Press, 2004.

Fitch, W. Tecumseh. "Musical Protolanguage: Darwin's Theory of Language Evolution Revisited." *Language Learning and Development* 7, (2009): 253-262.

Fitch, W. Tecumseh. "Rhythmic cognition in humans and animals: distinguishing meter and pulse perception." *Frontiers in Systems Neuroscience* 7, (2013): 68.

Fitch, W. Tecumseh. "The biology and evolution of music: A comparative perspective." *Cognition* 100, (2006): 173-215.

Fitch, W. Tecumseh. "The evolution of language: a comparative review." *Biology and Philosophy* 20, no. 2-3 (2005a): 193-203.

Fitch, W. Tecumseh. "The evolution of Music in Comparative Perspective." *Annals of the New York Academy of Sciences* 1060, (2005b): 29-49.

Fitch, W. Tecumseh. "The evolution of speech: a comparative review." *Trends in Cognitive Sciences* 4, no. 7 (2000b): 258-267.

Fitch, W. Tecumseh. "The evolution of syntax: an exaptationist perspective." *Frontiers in evolutionary neuroscience* 3, (2011): 9.

Fitch, W. Tecumseh. "The phonetic potential of nonhuman vocal tracts: Comparative cineradiographic observations of vocalizing animals." *Phonetica* 57, no. 2-4 (2000a): 205-218.

Fitch, W. Tecumseh. "Vocal tract length and formant frequency dispersion correlate with body size in rhesus macaques." *Journal of Acoustical Society of America* 102, (1997): 1213-1222.

Fitch, W. Tecumseh. 2010. *The Evolution of Language*. Cambridge: Cambridge University Press.

Flohr, John W., and Colwyn Trevarthen. "Music learning in childhood: Early developments of a musical brain and body." In *Neurosciences in music pedagogy*, edited by Wilfried Gruhn and Francis H. Rauscher, 53-100. New York: Nova Biomedical Books, 2007.

Fo, Dario. 1977. *Manuale minimo dell'attore*. Torino: Einaudi.

Fox, Charles W., Derek A. Roff, and Daphne J. Fairbair. 2001. *Evolutionary Ecology. Concepts and Case Studies*. New York: Cambridge University Press.

Frankl-Vilches, Carolina, and Manfred Gahr. "Androgen and estrogen sensitivity of bird song: a comparative view on gene regulatory levels." *Journal of Comparative Physiology A* 204, no. 1 (2018): 113-126.

Fritz, Thomas, Sebastian Jentschke, Nathalie Gosselin, Daniela Sammler, Isabelle Peretz, Robert Turner, Angela D. Friederici, and Stefan Koelsch. "Universal recognition of three basic emotions in music." *Current biology* 19, no. 7 (2009): 573-576.

Gamba, Marco, and Cristina Giacoma. "Key issues in the study of primate acoustic signals." *Journal of Anthropological Science* 83, (2005): 61-87.

Gamba, Marco, Camilla Colombo, and Cristina Giacoma. "Acoustic cues to caller identity in lemurs: a case study." *Journal of Ethology* 30, no. 1 (2012): 191-196.

Gamba, Marco, Livio Favaro, Valeria Torti, Viviana Sorrentino, and Cristina Giacoma. "Vocal tract flexibility and variation in the vocal output in wild Indris." *Bioacoustics: The International Journal of Animal Sound and its Recording* 20, (2011): 251-266.

Gamba, Marco, Valeria Torti, Longondraza Miaretsoa, Daria Valente, Chiara De Gregorio, Martina Tubito, Martina Zarantonello, Vittorio L. Bianco, Livio Favaro, Olivier Friard, and Cristina Giacoma. "Primate songs and their relevance in the study of language evolution." In *The Evolution of Language - Proceedings of the 12th International Conference on the Evolution of Language (Evolang12)*, edited by Christine Cuskley, Hannah Little, Andrea Ravignani, Molly Flaherty, Luke McCrohon, and Tessa Verhoef, 134-136. Toruń, Poland: Niclolaus Copernicus University, 2018.

Gamba, Marco, Valeria Torti, Vittoria Estienne, Rose M. Randrianarison, Daria Valente, Paolo Rovara, Giovanna Bonadonna, Olivier Friard, and Cristina Giacoma. "Affiliations expand The Indris Have Got Rhythm! Timing and Pitch

Variation of a Primate Song Examined between Sexes and Age Classes." *Frontiers in Neuroscience* 10, (2016): 249.

Gamba, Marco. "Vocal tract-related cues across human and nonhuman signals." *Reti, Saperi, Linguaggi. Italian Journal of Cognitive Science* 1, (2014): 49-68.

Garamszegi, László Z., Denitza Z. Pavlova, Marcel Eens, and Anders P. Møller. "The evolution of song in female birds in Europe." *Behavioral Ecology* 18, (2007): 86-96.

Garcia, Maxime, and Livio Favaro. "Animal vocal communication: function, structures, and production mechanisms." *Current Zoology* 63, no. 4 (2017): 417-419.

Gardner, Howard, and Dennie Wolf. "Waves and streams of symbolization: Notes on the development of symbolic capacities in young children." In *The Acquisition of Symbolic Skills*, edited by John Sloboda, 19-42. Boston: Springer, 1983.

Gardner, R. Allen, and Beatrice T. Gardner. "Teaching Sign Language to a Chimpanzee." *Science* 165, (1969): 664-672.

Gardner, Timothy J., Felix Naef, and Fernando Nottebohm. "Freedom and rules: the acquisition and reprogramming of a bird's learned song." *Science* 308, no. 5724 (2005): 1046-1049.

Gazzaniga, Michael S. 2009. *Human: The Science Behind What Makes Your Brain Unique*. New York: Harper Collins Publishers.

Geissmann, Thomas, and Vincent Nijman. "Calling in wild silvery gibbons (*Hylobates moloch*) in Java (Indonesia): Behavior, phylogeny and conservation." *American Journal of Primatology* 68, (2006): 1-19.

Geissmann, Thomas. "Duet-Splitting and the evolution of gibbon songs." *Biology Review* 77, (2002): 57-76.

Geissmann, Thomas. "Evolution of Communication in Gibbons (Hylobatidae)." Ph.D. diss., University of Zurich, 1993.

Gensini, Stefano. "Comunicazione animale e "soglia" semiotica. Un tema da ripensare." *Syzetesis* VI, no. 2 (2019): 341-362.

Gentile, Giovanni. 1931. *La filosofia dell'arte*. Milano: Treves.

Ghanzanfar, Asif., and Drew Rendall. "The evolution of human vocal production." *Current Biology* 18, (2008): 457-460.

Ghazanfar, Asif A., and Daniel Y. Takahashi. "The evo-devo of vocal communication: Insights from marmoset monkeys." In *Evolution of Nervous Systems: Second Edition*, edited by Jon H. Kaas, 317-324. Amsterdam: Elsevier Inc., 2016.

Ghazanfar, Asif A., and Marc D. Hauser. "The neuroethology of primate vocal communication: substrates for the evolution of speech." *Trends in Cognitive Science* 3, (1999): 377-384.

Ghazanfar, Asif A., Daniel Y. Takahashi, Yisi S. Zhang, and Jeremy I Borjon. "Marmoset Monkey Vocal Communication: Common Developmental Trajectories with Humans and Possible Mechanisms." In *Minnesota Symposia on Child Psychology: Development of the Social Brain*, edited by Jed T. Elison, and Maria D. Sera, 87-112. Hoboken, New Yersey: John Wiley & Sons, 2018.

Giacoma, Cristina, Viviana Sorrentino, Clement Rabarivola, and Marco Gamba. "Sex differences in the song of Indri." *International Journal of Primatology* 31, (2010): 539-551.

Giannattasio, Francesco. 1998. *Il concetto di musica: Contributi e prospettive della ricerca etnomusicologica*. Roma: Bulloni.

Gibbs, Raymond W. "Embodied experience and linguistic meaning." *Brain and language* 84, no. 1 (2003): 1-15.

Gibson, Kathleen R. "Talking about birds, bees, and primates, too: implications for language evolution." In *The Evolution of Language. Proceedings of the 8th International Conference (EVOLANG8)*, edited by Andrew D. M. Smith, Marieke Schouwstra, Bart de Boer, and Kenny Smith, 153-159. Singapore: World Scientific Publishing, 2010.

Gifford, Gordon W., Katherine A. MacLean, Marc D. Hauser, and Yale E. Cohen. "The Neurophysiology of Functionally Meaningful Categories: Macaque Ventrolateral Prefrontal Cortex Plays a Critical Role in Spontaneous Categorization of Species-Specific Vocalizations." *Journal of Cognitive Neuroscience* 17, no. 9 (2005): 1471-1482.

Gill, Sharon A., and Andrea M. K. Bierema. "On the meaning of alarm calls: A review of functional reference in avian alarm calling." *Ethology* 119, no. 6 (2013): 449-461.

Glaser, Susan. "The missing link: Connections between musical and linguistic prosody." *Contemporary Music Review* 19, no. 3 (2000): 129 -154.

Gleitmen, Lila R., and Eric Wanner. "Language acquisition: The state of the art." In *Language acquisition: The state of the art*, edited by Eric Wanner and Lila R. Gleitman, 3-48. Cambridge: Cambridge University Press, 1982.

Glenberg, Arthur M., and Vittorio Gallese. "Action-based language: a theory of language acquisition, comprehension, and production." *Cortex* 48, no. 7 (2011): 905-922.

Goldstein, Michael H., and Jennifer A. Schwade. "Social feedback to infants' babbling facilitates rapid phonological learning." *Psychological science* 19, no. 5 (2008): 515-523.

Gonzalez-Voyer, Alejandro, and Niclas Kolm. "Parental care and investment." *eLS*, (2010):1-8.

Goodall, Jane. 1986. *The Chimpanzees of Gombe - Patterns of Behaviour*. Massachusetts: Belknap Press of Harvard University.

Gould, James L., and Peter Marler. "Apprendimento e istinto." *Le Scienze* 38, no. 223 (1987): 44-55.

Gould, Stephen J. "A developmental constraint in Cerion, with comments on the definition and interpretation of constraint in evolution." *Evolution* 43, (1989): 516-539.

Gould, Stephen J. "The evolutionary biology of constraint." *Daedalus* 109, (1980): 39-52.

Gould, Stephen J., and Elisabeth Vrba. "Exaptation - A missing term in the science of form." *Paleobiology* 8, no. 1 (1982): 4-15.

Gould, Stephen J., and Niles Eldredge. "Punctuated equilibria: the tempo and mode of evolution reconsidered." *Paleobiology* 3, no. 2 (1977): 115-151.

Gould, Stephen J., and Richard Lewontin. "The spandrels of San Marco and the Panglossian paradigm: A critique of the adaptationist programme." *Proceedings of the Royal Society of London B* 205, no. 1161, (1979): 581-598.

Granier-Deferre, Carolyn, Aurélie Ribeiro, Anne-Yvonne Jacquet, and Sophie Bassereau. "Near-term fetuses process temporal features of speech." *Developmental Science* 14, no. 2 (2011): 336-352.

Greenewalt, Crawford H. 1968. *Bird Song: Acoustics and Physiology*. Washington: Smithsonian Institution Press.

Greenspan, Stanley I., and Stuart G. Shanker. 2004. *The First Idea. How Symbols, Language, and Intelligence Evolved from Our Primate Ancestors to Modern Humans*. Cambridge, MA: Da Capo Press.

Greimas, Algirdas J. 1966. *Sémantique structural*. Paris: Larousse.

Grieser, DiAnne L., and Patricia K. Kuhl. "Maternal speech to infants in a tonal language: Support for universal prosodic features in motherese." *Developmental Psychology* 24, no. 1 (1988): 14-20.

Griffin, Donald R. 1992. *Animal Minds: Beyond Cognition to Consciousness*. London: University of Chicago Press.

Griffin, Donald R. *The Question of Animal Awareness. Evolutionary Continuity of Mental Experience*. New York: Rockfeller University Press, 1976.

Griffiths, Paul E. 1997. *What Emotions Really Are. The Problem of Psychological Categories*. London: The University of Chicago Press.

Grimaldi, Mirko. 2019. *Il cervello fonologico*. Roma: Carocci.

Güntürkün, Onur, Monika Güntürkün, and Constanze Hahn. "Whistled Turkish alters language asymmetries." *Current Biology* 25, no. 16 (2015): R706-R708.

Gussenhoven, Carlos. 2004. *The Phonology of Tone and Intonation*. Cambridge: Cambridge University Press.

Hagoort, Peter, Lea Hald, Marcel Bastiaansen, and Karl M. Petersson. "Integration of word meaning and world knowledge in language comprehension." *Science* 304, no. 5669 (2004): 438-441.

Haimoff, Elliott H. "Convergence in the duetting of monogamous Old World primates." *Journal of Human Evolution* 15, no. 1 (1986): 51-59.

Haimoff, Elliott H. 1983. *Gibbon Songs: An Acoustical, Organizational, and Behavioural Analysis*. Cambridge: Cambridge University Press.

Hall, Brian K. 1999. *Evolutionary Developmental Biology*. Second Edition. Dordrecht: Kluwer Academic.

Hall, Michelle L. "Convergent vocal strategies of males and females are consistent with a cooperative function of duetting in Australian magpie-larks." *Behaviour* 143, (2006): 425-449.

Hamilton, Andy. 2007. *Aesthetics and Music*. UK: Bloomsbury Publishing.

Hamilton, William D. "Innate social aptitudes of man: an approach from evolutionary genetics." *Biosocial Anthropology* 133, (1975): 115-132.

Hamilton, William D. "The genetical evolution of social behaviour." *Journal of Theoretical Biology* 7, (1964): 1-16.

Hanslick, Eduard. 1854. *Vom Musikalisch-Schönen*. Leipzig: R. Weigel.

Hanson, Howard. "Some objective studies of rhythm in music." *American Journal of Psychiatry* 101, no. 3 (1944): 364-369.

Hara, Erina, Miriam V. Rivas, James M. Ward, Kazuo Okanoya, and Erich D. Jarvis. "Convergent Differential Regulation of Parvalbumin in the Brains of Vocal Learners." *PLoS One* 7, no. 1 (2012): e29457.

Hari, Riitta, Linda Henriksson, Sanna, Malinen, and Lauri Parkkonen. "Centrality of social interaction in human brain function." *Neuron* 88, (2015): 181-193.

Hart Johan't, René Collier, and Antonie Cohen. 2006. *A Perceptual Study of Intonation: An Experimental-phonetic Approach to Speech Melody*. Cambridge: Cambridge University Press.

Harwood, Dane L. "Universalism music: A perspective from cognitive psychology." *Ethnomusicology*, (1976): 521-533.

Hatfield, Elaine, John T. Cacioppo, and Richard L. Rapson. 1994. *Emotional Contagion. Studies in Emotion and Social Interaction*. Cambridge: Cambridge University Press.

Hausen, Maija, Ritva Torppa, Viljami R. Salmela, Martti Vainio, and Teppo Särkämö. "Music and speech prosody: A common rhythm." *Frontiers in Psychology* 4, (2013): 566.

Hauser, Marc D. "Functional referents and acoustic similarity: Field playback experiments with rhesus monkeys." *Animal Behaviour* 55, (1998): 1647-1658.

Hauser, Marc D. "Review of "How monkey se the world: inside the mind of another species" by Cheney D. L., Seyfarth R. M." *Ethology* 89, (1992): 170-171.

Hauser, Marc D. 1996. *The Evolution of Communication*. Cambridge: MIT Press.

Hauser, Marc D., and Elizabeth Spelke. "Evolutionary and Developmental Foundations of Human Knowledge: A Case Study of Mathematics." In *The Cognitive Neurosciences*, edited by Michael S. Gazzaniga, 853-864. Cambridge, MA: The MIT Press, 2004.

Hauser, Marc D., and Josh McDermott. "The evolution of the music faculty: A comparative perspective." *Nature Neuroscience* 6, (2003): 663-668.

Hauser, Marc D., and W. Tecumseh Fitch. "What are the uniquely human components of the language faculty?." *Studies in the Evolution of Language* 3, (2003): 158-181.

Hauser, Marc D., Charles Yang, Robert C. Berwick, Ian Tattersall, Michael J. Ryan, Jeffrey Watumull, Noam Chomsky, and Richard C. Lewontin. "The mystery of language evolution." *Frontiers in Psychology* 5, no. 401 (2014): 401.

Hauser, Marc D., Noam Chomsky, and Tecumseh W. Fitch. "The faculty of language: what is it, who has it, and how did it evolve?." *Science* 298, no. 5598 (2002): 1569-1579.

Hayashi, Misato, and Tetsuro Matsuzawa. "Mother-infant interactions in captive and wild chimpanzees." *Infant Behavior and Development* 48, (2017): 20-29.

Hayes, Cathy. 1951. *The Ape in Our House*. New York: Harper & Row.

Heffner, Christopher C., and Robert L. Slevc. "Prosodic structure as a parallel to musical structure." *Frontiers in psychology* 6, (2015): 1962.

Hewitt, Gwen, Ann MacLarnon, and Kate E. Jones. "The functions of laryngeal air sacs in primates: A new hypothesis." *Folia Primatologica* 73, no. 2-3 (2002): 70-94.

Hodges, Donald A. "Why are we musical? Speculations on an evolutionary plausibilty for musical behavior." *Bulletin of the Council for Research in Music Education* 99, (1989): 7-22.

Hoeschele, Marisa, Hugo Merchant, Yukiko Kikuchi, Yuko Hattori, and Carel ten Cate. "Searching for the origins of musicality across species." *Philosophical Transactions of the Royal Society B* 370, no. 1664 (2015): 20140094.

Hölldobler, Bert, and Edward O. Wilson. *The Ants.* Cambridge (MA): Harvard University Press, 1990.

Hölldobler, Bert. "Evolution of insect communication." In *Insect Communication. 12th Symposium of the Royal Entomological Society of London*, edited by Trevor Lewis, 349-377. London: Academic Press, 1984.

Honing, Henkjan, Carel ten Cate, Isabelle Peretz, and Sandra E. Trehub. "Without it no music: Cognition, biology and evolution of musicality." *Philosophical Transactions of the Royal Society B* 370, no. 1664 (2015): 20140088.

Honing, Henkjan. 2019. *The Evolving Animal Orchestra: In Search of What Makes Us Musical.* Cambridge (MA): MIT Press.

Honing, Henkjan. "On the biological basis of musicality." *Annals of the New York Academy of Sciences* 1423, no. 1 (2018): 51-56.

Honing, Henkjan. 2013. *Musical Cognition: A Science of Listening.* UK: Routledge.

Horn, Andrew G., Marty L. Leonard, and Daniel M. Weary, "Oxygen consumption during crowing by roosters: Talk is cheap." *Animal Behaviour* 50, (1995): 1171-1175.

Hrdy, Sarah Blaffer. 2011. *Mothers and Others.* Cambridge, (MA): Harvard University Press.

Hunyadi, László. "Grouping, the cognitive basis of recursion in language." *Argumentum* 2, (2006): 67-114.

Huotilainen, Minna. "A new dimension on foetal language learning." *Acta Paediatrica* 102, no. 2 (2013): 102-103.

Huron, David. "Is music an evolutionary adaptation?." Annals of the New York Academy of sciences 930, no. 1 (2001): 43-61.

Huron, David. 2008. *Sweet anticipation: Music and the Psychology of Expectation.* Cambridge: MIT Press.

Ilie, Gabriella, and William Forde Thompson. "A comparison of acoustic cues in music and speech for three dimensions of affect." *Music Perception* 23, no. 4 (2006): 319-330.

Imberty, Michel, and Giuseppe Buzzanca. "Cognitivistic perspectives in modern musical psychology." *Rivista italiana di musicologia* 35, no. 1/2, (2000): 453-484.

Imberty, Michel. 1986. *Entendre la musique. Sémantique psychologique de la musique.* Paris: Dunode.

Jablonka Eva, Simona Ginsburg, and Daniel Dor. "The co-evolution of language and emotions." *Philosophical transactions of the Royal Society of London B* 367, no. 1599 (2012): 2152-2159.

Jackendoff, Ray. "Parallels and Nonparallels between Language and Music." *Music Perception* 26, no. 3 (2009): 195-204.

Jakobson, Roman. 1973. *Essais de linguistique générale.* Paris: Les Editions de Minuit.

Janik, Vincent M., and Peter J. B. Slater. "The different roles of social learning in vocal communication." *Animal Behaviour* 60, (2000): 1-11.

Jankelevič, Vladimir. 1961. *La musique et l'ineffable*. Paris: Éditions du Seuil.

Jarvis, Erich D. "Learned birdsong and the neurobiology of human language." *Annals of the New York Academy of Sciences* 1016, (2004): 749-777.

Jarvis, Erich D., "S01-5 Evolution of brain structures for vocal learning in birds: a synopsis." *Acta Zoologica Sinica* 52, (2006): 85-89.

Jarvis, Erich D., Onur Güntürkün, Laura Bruce, András Csillag, Harvey Karten, Wayne Kuenzel, Loreta Medina, George Paxinos, David J. Perkel, Toru Shimizu, Georg Striedter, J. Martin Wild, Gregory F. Ball, Jennifer Dugas-Ford, Sarah E. Durand, Gerald E. Hough, Scott Husband, Lubica Kubikova, Diane W. Lee, Claudio V. Mello, Alice Powers, Connie Siang, Tom V. Smulders, Kazuhiro Wada, Stephanie A. White, Keiko Yamamoto, Jing Yu, Anton Reiner and Ann B. Butler. "Avian brains and a new understanding of vertebrate brain evolution." *Nature Reviews Neuroscience* 6, no. 2 (2005): 151-159.

Jespersen, Otto. 1922. *Language, Its Nature, Development, and Origin*. New York: W. W. Norton & Company.

Johnson, Mark. 1987. *The Body in the Mind: The Bodily Basis of Meaning, Imagination, and Reason*. Chicago: University of Chicago Press.

Joliveau, Elodie, John Smith, and Joe Wolfe. "Acoustics: tuning of vocal tract resonance by sopranos." *Nature* 427, (2004): 116.

Joliveau, Elodie, John Smith, and Joe Wolfe. "Vocal tract resonances in singing: The soprano voice." *The Journal of the Acoustical Society of America* 116, no. 4 (2004): 2434-2439.

Jordan, Daniel S., and Roger N. Shepard. "Tonal schemas: Evidence obtained by probing distorted musical scales." *Perception & Psychophysics* 41, no. 6 (1987): 489-504.

Jun, Sun-Ah, ed. *Prosodic Typology: The Phonology of Intonation and Phrasing (Vol. 1)*. New York: Oxford University Press, 2007.

Jürgens, Uwe. "Neural pathways underlying vocal control." *Neuroscience & Biobehavioral Reviews* 26, no. 2 (2002): 235-258.

Jusczyk, Peter W., Anne Cutler, and Nancy J. Redanz. "Infants' preferences for the predominant stress patterns of English words." *Papers and Reports on Child Language Development* 64, (1993): 675-687.

Juslin, Patrik N., and Petri Laukka. "Communication of emotions in vocal expression and music performance: Different channels, same code?." *Psychological Bulletin* 129, no. 5 (2003): 770-814.

Kania, Andrew. "Music." In *The Routledge Companion to Aesthetics*, edited by Gaut Berys, and Dominic Lopes, 639-648. New York: Routledge, 2013.

Kanwal, Jagmeet S., Sumiko Matsumura, Kevin Ohlemiller, and Nobuo Suga. "Analysis of acoustic elements and syntax in communication sounds emitted by mustached bats." *The Journal of the Acoustical Society of America* 96, no. 3 (1994): 1229-1254.

Karmiloff, Kyra, and Annette Karmiloff-Smith. 2002. *Sentieri del linguaggio*. Milano: McGraw-Hill Italia.

Karpf, Anne. 2006. *The Human Voice. How This Extraordinary Instrument Reveals Essential Clues About Who We Are*. USA: Bloomsbury.

Kauffman, Stuart. 2000. *Investigation*. Oxford: Oxford University Press.

Kazanina, Nina, Jeffrey S. Bowers, and William Idsardi. "Phonemes: Lexical access and beyond." *Psychonomic Bulletin & Review* 25, no. 2 (2018): 560-585.

Kewley-Port Diane, and Charles S. Watson. "Formant-frequency discrimination for isolated English vowels." *Journal of the Acoustical Society of America* 95, (1994): 485-496.

Kingstone, Alan, Daniel Smilek, and John D. Eastwood. "Cognitive ethology: A new approach for studying human cognition." *British Journal of Psychology* 99, no. 3 (2008): 317-340.

Kircher, Athanasius. 1650. *Musurgia universalis, sive Ars magna consoni et dissoni in X libros digesta*. Roma: Corbelletti.

Kisilevsky, Barbara S., Sylvia M. J. Hains, Kang Lee, Xing Xie, Hefeng Huang, Hai Hui Ye, Ke Zhang, and Zengping Wang. "Effects of experience on fetal voice recognition." *Psychological Science* 14, no. 3 (2003): 220-224.

Kitchen Dawn M., Thore J. Bergman, Dorothy L. Cheney, James R. Nicholson, and Robert M. Seyfarth. "Comparing responses of four ungulate species to playbacks of baboon alarm calls." *Animal Cognition* 13, no. 6 (2010): 861-870.

Koda, Hiroki, Alban Lemasson, Chisako Oyakawa, Joko Pamungkas, and Nobuo Masataka. "Possible role of mother-daughter vocal interactions on the development of species-specific song in gibbons." *PloS One* 8, no. 8 (2013): e71432.

Koda, Hiroki, Takeshi Nishimura, Isao T. Tokuda, Chisako Oyakawa, Toshikuni Nihonmatsu, and Nobuo Masataka. "Soprano singing in gibbons." *American Journal of Physical Anthropology* 149, no. 3 (2012): 347-355.

Koelsch, Stefan, Elisabeth Kasper, Daniela Sammler, Katrin Schulze, Thomas Gunter, and Angela D. Friederici. "Music, language and meaning: brain signatures of semantic processing." *Nature Neuroscience* 7, (2004): 302-307.

Koelsch, Stefan, Thomas C. Gunter, Matthias Wittfoth, and Daniela Sammler. "Interaction between syntax processing in language and in music: An ERP study." *Journal of Cognitive Neuroscience* 17, no. 10 (2005): 1565-1577.

Koelsch, Stefan. "Toward a neural basis of music perception–a review and updated model." *Frontiers in Psychology* 2, (2011): 110.

Kotz, Sonja A., Andrea Ravignani, and Tecumseh W. Fitch. "The Evolution of Rhythm Processing." *Trends in Cognitive Sciences* 22, no. 10 (2018): 896-910.

Krams, Indrikis, Tatjana Krama, Todd M. Freeberg, Cecilia Kullberg, and Jeffrey R. Lucas. "Linking social complexity and vocal complexity: a parid perspective." *Philosophical Transactions of the Royal Society B* 367, (2012): 1879-1891.

Kreiman, Jody, and Diana Sidtis. 2011. *Foundations of Voice Studies: An Interdisciplinary Approach to Voice Production and Perception*. UK: Wiley Blackwell.

Kristeller, Paul Oskar. "The modern system of the arts: A study in the history of aesthetics part I." *Journal of the History of Ideas* 12, no. 4 (1951): 496-527.

Kroodsma, Donald E., and Bruce E. Byers. "The Function(s) of Bird Song". *American Zoologist* 31, no 2 (2015): 318-328.

Kroodsma, Donald E., and Hiroshi Momose. "Songs of the Japanese population of the winter wren (Troglodytes troglodytes)." *Condor* 93, (1991): 424-432.

Krumhansl, Carol L. "Perceiving tonal structure in music: The complex mental activity by which listeners distinguish subtle relations among tones, chords, and keys in Western tonal music offers new territory for cognitive psychology." *American Scientist* 73, no. 4 (1985): 371-378.

Krumhansl, Carol L. "Rhythm and pitch in music cognition". *Psychological Bulletin* 126, no. 1 (2000): 159-179.

Kubikova, Lubica, Elena A. Turner, and Erich D. Jarvis. "The pallial basal ganglia pathway modulates the behaviourally driven gene expression of the motor pathway." *European Journal of Neuroscience* 25, no. 7 (2007): 2145-2160.

Kuhl, Patricia K. "Auditory perception and the evolution of speech." *Human Evolution* 3, (1988): 19-43.

Kuhl, Patricia K. "Early language acquisition: cracking the speech code." *Nature Reviews Neuroscience* 5, no. 11 (2004): 831-843.

Kuhl, Patricia K., Erica Stevenson, Akiko Hayashi, Toshisada Deguchi, Shigeru Kiritani, and Paul Iverson. "Infants show a facilitation effect for native language phonrc perception between 5 and 12 months." *Developmental Science* 9, no. 2 (2006): 13-21.

Kulahci, Ipek, Daniel I. Rubinstein, and Asif A. Ghazanfar. "Lemurs groom-at-a-distance through vocal networks." *Animal Behavior* 110, (2015): 179-186.

Kvarnemo, Charlotta. "Evolution and maintenance of male care: is increased paternity a neglected benefit of care?" *Behavioral Ecology* 17, no. 1 (2006): 144-148.

Lachlan, Robert F., Oliver Ratmann, and Stephen Nowicki. "Cultural conformity generates extremely stable traditions in bird song." *Nature Communications* 9, no. 1 (2018): 1-9.

Lachmann, Michael, Szabolcs Számadó, and Carl T. Bergstrom. "Cost and conflict in animal signals and human language." *PNAS* 98, no. 23 (2001): 13189-13194.

Lagaay, Alice. "Between sound and silence: Voice in the history of psychoanalysis." *Episteme* 1, no. 1, (2008): 53-62.

Lahav, Amir, Elliot Saltzman, and Gottfried Schlaug. "Action representation of sound: audiomotor recognition network while listening to newly acquired actions." *Journal of Neuroscience* 27, no. 2 (2007): 308-314.

Lakoff, George, and Mark Johnson. 1999. *Philosophy in the Flesh: The Embodied Mind and its Challenge to Western Thought*. New York: Basic books.

Lameira, Adriano R., Madeleine E. Hardus, Alexander Mielke, Serge A. Wich, and Robert W. Shumaker, "Vocal fold control beyond the species-specific repertoire in an orangutan." *Scientific Reports* 6, no. 30315 (2016): 1-10.

Langer, Jonas. 1969. *Theories of Development*. New York: Holt Rinehart and Winston Inc.

Langus, Alan, Erika Marchetto, Ricardo A. H. Bion, and Marina Nespor. "Can prosody be used to discover hierarchical structure in continuous speech?" *Journal of Memory and Language* 66, no. 1, (2012): 285-306.

Laubichler, Manfred. "A Constrained View of Evo-Devo's Roots." *Science* 309, (2005): 1019-1020.

Lee, Yune S., Petr Janata, Carlton Frost, Michael Hanke, and Richard Granger. "Investigation of melodic contour processing in the brain using multivariate pattern-based fMRI." *Neuroimage* 57, no. 1 (2011): 293-300.

Leman, Marc, and Pieter-Jan Maes. "The Role of Embodiment in the Perception of Music." *Empirical Musicology Review* 9, no. 3-4 (2015): 236-246.

Leman, Marc. 2007. *Embodied Music Cognition*. Cambridge MA: MIT Press.

Leman, Marc. 2017. *The Routledge Companion to Embodied Music Interaction*. New York: Routledge.

Lerdahl, Fred. "Musical syntax and its relation to linguistic syntax." In *Language, Music, and the Brain*, edited by Michael A. Arbib, 257-272. London: MIT Press, 2013.

Lerdhal, Fred, and Ray Jackendoff. 1983. *The Generative Theory of Tonal Musical*. Cambridge: MIT Press.

Leroi-Gourhan, Andrè. 1964. *Le geste et la parole (Vol. 2)*. Paris: Albin Michel.

Lesaffre, Micheline, Pieter-Jan Maes, and Marc Leman, eds. *The Routledge Companion to Embodied Music Interaction*. New York, NY: Routledge, 2017.

Levinson, Jerrold. 2011. *Music, art, and metaphysics*. New York: Oxford University Press.

Levinson, Stephen C. "Turn-taking in Human Communication - Origins and Implications for Language Processing." *Trends in Cognitive Sciences* 20, no. 1 (2016): 6-14.

Levitin, Daniel J. 2006. *This is Your Brain on Music: The Science of a Human Obsession*. New York: Penguin.

Levy, Florence. "Mirror neurons, birdsong and human language: A hypothesis." *Frontiers in Psychiatry* 2, (2012): 1-7.

Lieberman, Philip, and Robert McCarthy. "Tracking the evolution of language and speech: Comparing vocal tracts to identify speech capabilities." *Expedition: The Magazine of the University of Pennsylvania* 49, no. 2 (2007): 15-20.

Lieberman, Philip, and Sheila E. Blumstein, 1988. *Speech Physiology, Speech Perception, and Acoustic Phonetics*. Cambridge: Cambridge University Press.

Lieberman, Philip. "Limits on tongue deformation. Diana monkey formants and the impossible vocal tract shapes." *Journal of Human Evolution* 50, (2006): 219-221.

Lieberman, Philip. "Motor control, speech, and the evolution of human language." In *Language Evolution*, edited by Morten H. Christiansen, and Simon Kirby, 255-271. Oxford: Oxford University Press, 2003.

Lieberman, Philip. "The evolution of human speech: Its anatomical and neural bases." *Current Anthropology* 48, no. 1 (2007): 39-66.

Lieberman, Philip. "The evolution of language and thought." *Journal of Anthropological Sciences* 94, (2016): 127-146.

Lieberman, Philip. 1984. *The Biology and Evolution of Language*. Cambridge (MA): Harvard University Press.

Lieberman, Philip. 1991. *Uniquely Human. The Evolution of Speech, Thought, and Selfless Behavior*. Cambridge (MA): Harvard University Press.

Livingstone, Frank B. "Did the Australopithecines sing?." *Current Anthropology* 14, (1973): 25-29.

Lo Piparo, Franco. 2003. *Aristotele e il linguaggio. Cosa fa di una lingua una lingua.* Roma-Bari: Laterza.

Locke, Simeon, and Lucia Kellar. "Categorical perception in a non-linguistic mode." *Cortex* 9, no. 4 (1973): 355-369.

Lomax, Alan. "Universals in song." *The World of Music* 19, no. 1-2 (1977): 117-130.

Lorenz, Konrad. 1978. *Vergleichende Verhaltensforschung: Grundlagen der Ethologie.* Berlin: Springer.

Luef, Eva Maria, and Katja Liebal. "Infant-Directed Communication in Lowland Gorillas (Gorilla gorilla): Do Older Animals Scaffold Communicative Competence in Infants?." *American Journal of Primatology* 74, no. 9 (2012): 841-852.

Luef, Eva Maria, Thomas Breuer, and Simone Pika. "Food-Associated Calling in Gorillas (*Gorilla g. gorilla*) in the Wild." *PLoS One* 11, no. 2 (2016): e0144197.

Ma, Weiyi, Anna Fiveash, and William Forde Thompson. "Spontaneous emergence of language-like and music-like vocalizations from an artificial protolanguage." *Semiotica*, no. 229 (2019): 1-23.

Mâche, François Bernard. 1992. *Musica, mito, natura.* Bologna: Cappelli.

Mado Proverbio, Alice, Andrea Orlandi, and Francesca Pisanu. "Brain processing of consonance/dissonance in musicians and controls: a hemispheric asymmetry revisited." *European Journal of Neuroscience* 44, no. 6 (2016): 2340-2356.

Mado Proverbio, Alice. 2019. *Neuroscienze cognitive della musica. Il cervello musicale tra arte e scienza.* Bologna: Zanichelli.

Maeder, Costantino, and Mark Reybrouck (eds.). *Music, analysis, experience: New perspectives in musical semiotics.* Leuven: Leuven University Press, 2015.

Maestripieri, Dario, and Josep Call. "Mother-infant communication in primates." *Advances in the Study of Behavior* 25, (1996): 613-642.

Magno Caldognetto, Emanuela, Piero Cosi, Carlo Drioli, Graziano Tisato, and Federica Cavicchio. "Modifications of phonetic labial targets in emotive speech: effects of the co-production of speech and emotions." *Speech Communication* 44, no. 1- 4 (2004): 173-185.

Magrath, Robert D., Dirk Platzen, and Junko Kondo. "From nestling calls to fledgling silence: adaptive timing of change in response to aerial alarm calls." *Proceedings of the Royal Society B* 273, no. 1599 (2006): 2335-2341.

Maretti, Giovanna, Viviana Sorrentino, Andriamasitoly Finomana, Marco Gamba, and Cristina Giacoma. "Not just a pretty song: an overview of the vocal repertoire of Indri indri." *Journal of Anthropological Sciences* 88, (2010): 151-165.

Marler, Peter, Alfred Dufty, and Roberta Pickert. "Vocal communication in the domestic chicken: I. Does a sender communicate information about the quality of a food referent to a receiver?." *Animal Behaviour* 34, (1986):188-193.

Marler, Peter, and Linda Hobbett. "Individuality in a long-range vocalization of wild chimpanzees." *Zeitschrift fur Tierpsychologie* 38, (1975): 97-109.

Marler, Peter. "Functions of arousal and emotion in primate communication: A semiotic approach." *Topics in Primatology* 1, (1992): 235-248.

Marler, Peter. "On the origin of speech from animal sounds." In *The Role of Speech in Language*, edited by James F. Kavanagh, and James Cutting, 11-37. Cambridge, MA: MIT Press, 1975.

Marler, Peter. "Origin of Music and Speech: Insight from Animals." In *The Origins of Music*, edited by Nils L. Wallin, Bjon Merker, and Steven Brown, 31-48. Cambridge: MIT Press, 2000.

Marshall, John C. "The descent of the larynx." *Nature* 338, (1989): 702-703.

Martinelli, Dario. 2011. *Quando la musica è bestiale per davvero. Studiare e capire la zoomusicologia.* Roma: Aracne.

Marx, Viola, and Emese Nagy. "Fetal behavioural responses to maternal voice and touch." *PloS one* 10, no. 6 (2015): e0129118.

Masataka, Nobuo. "Music, Evolution and Language." *Developmental Science* 10, no. 1 (2007): 35-39.

Masataka, Nobuo. 2003. *The Onset of Language.* Cambridge: Cambridge University Press.

Matsuda, Yoshi-Taka, Kenichi Ueno, Kang Cheng, Yukuo Konishi, Reiko Mazuka, and Kazuo Okanoya. "Auditory observation of infant-directed speech by mothers: experience-dependent interaction between language and emotion in the basal ganglia." *Frontiers in Human Neuroscience* 8, no. 907 (2014): 907.

Matsuzawa, Tetsuro. "Evolutionary Origins of the Human Mother-Infant Relationship." In *Cognitive Development in Chimpanzees*, edited by Tetsuro Matsuzawa, Masaki Tomonaga, and Masayuki Tanaka, 127-141. Tokyo: Springer, 2006.

Mattingly, Ignatius G. "The global character of phonetic gestures." *Journal of Phonetics* 18, no. 3 (1990): 445-452.

Maynard Smith, John, Richard Burian, Stuart Kauffman, Pere Alberch, John Campbell, Brian Goodwin, Russell Lande, David Raup, and Lewis Wolpert. "Developmental constraints and evolution." *Quarterly Review of Biology* 60, (1985): 265-287.

McCarty, John P. "The energetic costs of begging in nestling passerines." *The Auk* 113, (1996): 178-188.

McComb, Katie, and Stuart Semple. "Co-evolution of vocal communication and sociality in primates." *Biology Letters* 1, (2005): 381-385.

McDermott, Josh H., and Andrew J. Oxenham. "Music perception, pitch, and the auditory system." *Current Opinion in Neurobiology* 18, no. 4 (2008): 452-463.

Mehler, Jacques, Josiane Bertoncini, Michele Barriere, and Dora Jassik-Gerschenfeld. "Infant recognition of mother's voice. *Perception* 7, no. 5 (1978): 491-497.

Mehler, Jacques, Peter Jusczyk, Ghislaine Lambertz, Nilofar Halsted, Bertoncini Josiane, and Claudine Amiel-Tison. "A precursor of language acquisition in young infants." *Cognition* 29, no. 2 (1988): 143-178.

Mehr, Samuel A., Manvir Singh, Dean Knox, Daniel M. Ketter, Daniel Pickens-Jones, S. Atwood, Christopher Lucas, Nori Jacoby, Alena A. Egner, Erin J.

Hopkins, Rhea M. Howard, Joshua K. Hartshorne, Mariela V. Jennings, Jan Simson, Constance M. Bainbridge, Steven Pinker, Timothy J. O'Donnell, Max M. Krasnow, and Luke Glowacki. "Universality and diversity in human song." *Science* 366, no. 6468 (2019): eaax0868.

Menary, Richard. "Introduction to the special issue on 4E cognition." *Phenomenology and the Cognitive Sciences* 9, no. 4 (2010): 459-463.

Menary, Richard. 2010. *The Extended Mind*. Cambridge, MA: MIT Press.

Menninghaus, Winfried. "La teoria darwiniana sulla musica e la retorica." *Rivista di estetica* 54, no. 1 (2013): 35-156.

Merker, Bjorn, Iain Morley, and Willem Zuidema. "Five fundamental constraints on theories of the origins of music." *Philosophical Transactions of the Royal Society B* 370, no. 1664 (2015): 20140095.

Merleau-Ponty, Maurice. 1945. *Phénoménologie de la perception*. Paris: Gallimard.

Merriam, Alan P. 1964. *The Anthropology of Music*. Evanston: Northwestern University Press.

Meuthen, Denis, Sebastian A. Baldauf, and Timo Thünken. "Evolution of alarm cues: a role for kin selection." *F1000 Research* 1, no. 27 (2014): 1-27.

Meyer, Julien. "Bioacoustics of human whistled languages: an alternative approach to the cognitive processes of language." *Anais da Academia Brasileira de Ciências* 76, no. 2 (2004): 406-412.

Meyer, Julien. 2015. *Whistled languages. A Worldwide Inquiry on Human Whistled Speech*. Heidelberg, Germany; New York, NY, USA: Springer.

Meyer, Leonard. 1956. *Emotion and Meaning in Music*. Chicago: University of Chicago Press.

Meyer, Martin, Matthias Keller, and Nathalie Giroud. "Suprasegmental speech prosody and the human brain." In *The Oxford handbook of voice perception*, edited by Frühholz, Sascha, and Pascal Belin, 143-165. New York: Oxford University Press, 2018.

Miall, David S., and Don Kuiken. "Foregrounding, Defamiliarization, and Affect: Response to Literary Stories." *Poetics* 22, (1994): 389-407.

Miall, David S., and Ellen Dissanayake. "The poetics of babytalk." *Human Nature* 14, no. 4 (2003): 337-364.

Migliaccio, Carlo. "Il Positivismo e la musica". In *Introduzione alla filosofia della musica*, edited by Carlo Migliaccio, 114-129. Novara: UTET, 2009.

Miller, Geoffrey. "Evolution of music through sexual selection." In *The Origins of Music*, edited by Nils Wallin, Bjorn Merker, and Steven Brown, 329-360. Cambridge: MIT Press, 2000.

Miller, Geoffrey. 2000. *The Mating Mind: How Sexual Choice Shaped the Evolution of Human Nature*. New York: Anchor Books.

Millotte, Severine, Roger Wales, Emmanuel Dupoux, and Anne Christophe. "Can prosodic cues and function words guide syntactic processing and acquisition." In *Speech Prosody: 3rd International Conference*, edited by Rüdiger Hofmann, and Hansjörg Mixdorff. Dresden: TUD Press, 2006.

Minelli, Alessandro. "Biological systematics in the Evo-Devo era." *European Journal of Taxonomy* 125, (2015): 1-23.

Minelli, Alessandro. 2007. *Forme del divenire. Evo-devo: La biologia evoluzionistica dello sviluppo*. Torino: Einaudi.

Mitani, John C., and Jennifer Stuht. "The evolution of nonhuman primate loud calls: Acoustic adaptation for long-distance transmission." *Primates* 39, (1998): 171-182.

Mitani, John C., and Kari L. Brandt. "Social factors influence the acoustic variability in the long-distance calls of male chimpanzees." *Ethology* 96, (1994): 233-252.

Mithen, Steven. "Handaxes: The First Aesthetic Artefacts." In *Evolutionary Aesthetics*, edited by Eckart Voland, and Karl Grammer, 261-275. Heidelberg: Springer, 2003.

Mithen, Steven. 1999. *The Prehistory of the Mind: The Cognitive Origins of Art, Religion and Science*. London: Thames and Hudson.

Mithen, Steven. 2005. *The Singing Neanderthals: The Origins of Music, Language, Mind, and Body*. Cambridge, MA: Harvard University Press.

Mitterer, Holger, Taehong Cho, and Sahyang Kim. "How does prosody influence speech categorization?." *Journal of Phonetics* 54, (2016): 68-79.

Mol, Carien, Aoju Chen, René W. J. Kager, and Sita M. Ter Haar. "Prosody in birdsong: A review and perspective." *Neuroscience & Biobehavioral Reviews* 81, (2017): 167-180.

Molino, Jean. "Fait musical et sémiologie de la musique." *Musique en jeu* 17, (1975): 37-62.

Monnot, Marilee, Robert Foley, and Elliott Ross. "Affective prosody: Whence motherese." *Behavioral and Brain Sciences* 27, no. 4 (2004): 518-519.

Moon, Christine, Hugo Lagercrantz, and Patricia K. Kuhl. "Language experienced in utero affects vowel perception after birth: A two-country study." *Acta Paediatrica* 102, no. 2 (2013): 156-160.

Moon, Seung-Jae, and Bjorn Lindblom. "Two experiments on oxygen consumption during speech production: vocal effort and speaking tempo." *Proceedings of the 15th International Congress of Phonetic Sciences*, (2003): 3129-3132.

Morgan, James L., and Elissa L. Newport. "The role of constituent structure in the induction of an artificial language." *Journal of Verbal Learning and Verbal Behavior* 20, no. 1 (1981): 67-85.

Morley, Iain. "A multi-disciplinary approach to the origins of music: perspectives from anthropology, archaeology, cognition and behaviour." *Journal of Anthropological Science* 92, (2013): 147-177.

Morley, Iain. 2013. *The Prehistory of Music: Human Evolution, Archaeology, and the Origins of Musicality*. Oxford: Oxford University Press.

Morris, Charles William. 1938. *Foundations of the Theory of Signs*. Chicago: Chicago University Press.

Morris, Charles William. 1946. *Signs, Language, and Behavior*. New York: Prentice Hall.

Morton, Eugene S. "Ecological sources of selection on avian sounds." *The American Naturalist* 109, no. 965 (1975): 17-34.

Munhall, Kevin, and Anders Löfqvist. "Gestural aggregation in speech: Laryngeal gestures." *Journal of Phonetics* 20, no. 1 (1992): 111-126.

Muscelli, Cristiano. "Tra parola e canto. La voce tra fenomeno e oggetto pulsionale." *Rivista di estetica* 66, (2017): 210-223.

Näätänen, Risto, Petri Paavilainen, Teemu Rinne, and Kimmo Alho. "The mismatch negativity (MMN) in basic research of central auditory processing: a review." *Clinical Neurophysiology* 118, no. 12 (2007): 2544 -2590.

Naoi, Nozomi, Shigeru Watanabe, Kikuo Maekawa, and Junko Hibiya. "Prosody discrimination by songbirds (Padda oryzivora)." *PLoS One* 7, no. 10 (2012): e47446.

Narmour, Eugene. 1990. *The Analysis and Cognition of Basic Melodic Structures: The Implication-realization Model.* Chicago, IL: University of Chicago Press.

Nattiez, Jean Jacques. 1987. *Musicologie générale et sémiologie.* Paris: Christian Bourgois Editeur.

Nattiez, Jean-Jacques, and Roberta Faroldi. "Modelli linguistici e analisi delle strutture musicali." *Rivista italiana di musicologia* 35, no. 1-2 (2000): 321-377.

Nattiez, Jean-Jacques. "La linguistique: voie nouvelle pour l'analyse musicale?'." *Cahiers canadiens de musique* 4, (1972): 101-115.

Nattiez, Jean-Jacques. "Sémiologie et sémiographie musicale." *Musique en Jeu* 13, (1973): 78-85.

Nattiez, Jean-Jacques. 1975. *Fondements d'une sémiologie de la musique.* Paris: Union Générale d'Editions.

Nearey, Terrance M. "Vowel-space normalization procedures and phone-preserving transformations of synthetic vowels." *The Journal of the Acoustical Society of America* 74, S1, (1983): S17.

Negus, Victor E. "The function of the epiglottis." *Journal of Anatomy.* 62, no. 1 (1927): 1-8.

Negus, Victor E. 1949. *The Comparative Anatomy and Physiology of the Larynx.* London: William Heineman Medical Books.

Nespor, Marina. 1993. *Fonologia.* Bologna: Il Mulino.

Nesse, Randolph M. "Evolutionary explanations of emotions." *Human Nature* 1, no. 3, (1990): 261-289.

Nettl, Bruno. "An ethnomusicologist contemplates universals in musical sound and musical culture." In *The Origins of Music,* edited by Nils L. Wallin, Bjon Merker, and Steven Brown, 463-472. Cambridge: MIT Press, 2000.

Newen, Albert, Leon De Bruin, and Shaun Gallagher, eds. *The Oxford Handbook of 4E Cognition.* Oxford University Press, 2018.

Newman, John D. "Motherese by any other name: Mother-infant communication in non-hominin mammals." *Behavioral Brain Sciences* 27, no. 4 (2004): 519-520.

Nguyen, Noël, and Véronique Delvaux. "Role of imitation in the emergence of phonological systems." *Journal of Phonetics* 53, (2016): 46-54.

Nieminen, Sirke, Eva Istók, Elvira Brattico, and Mari Tervaniemi. "The development of the aesthetic experience of music: preference, emotions, and beauty." *Musicae Scientiae* 16, no. 3 (2012): 372-391.

Nietzsche, Friedrich. 1872. *Die Geburt der Tragödie aus dem Geiste der Musik.* Leipzig: Verlag von E. W. Fritzsch.

Nietzsche, Friedrich. 1878. *Menschliches, Allzumenschliches. Ein Buch für freie Geister.* Chemnitz: Verlag von Ernst Schmeitzner.

Nishimura, Takeshi. "The descended larynx and the descending larynx." *Anthropological Science* (2018): 180301.

Noë, Alva. "Conscious reference." *The Philosophical Quarterly* 59, no. 236 (2009): 470-482.

Noë, Alva. 2004. *Action in Perception.* Cambridge: MIT Press.

Nottebohm, Fernando. "A zoologist' s view of some language phenomena, with particular emphasis on vocal learning." In *Foundations of language development*, edited by Eric H., Lenneberg, and Elizabeth Lenneberg, 61-103. New York: Academic Press, 1975.

Nottebohm, Fernando. "The Search for Neural Mechanisms That Define the Sensitive Period for Song Learning in Birds." *Netherlands Journal of Zoology* 43, no. 1-2 (1993): 193-234.

Nowicki, Stephen, and William A. Searcy. "The evolution of vocal learning." *Current Opinion in Neurobiology* 28, (2014): 48-53.

O'Regan, J. Kevin, and Alva Noë. "A sensorimotor account of vision and visual consciousness." *Behavioral and Brain Sciences* 24, no. 5, (2001): 939-973.

O'Regan, J. Kevin, and Alva Noë. "What it is like to see: A sensorimotor theory of perceptual experience." *Synthese* 129, no. 1 (2001): 79-103.

Odom, Karan J., Michelle L. Hall. Katharina Riebel, Kevin E. Omland, and Naomi E. Langmore. "Female song is widespread and ancestral in songbirds." *Nature Communications* 5, no. 1 (2014): 1-6.

Ohala, John J. "Ethological theory and the expression of emotions in the voice." *Proceeding of Fourth International Conference on Spoken Language Processing* 3, (1996): 1812-1815.

Okanoya, Kazuo. "Sexual Display as a Syntactical Vehicle: The Evolution of Syntax in Birdsong and Human Language through Sexual Selection." In *The Transition to Language*, edited by Allison Wray, 46-63. Oxford: Oxford University Press, 2002.

Okanoya, Kazuo. "Song Syntax in Bengalese Finches: Proximate and Ultimate Analyses." *Advances in the Study of Behavior* 14, (2004): 297-346.

Oliveira, Dag, and Ades C. "Long-distance calls in Neotropical primates." *An Acad Bras Cienc* 76, (2004): 393-398.

Oliveira, Dilmar A. G., and César Ades. "Long-distance calls in Neotropical primates." *Anais da Academia Brasileira de Ciências* 76, no. 2 (2004): 393-398.

Ostwald, Peter F. 1973. *The Semiotics of Humans Sounds.* Mouton: The Hague.

Owings, Donald H., and Eugene S. Morton. 1998. *Animal Vocal Communication: A new approach.* Cambridge: Cambridge University Press.

Pacherie, Elisabeth. "The Phenomenology of Joint Action: Self-Agency versus Joint Agency." In *Joint attention: New Developments in Psychology, Philosophy of Mind, and Social Neuroscience*, edited by Axel Seemann, 343-390. Cambridge: MIT Press, 2011.

Palombit, Ryne A. "Friendship" with males. A female counterstrategy to infanticide in the Okavango Chacma Baboons." In *Sexual Coercion in Primates and Humans. An Evolutionary Perspective on Male Aggression*

Against Females, edited by Martin N. Muller, and Richard W. Wrangham, 377-409. Cambridge, MA: Harvard University Press, 2009.

Parlato-Oliveira, Erika, Catherine Saint-Georges, David Cohen, Hugues Pellerin, Isabella Marques Pereira, Catherine Fouillet, Mohamed Chetouani, Marc Dommergues and Sylvie Viaux-Savelon. ""Motherese" Prosody in Fetal-Directed Speech: An Exploratory Study Using Automatic Social Signal Processing." *Frontiers in Psychology* 12, (2021): 649.

Parncutt, Richard. "Mother schema, obstetric dilemma, and the origin of behavioral modernity." *Behavioral Sciences* 9, no. 12 (2019): 142.

Patel, Aniruddh D. "Language, music, syntax and the brain." *Nature Neuroscience* 6, (2003): 674-681.

Patel, Aniruddh D. "Musical rhythm, linguistic rhythm, and human evolution." *Music Percept* 24, (2006): 99-104.

Patel, Aniruddh D. "Rhythm in language and music: parallels and differences." *Annals of the New York Academy of Sciences* 999, no. 1 (2003): 140-143.

Patel, Aniruddh D. "The evolutionary biology of musical rhythm: was Darwin wrong?." *PLoS Biology* 12, no. 3 (2014): e1001821.

Patel, Aniruddh D., 2008. *Music, Language, and the Brain.* Oxford: Oxford University Press.

Patel, Aniruddh D., and Steven M. Demorest. "Comparative Music Cognition: Cross-Species and Cross-Cultural Studies". In *Psychology of Music*, edited by Diana Deutsch, 647-681. New York: Elsevier, 2013.

Patel, Aniruddh D., Isabelle Peretz, Mark Tramo, and Raymonde Labreque. "Processing prosodic and musical patterns: a neuropsychological investigation. *Brain and language* 61, no. 1 (1998): 123-144.

Patel, Aniruddh D., John R. Iversen, Yanqing Chen, and Bruno H. Repp. "The influence of metricality and modality on synchronization with a beat." *Experimental Brain Research* 163, (2005): 226-238.

Payne, Roger. 1995. *Among Whales*. New York: Scribner Books.

Peirce, Charles. "Elements of logic." In *Collected Papers of Charles Sanders Peirce*, edited by Charles Hartshorne and Paul Weiss, 129-269. Cambridge: Harvard University Press, 1960.

Pell, Marc D., Abhishek Jaywant, Laura Monetta, and Sonja A. Kotz. "Emotional speech processing: disentangling the effects of prosody and semantic cues." *Cognition & Emotion* 25, (2011): 834-853.

Penn, Derek C., Keith J. Holyoak, and Daniel J. Povinelli. "Darwin's mistake: Explaining the discontinuity between human and nonhuman minds." *Behavioral and Brain Sciences* 31, no. 2 (2008): 109-130.

Pennisi, Antonino, and Alessandra Falzone. 2010. *Il prezzo del linguaggio. Evoluzione ed estinzione nelle scienze cognitive*. Bologna: Il Mulino.

Pennisi, Antonino, and Alessandra Falzone. 2016. *Darwinian Biolinguistics. Theory and History of a Naturalistic Philosophy of Language and Pragmatics*. Cham: Springer.

Pennisi, Antonino, and Alessandra Falzone. 2017. *Linguaggio, evoluzione e scienze cognitive: un'introduzione*. Roma-Messina: Corisco Edizioni.

Pennisi, Antonino. "Dimensions of the Bodily Creativity. For an Extended Theory of Performativity." In *The Extended Theory of Cognitive Creativity:*

Interdisciplinary Approaches to Performativity, edited by Antonino Pennisi, and Alessandra Falzone, 9-40. Cham, New York, London: Springer International Publishing, 2020.

Pennisi, Antonino. "Prospettive evoluzioniste nell'embodied cognition. Il cervello «inquilino del corpo»." *Reti, saperi, linguaggi* 3, no. 1 (2016): 179-201.

Pennisi, Antonino. 2014. *L'errore di Platone. Biopolitica, linguaggio e diritti civili in tempo di crisi*. Bologna: Il Mulino.

Pennisi, Antonino. *Che ne sarà dei corpi? Spinoza e i misteri della cognizione incarnata*. Bologna: Il Mulino, 2021.

Pepperberg, Irene M. "Grey Parrots do not always 'parrot': the roles of imitation and phonological awareness in the creation of new labels from existing vocalizations." *Language Sciences* 29, (2007): 1-13.

Peretz, Isabelle, and Max Coltheart. "Modularity of music processing." *Nature Neuroscience* 6, (2003): 688-691.

Peretz, Isabelle. "Neurobiology of congenital amusia." *Trends in Cognitive Sciences* 20, no. 11 (2016): 857-867.

Peretz, Isabelle. "The nature of music from a biological perspective." *Cognition* 100, no. 1, (2006): 1-32.

Perruchet, Pierre, and Bénédicte Poulin-Charronnat. "Challenging prior evidence for a shared syntactic processor for language and music." *Psychonomic Bulletin & Review* 20, no. 2 (2013): 310-317.

Peters, Ann M. 1983. *The Units of Language Acquisition*. New York: Cambridge University Press.

Petersen, Michael R., Michael D. Beecher, Stephen R. Zoloth, Steven Green, Peter R. Marler, David B. Moody, and William C. Stebbins. "Neural lateralization of species-specific vocalizations by Japanese macaques (Macaca fuscata)". *Science* 202, (1978): 324-327.

Petkov, Christopher I., and Erich D. Jarvis. "Birds, primates, and spoken language origins: behavioral phenotypes and neurobiological substrates." *Frontiers in Evolutionary Neuroscience* 4, no. 12 (2012): 1-24.

Pfenning, Andreas R., Erina Hara, Osceola Whitney, Miriam V. Rivas, Rui Wang, Petra L. Roulhac, Jason T. Howard, Morgan Wirthlin, Peter V. Lovell, Ganeshkumar Ganapathy, Jacquelyn Mouncastle, M. Arthur Moseley, J. Will Thompson, Erik J. Soderblom, Atsushi Iriki, Masaki Kato, M. Thomas P. Gilbert, Guojie Zhang, Trygve Bakken, Angie Bongaarts, Amy Bernard, Ed Lein, Claudio V. Mello, Alexander J. Hartemink, Erich D. Jarvis. "Convergent transcriptional specializations in the brains of humans and song-learning birds". *Science* 346, no. 6215 (2014): 1256846.

Piaget, Jean. 1945. *La formation du Symbole chez l'enfant*. Neuchâtel: Delachaux et Niestlé.

Pievani, Telmo. "Between skeptics and adaptationists: new prospects for human language evolution." *Ciência & Ambiente* 48, (2014): 149-163.

Pievani, Telmo. 2005. *Introduzione alla filosofia della biologia*. Bari: Laterza.

Pilastro, Andrea. 2007. *Sesso ed evoluzione. La straordinaria storia evolutiva della riproduzione sessuale*. Milano: Bompiani.

Pinker, Steven. 1997. *How the Mind Works*. New York: Norton.

Pisanski, Katarzyna, Valentina Cartei, Carolyn McGettigan, Jordan Raine, and David Reby. "Voice modulation: a window into the origins of human vocal control?." *Trends in Cognitive Sciences* 20, no. 4 (2016): 304-318.

Pistorio, Ashley, Brett Vintch, and Xiaoqin Wang. "Acoustic analyses of vocal development in a New World primate, the common marmoset (*Callithrix jacchus*)." *Journal of the Acoustical Society America* 120, (2006): 1655-1670.

Plakke, Bethany, and Lizabeth M. Romanski. "Auditory connections and functions of prefrontal cortex." *Frontiers in neuroscience* 8, (2014): 199.

Ploog, Detlev. "Homo sapiens?. The speciation of modern Homo sapiens." In *The Speciation of Modern Homo Sapiens*, edited by Tim J. Crow, 121-135. Oxford: Oxford University Press, 2002.

Pollock, Jonathan I. "Field observations on Indri indri: A preliminary report". In *Lemur biology* edited by Ian Tattersall, and Robert W. Sussman, 287-311. New York and London: Plenum Press, 1975.

Pollock, Jonathan I. "The song of the Indris (Indri Indri; Primates: Lemuroidea): Natural History, Form, and Function." *International Journal of Primatology* 7, no. 3 (1986): 225-264.

Pomberger, Thomas, Cristina Risueno-Segovia, Julia Löschner, and Steffen R. Hage. "Precise motor control enables rapid flexibility in vocal behavior of marmoset monkeys." *Current Biology* 28, no. 5 (2018): 788-794.

Power, Camilla. "Old wives' tales: the gossip hypothesis and the reliability of cheap signals." In *Approaches to the Evolution of Language*, edited by Chris Knight, James Hurford, and Michael Studdert-Kennedy, 157-199. Cambridge, MA: Cambridge University Press, 1998.

Prather, Jonathan F., Susan Peters, Stephen Nowicki, and Richard Mooney. "Precise auditory-vocal mirroring in neurons for learned vocal communication." *Nature* 451, (2008): 305-310.

Premack, David. 1986. *Gavagai! Or the Future History of the Animal Language Controversy*. Cambridge, MA: MIT Press.

Prinz, Jesse. "Is the mind really modular?" In *Contemporary Debates in Cognitive Science*, edited by Robert Stainton, 22-36. New York: Blackwell, 2005.

Proto, Teresa. "Prosody, melody and rhythm in vocal music: The problem of textsetting in a linguistic perspective." *Linguistics in the Netherlands* 32, no. 1 (2015): 116-129.

Proust, Joëlle. "The Evolution of Primate Communication and Metacommunication." *Mind & Language* 31, no. 2 (2016): 177-203.

Querleu, Denis, Xavier Renard, Fabienne Versyp, Laurence Paris-Delrue, and Gilles Crèpin. "Fetal hearing." *European Journal of Obstetrics & Gynecology and Reproductive Biology* 28, no. 3 (1988): 191-212.

Ramus, Franck, Marc D. Hauser, Cory Miller, Dylan Morris, and Jacques Mehler. "Language discrimination by human newborns and by cotton-top tamarin monkeys." *Science* 288, no. 5464 (2000): 349-351.

Rasmussen, Lois E. L. "Chemical communication: an integral part of functional Asian elephant (Elephas maximus) society." *Ecoscience* 5, no. 3 (1998): 410-426.

Rauschecker, Josef P. "Ventral and dorsal streams in the evolution of speech and language." *Frontiers in Evolutionary Neuroscience* 4, (2012): 7.

Rauschecker, Josef P., and Sophie K. Scott. "Maps and streams in the auditory cortex: Nonhuman primates illuminate human speech processing." *Nature* 12, no. 6 (2009): 718-724.

Ravignani, Andrea, Mauricio Martins, and W. Tecumseh Fitch. "Vocal learning, prosody, and basal ganglia: Don't underestimate their complexity." *Behavioral and Brain Sciences* 37, no. 6 (2014): 570-571.

Read, Andrew F., and Daniel M. Weary. "Sexual selection and the evolution of bird song: a test of the Hamilton-Zuk hypothesis." *Behavioral Ecology and Sociobiology* 26, no. 1 (1990): 47-56.

Reiner, Anton, David J. Perkel, Claudio V. Mello, and Erich D. Jarvis. "Songbirds and the Revised Avian Brain Nomenclature." *Annals of the New York Academy of Sciences* 1016, (2004): 77-108.

Rendall, Drew, Michael J. Owren, and Michael J. Ryan. "What do animal signals mean?" *Animal Behaviour* 78, no. 2 (2009): 233-240.

Rendall, Drew. "Acoustic correlates of caller identity and affect intensity in the vowel-like grunt vocalizations of baboons." *The Journal of the Acoustical Society of America* 113, no. 6 (2003): 3390-3402.

Reybrouck, Mark. "Biological roots of musical epistemology: Functional cycles, Umwelt, and enactive listening." *Semiotica* 134, (2001): 599-633.

Reybrouck, Mark. 2021. *Musical Sense-making. Enaction, Experience, and Computation*. Abingdon-New York: Routledge.

Reynolds, Vernon. "Some behavioral comparisons between the chimpanzee and the mountain gorilla in the wild." *American Anthropologist* 67, (1965): 691-706.

Rialland, Annie. "Question prosody: An African perspective." *Tones and Tunes* 1, (2007): 35-64.

Richman, Bruce. "How music fixed nonsense into significant formulas: On rhythm, repetition, and meaning." In *The Origins of Music*, edited by Nils Wallin, Bjon Merker, and Steven Brown, 301-314. Cambridge, MA: The MIT Press, 2000.

Richman, Bruce. "Rhythm and melody in gelada vocal exchanges." *Primates* 28, no. 2 (1987): 199-223.

Rodseth, Lars, Richard W. Wrangham, Alisa Harrigan, and Barbara B. Smuts. "The human community as a primate society." *Current Anthropology* 32, (1991): 429-433.

Roederer, Juan G. "The search for a survival value of music." *Music Perception* 13, (1984): 350-356.

Rogers, Danny I. "Podiceps cristatus Great crested grebe." In *Handbook of Australian, New Zealand and Antarctic Birds. Volume 1. Ratites to Ducks*, edited by Stephen Marchant, and Peter J. Higgins, 115-124. Melbourne: Oxford University Press, 1990.

Rorty, Richard. 1967. *The Linguistic Turn. Recent Essays in Philosophical Method*. Chicago: The University of Chicago Press.

Rosenblatt, Jay S., and Charles T. Snowdon. 1996. *Parental Care: Evolution, Mechanisms, and Adaptive Significance*. San Diego: Academic Press.

Rosier, Renee L., and Tracy Langkilde. "Behavior under risk: How animals avoid becoming dinner." *Nature Education Knowledge* 2, (2011): 8.

Rotilio, Giuseppe. "L'alimentazione degli ominidi fino alla rivoluzione agropastorale del Neolitico." In *In carne e ossa. DNA, cibo e culture dell'uomo preistorico*, edited by Gianfranco Biondi, Fabio Martini, Giuseppe Rotilio, and Olga Rickards, 83-145. Roma-Bari: Laterza, 2006.

Roughgarden, Joan. "The social selection alternative to sexual selection." *Philosophical Transactions of the Royal Society B* 367, no. 1600: (2012): 2294-2303.

Rowlands, Mark. *The New Science of the Mind: From Extended Mind to Embodied Phenomenology*. Cambridge, MA: MIT Press, 2010.

Royle, Nick J., Per T. Smiseth, and Mathias Kölliker (eds.). *The Evolution of Parental Care*. Oxford: Oxford University Press, 2012.

Rumpf, Marion, and Barbara Tzschentke. "Perinatal acoustic communication in birds: Why do birds vocalize in the egg?." *The Open Ornithology Journal* 3, (2010): 141-149.

Russell, Jamie L., Joseph M. McIntyre, William D. Hopkins, and Jared P. Taglialatela. "Vocal learning of a communicative signal in captive chimpanzees, Pan troglodytes." *Brain and Language* 127, no. 3 (2013): 520-525.

Ruwet, Nicolas. "Musicologie et linguistique". *Revue internationale des sciences sociales* XIX, no. 1 (1967): 85-93.

Sacks, Oliver. 2008. *Musicophilia: Tales of Music and the Brain*. New York: Vintage Books.

Saint-Georges Catherine, Mohamed Chetouani, Raquel Cassel, Fabio Apicella, Ammar Mahdhaoui, Filippo Muratori, Marie-Christine Laznik, and David Cohen. "Motherese in interaction: at the cross-road of emotion and cognition? (a systematic review)." *PLoS One* 8, (2013): e78103.

Saltzman, Elliot L., and Kevin G. Munhall. "A dynamical approach to gestural patterning in speech production." *Ecological Psychology* 1, no. 4 (1989): 333-382.

Sander, David, Didier Grandjean, Gilles Pourtois, Sophie Schwartz, Mohamed L. Seghier, Klaus R. Scherer, Patrik Vuilleumier. "Emotion and attention interactions in social cognition: brain regions involved in processing anger prosody." *Neuroimage* 28, (2005): 848-858.

Sarà, Michele. "Biological evolution: An holistic organism-centered approach." *Rivista di Biologia/Biology Forum* 86, (1993): 347-359.

Saussure, Ferdinand De. 1955. *Cours de linguistique générale*. Payot: Paris.

Saussure, Ferdinand De. 2002. *Écrits de linguistique générale*. Paris: Gallimard.

Sawyer, Keith. "The semiotics of improvisation: The pragmatics of musical and verbal performance." *Semiotica. Journal of the International Association for Semiotic Studies* 108, no. 3-4 (2009): 269-306.

Scarantino, Andrea, and Zanna Clay. "Contextually variable signals can be functionally referential." *Animal Behaviour* 100, (2015): e1- e8.

Schachner, Adena, Timothy F. Brady, Irene M. Pepperberg, and Marc D. Hauser. "Spontaneous motor entrainment to music in multiple vocal mimicking species." *Current Biology* 19, no. 10 (2009): 831-836.

Schel, Anne Marijke, Simon W. Townsend, Zarin Machanda, Klaus Zuberbühler, and Katie E. Slocombe. "Chimpanzee alarm call production meets key criteria for intentionality." *PloS One* 8, no. 10 (2013): e76674.

Schellenberg, E. Glenn, and Sandra E. Trehub. "Culture-general and culture-specific factors in the discrimination of melodies." *Journal of Experimental Child Psychology* 74, no. 2 (1999): 107-127.

Schenker, Heinrich. 1935. *Der Freie Satz*. New York: Longman.

Scherer, Klaus R. "Emotion expression in speech and music." In *Music, Language, Speech, and Brain*, edited by Sundberg Johan, Lennart Nord and Rolf Carlson, 146-156. London: Palgrave, 1991.

Scherer, Klaus R., Marcel R. Zentner, and Annekathrin Schacht. "Emotional states generated by music: An exploratory study of music experts." *Musicae Scientiae* 5, no. 1 (2001): 149-171.

Schiavio, Andrea, Damiano Menin, and Jakub Matyja. "Music in the flesh: Embodied simulation in musical understanding." *Psychomusicology: Music, Mind, and Brain* 24, no. 4 (2014): 340.

Schiavio, Andrea, Dylan van der Schyff, Julian Cespedes-Guevara, and Mark Reybrouck. "Enacting musical emotions. Sense-making, dynamic systems, and the embodied mind." *Phenomenology and the Cognitive Sciences* 16, no. 5 (2017): 785-809.

Schilbach, Leonhard, Bert Timmermans, Vasudevi Reddy, Alan Costall, Gary Bente, Tobias Schlicht and Kai Vogeley. "Toward a second-person neuroscience 1." *Behavioral and brain sciences* 36, no. 4 (2013): 393-414.

Schindler, Antonio, Irene Vernero, and Elena Aimar. "Fisiologia della percezione uditiva." In *Allenamento della percezione uditiva nei bambini con impianto cocleare*, edited by Elena Aimar, Antonio Schindler, and Irene Vernero, 13-39. Milano: Springer, 2009.

Schön, Daniele, Lilach Akiva-Kabiri, and Tomaso Vecchi. 2007. *Psicologia della musica*. Roma: Carocci.

Schopenhauer, Arthur. 1819. *Die Welt als Wille und Vorstellung*. Leipzig: F. M. Brodhaus.

Schore, Allan N. "Attachment and the regulation of the right brain." *Attachment & Human Development* 2, no. 1 (2000): 23-47.

Schusterman, Ronald. J. "Vocal learning in mammals with special emphasis on pinnipeds." In *The Evolution of Communicative Flexibility: Complexity, Creativity, and Adaptability in Human and Animal Communication*, edited by Kimbrough D. Oller, and Ulrike Griebel, 41-70. Cambridge (MA): MIT Press, 2008.

Schwartz, David A., Catherine Q. Howe, and Dale Purves. "The statistical structure of human speech sounds predicts musical universals." *Journal of Neuroscience* 23, no. 18 (2003): 7160-7168.

Scott-Phillips Thom. 2015. *Speaking our Minds*. London, UK: Palgrave Macmillan.

Scruton, Roger. 1999. *The Aesthetics of Music*. New York: Oxford University Press.

Seashore, Carl E. 1938. *Psychology of Music*. New York - London: McGraw-Hill Book Company.

Sebastian-Gallés, Núria, Emmanuel Dupoux, Juan Segui, and Jacques Mahler. "Contrasting syllabic effects in Catalan and Spanish." *Journal of Memory and Language* 31, (1992): 18-32.

Sebeok, Thomas A. "Animal Communication." *Science* 147, (1965): 1006-1014.

Sebeok, Thomas A. (ed.) *Animal Communication. Techniques of Study and Results of Research.* Bloomington: Indiana University Press, 1968.

Seifert, Uwe, Paul F. M. J. Verschure, Michael A. Arbib, Annabel J. Cohen, Leonardo Fogassi, Thomas Fritz, Gina Kuperberg, Jônatas Manzolli, and Nikki Rickard. "Semantics of Internal and External Worlds". In *Language, Music, and the Brain: A Mysterious Relationship,* edited by Michael A. Arbib, 203-229. Cambridge, MA: MIT Press, 2013.

Seyfarth, Robert M., and Cheney Dorothy L. "The origin of meaning in animal signals." *Animal Behaviour* 124, (2017): 339-346.

Seyfarth, Robert M., and Dorothy L. Cheney. "Meaning and emotion in animal vocalizations." *Annals of the New York Academy of Sciences,* (2003): 32-55.

Seyfarth, Robert M., and Dorothy L. Cheney. "The ontogeny of vervet monkey alarm-calling behavior: A preliminary report." *Zeitschrift fur Tierpychologie* 49, (1980): 381-405.

Seyfarth, Robert M., Dorothy L. Cheney, and Peter Marler. "Vervet monkey alarm calls: semantic communication in a free-ranging primate." *Animal Behaviour* 28, no. 4 (1980): 1070-1094.

Shapiro, Lawrence. 2004. *The Mind Incarnate.* Cambridge: MIT Press

Sheldon, Ben C., and Simon Verhulst. "Ecological immunology: costly parasite defences and trade-offs in evolutionary ecology." *Trends in ecology & evolution* 11, no. 8 (1996): 317-321.

Siegel, Jane A., and William Siegel. "Categorical perception of tonal intervals: Musicians can't tell sharp from flat." *Perception & Psychophysics* 21, no. 5 (1977): 399-407.

Sievers, Christine, Markus Wild, and Thibaud Gruber. "Intentionality and flexibility in animal communication." In *The Routledge Handbook of Philosophy of Animal Minds,* edited by Kristin Andrews and Jacob Beck, 333-342. London: Taylor & Francis, 2017.

Simonyan, Kristina, and Barry Horwitz. "Laryngeal motor cortex and control of speech in humans." *The Neuroscientist* 17, no. 2 (2011): 197-208.

Simonyan, Kristina, John Ostuni, Christy L. Ludlow, and Barry Horwitz. "Functional but not structural networks of the human laryngeal motor cortex show left hemispheric lateralization during syllable but not breathing production." *Journal of Neuroscience* 29, no. 47 (2009): 14912-14923.

Slater, Peter J. B., and Nigel I. Mann, "Why do the females of many bird species sing in the tropics?" *Journal of Avian Biology* 35, (2004): 289-294.

Sloboda, John A. 1985. *The Musical Mind. The Cognitive Psychology of Music.* Oxford: Oxford University Press.

Smith, William J. 1977. *The Behavior of Communicating: An Ethological Approach.* Cambridge, MA: Harvard University Press.

Snowdon, Charles T. "Sexual selection and communication." In *Sexual Selection in Primates: New and Comparative Perspectives,* edited by Peter M.

Kappeler, and Carel van Schaik, 57-70. Cambridge: Cambridge University Press, 2004.

Sorrentino, Viviana, Marco Gamba, and Cristina Giacoma. "A quantitative description of the vocal types emitted in the indri's song." In *Leaping Ahead*, edited by Judith Masters, Marco Gamba, and Fabien Génin, 315-322. New York: Springer, 2013.

Spelke, Elizabeth, and Katherine Kinzler. "Core knowledge." *Developmental Science*, no. 10 (2007): 89-96.

Spelke, Elizabeth. "Innateness, Learning, and Rationality." *Child Development Perspectives* 3, no. 2 (2009): 96-98.

Srikosamatara, Sompoad. "Imitation of vocal duet by a widow of the pileated gibbon (Hylobates pileatus) in Southeast Thailand." *International Journal of Primatology* 3, (1982): 336.

Stafford, Kathleen M., Christopher G. Fox, and David S. Clark. "Long-range acoustic detection and localization of blue whale calls in the northeast Pacific Ocean." *The Journal of the Acoustical Society of America* 104, no. 6 (1998): 3616-3625.

Stanton, Margaret A., Elizabeth V. Lonsdorf, Anne E. Pusey, Jane Goodall, and Carson M. Murray. "Maternal behavior by birth order in wild chimpanzees (Pan troglodytes) increased investment by first-time mothers." *Current anthropology* 55, no. 4 (2014): 483-489.

Stearns, Steven C., "Natural selection and fitness, adaptation and constraint." In *Patterns and Processes in the History of Life*, edited by David M Raup, and David Jablonski, 23-44. New York: Springer-Verlag, 1986.

Stefani, Gino, Luca Marconi, and Franca Ferrari. 1990. *Gli intervalli musicali*. Milano: Bompiani.

Stefani, Gino. 1976. *Introduzione alla semiotica della musica*. Palermo: Sellerio.

Stefani, Gino. 1982. *La competenza musicale*. Bologna: CLUEB.

Steinbeis, Nikolaus, and Stefan Koelsch. "Shared neural resources between music and language indicate semantic processing of musical tension-resolution patterns." *Cerebral Cortex* 18, no. 5 (2008): 1169-1178.

Stern, Daniel N. 1985. *The Interpersonal World of the Infant: A View from Psychoanalysis and Developmental Psychology*. New York: Basic Books.

Stern, Theodore. "Drum and whistle "languages": An analysis of speech surrogates." *American Anthropologist* 59, no. 3 (1957): 487-506.

Studdert-Kennedy, Michael. "Evolutionary implications of the particulate principle: imitation and the dissociation of phonetic form from semantic function." In *The Evolutionary Emergence of Language*, edited by Chris Knight, Michael Studdert-Kennedy, and James R. Hurford, 161-176. Cambridge: Cambridge University Press, 2000.

Studdert-Kennedy, Michael. "Imitation and the emergence of segments." *Phonetica* 57, (2000): 275-283.

Sundberg, Johan, and Björn Lindblom. "Generative theories in language and music descriptions." *Cognition* 4, no. 1 (1976): 99-122.

Sundberg, Johan. "Formant technique in a professional female singer." *Acustica* 32, (1975): 89-96.

Sundberg, Johan. 1987. *The Science of the Singing Voice*. Dekalb: Northern Illinois University Press.

Sundberg, Johan. "Articulatory interpretation of the "singing formant"." *The Journal of the Acoustical Society of America* 55, no. 4 (1974): 838-844.

Swadesh, Morris. 2017. *The Origin and Diversification of Language*. New York: Routledge.

Swingley, Daniel. "Contributions of infant word learning to language development." *Philosophical Transactions of the Royal Society B* 364, no. 1536 (2009): 3617-3632.

Syal, Supriya, and Barbara L. Finlay. "Thinking outside the cortex: Social motivation in the evolution and development of language." *Developmental Science* 14, no. 2 (2011): 417-430.

Taglialatela, Jared P., Lisa Reamer, Steven J. Schapiro, and William D. Hopkins. "Social learning of a communicative signal in captive chimpanzees." *Biology Letters* 8, no. 4 (2012): 498-501.

Takahashi, Daniel Y., Alicia R. Fenley, and Asif A. Ghazanfar. "Early development of turn-taking with parents shapes vocal acoustics in infant marmoset monkeys." *Philosophical Transactions of the Royal Society B* 371, no. 1693 (2016): 20150370.

Takahashi, Daniel Y., Alicia R. Fenley, Yaoy Teramoto Kimura, Darshana Z. Narayanan, Jeremy I. Borjon, Peter Holmes, and Asif A. Ghazanfar. "The developmental dynamics of marmoset monkey vocal production." *Science* 349, (2015): 734-738.

Takahashi, Daniel Y., Darshana Z. Narayan, and Asif A. Ghazanfar. "Coupled oscillator dynamics of vocal turn-taking in monkeys." *Current Biology* 23, no. 21 (2013): 2162-2168.

Tarasti, Eero. 1994. *A Theory of Musical Semiotics*. Bloomington: Indiana University Press.

Tarasti, Eero. 2002. *Signs of Music: A Guide to Musical Semiotics*. Berlin: Walter de Gruyter.

Tattersall, Ian. 2012. *Masters of the Planet: The Search of our Human Origins*. London: Macmillan.

Taylor, Anna M., and David Reby. "The contribution of source-filter theory to mammal vocal communication research." *Journal of Zoology* 280, no. 3 (2010): 221-236.

Tchernichovski, Ofer, and Gary Marcus. "Vocal learning beyond imitation: mechanisms of adaptive vocal development in songbirds and human infants." *Current Opinion in Neurobiology* 28, (2014): 42-47.

Tchernichovski, Ofer, and Josh Wallman. "Neurons of imitation." *Nature* 451, no. 17 (2008): 249-250.

Tchernichovski, Ofer, and Josh Wallman. "Behavioural neuroscience: Neurons of imitation." *Nature* 451, (2008): 249-250.

ten Cate, Carel, Michelle Spierings, Jeroen Hubert, and Henkjan Honing. "Can birds perceive rhythmic patterns? A review and experiments on a songbird and a parrot species." *Frontiers in Psychology* 7, (2016): 730.

Thompson, Katerina V., Andrew J. Baker, and Anne M. Baker. "Parental care and behavioral development in captive mammals." In *Wild Mammals in*

Captivity: Principles and Techniques for Zoo Management, edited by Devra G. Kleiman, Katerina V. Thompson, and Charlotte Kirk Baer, 367-385. Chicago: Chicago University Press, 2010.

Thompson, Roger K. R. "Natural and relational concepts in animals." In *Comparative Approaches to Cognitive Science*, edited by Herbert L. Roitblat, and Jean-Arcady Meyer, 175 -224. Cambridge, MA: The MIT Press, 1995.

Thompson, William F., Manuela M. Marin, and Lauren Stewart. "Reduced sensitivity to emotional prosody in congenital amusia rekindles the musical protolanguage hypothesis." *Proceedings of the National Academy of Sciences* 109, no. 46 (2012): 19027-19032.

Thorpe, William H. 1961. *Bird Song: The Biology of Vocal Communication and Expression in Birds.* Cambridge: Cambridge University Press.

Tinbergen, Nikolass. 1951. *The Study of Instinct.* Oxford: Clarendon Press.

Tomasello, Michael. 1999. *The Cultural Origins of Human Cognition.* Cambridge, MA: Harvard University Press.

Tomasello, Michael. 2008. *Origins of Human Communication.* Cambridge, MA: MIT Press.

Toro, Juan M., Josep B. Trobalon, and Núria Sebastián-Gallés. "The use of prosodic cues in language discrimination tasks by rats." *Animal Cognition* 6, no. 2 (2003): 131-136.

Toro, Juan M., Marina Nespor, Jacques Mehler, and Luca Bonatti. "Finding words and rules in a speech stream: Functional differences between vowels and consonants." *Psychological Science* 19, no. 2 (2008): 137-144.

Torti, Valeria, Marco Gamba, Zo Hasina Rabemananjara, and Cristina Giacoma. "The songs of the indris (Mammalia: Primates: Indridae): contextual variation in the long-distance calls of a lemur." *Italian Journal of Zoology* 80, (2013): 596-607.

Townsend, Simon W., and Marta B. Manser. "Functionally referential communication in mammals: the past, present, and the future." *Ethology* 119, no. 1 (2013): 1-11.

Trainor, Laura J., Caren M. Austin, and Renée N. Desjardins. "Is infant-directed speech prosody a result of the vocal expression of emotion?." *Psychological Science* 11, (2000): 188-195.

Trehub, Sandra E. "Human processing predispositions and musical universals." In *The Origins of Music*, edited by Nils L. Wallin, Bjorn Merker, and Steven Brown, 427-448. Cambridge, MA: MIT Press, 2000.

Trehub, Sandra E. "Infants as musical connoisseurs." In *The Child as Musician: A Handbook of Musical Development*, edited by Gary McPherson, 33-49. Oxford: Oxford University Press, 2006.

Trehub, Sandra E. "The Developmental Origins of Musicality." *Nature Neuroscience* VI, no. 7 (2003): 669-673.

Trehub, Sandra E., Anna M. Unyk, and Laurel J. Trainor. "Maternal singing in cross-cultural perspective." *Infant Behavior and Development* 16, no. 3 (1993a): 285-295.

Trehub, Sandra E., Laurel J. Trainor, and Anna M. Unyk. "Music and speech processing in the first year of life." *Advances in Child Development and Behavior* 24, (1993b): 1-35.

Trevarthen, Colwyn. "Musicality and the intrinsic motive pulse: Evidence from human psychobiology and infant communication". *Musicae scientiae*, (1999): 157-213.

Trimble, Michael, and Dale Hesdorffer. "Music and the brain: the neuroscience of music and musical appreciation." *BJPsych international* 14, no. 2 (2017): 28-31.

Trivers, Robert L. "Parental investment and sexual selection." In *Sexual Selection and the Descent of Man, 1871-1971*, edited by Bernard Campbell, 136-179. Chicago: Aldine Publ. Co., 1972.

Trivers, Robert L. "Parent-offspring conflict." *American Zoologist* 14, (1974): 249-264.

Trivers, Robert L. "The evolution of reciprocal altruism." *Quarterly Review of Biology* 46, (1971): 35-57.

Trivers, Robert L. 1985. *Social Evolution*. Menlo Park, California: Benjamin/Cummings.

Tyack, Peter L. "A taxonomy for vocal learning." *Philosophical Transactions of the Royal Society B* 375, no. 1789 (2020): 20180406.

Tyack, Peter L. "Convergence of calls as animals form social bonds, active compensation for noisy communication channels, and the evolution of vocal learning in mammals." *Journal of Comparative Psychology* 122, (2008): 319-331.

Tyack, Peter L., and Christopher W. Clark. "Communication and acoustic behavior of dolphins and whales." In *Hearing by whales and dolphins*, edited by Arthur N. Popper, Richard R. Fay, and Whitlow Au, 156-224. New York: Springer, 2000.

Ujhelyi, Maria. "Is there any intermediate stage between animal communication and language?" *Journal of Theoretical Biology* 180, (1996): 71-76.

Vaissière, Jacqueline. "Phonetic explanations for cross-linguistic prosodic similarities." *Phonetica* 52, no. 3 (1995): 123-130.

van der Schyff, Dylan, and Andrea Schiavio. "Evolutionary Musicology Meets Embodied Cognition: Biocultural Coevolution and the Enactive Origins of Human Musicality." *Frontiers in Neuroscience* 11, (2017): 519.

Van Eijden, Theo M., and Stan J. Turkawski. "Morphology and physiology of masticatory muscle motor units." *Critical Reviews in Oral Biology & Medicine* 12, (2001): 76-91.

Vassilakis, Pantelis. "Auditory roughness as means of musical expression." *Selected Reports in Ethnomusicology* 12, (2005): 119-144.

Vattimo, Gianni. 2010. *Introduzione all'estetica*. Pisa: Edizioni ETS.

Viinikainen, Mikko, Jari Kätsyri, and Mikko Sams. "Representation of perceived sound valence in the human brain." *Human Brain Mapping* 33, no. 10 (2012): 2295-2305.

Virno, Paolo. 2003. *Scienze sociali e natura umana: facoltà di linguaggio, invariante biologico, rapporti di produzione*. Soveria Mannelli: Rubbettino Editore.

von Frisch, Karl. 1967. *The Dance Language and Orientation of Bees*. Cambridge (MA): Harvard University Press.

Vorperian, Houri K., and Ray D. Kent. "Vowel acoustic space development in children: A synthesis of acoustic and anatomic data." *Journal of Speech, Language, and Hearing Research* 50, no. 6 (2007): 1510-1545.

Wagner, Günter P. "The significance of developmental constraints for phenotypic evolution by natural selection." In *Population Genetics and Evolution*, edited by Gerdina de Jong, 222-229. Berlin Heidelberg: Springer-Verlag, 1988.

Wakefield, John C. (2020). *Intonational Morphology*. Singapore: Springer Nature.

Wallace, Alfred R. 1889. *Darwinism: An Exposition of the Theory of Natural Selection with Some of Its Applications*. London-New York: Macmillan.

Wallaschek, Richard. 2010. *Primitive Music*. Illinois: Sumner Press.

Wallin, Nils L. 1991. *Biomusicology: Neurophysiological, Neuropsychological, and Evolutionary Perspectives on the Origins and Purposes of Music*. New York: Pendragon Press.

Wang, Liang, Eliathamby Ambikairajah, and Eric H. C. Choi. "Automatic tonal and non-tonal language classification and language identification using prosodic information." *International Symposium on Chinese Spoken language Processing (ISCSLP)*, (2006): 485-496.

Wang, Rui, Chun- Chun Chen, Erina Hara, Miriam V. Rivas, Petra L. Roulhac, Jason T. Howard, Mukta Chakraborty, Jean-Nicolas Audet, and Erich D. Jarvis. "Convergent differential regulation of SLIT-ROBO axon guidance genes in the brains of vocal learners." *Journal of Comparative Neurology* 523, no. 6 (2015): 892-906.

Watson, Stuart K., Simon W. Townsend, Anne M. Schel, Claudia Wilke, Emma K. Wallace, Leveda Cheng, Victoria West, and Katie E. Slocombe. "Vocal learning in the functionally referential food grunts of chimpanzees." *Current Biology* 25, no. 4 (2015): 495-499.

Watzlawick, Paul, Janet B. Bavelas, and Don D. Jackson. 1967. *Pragmatics of Human Communication*. New York: W. W. Norton & Company,

Werner, Dennis. 1984. *Amazon Journey: An Anthropologist's Year Among Brazil's Mekranoti Indians*. New York: Simon and Schuster.

West, Hannah E. R., and Isabella Capellini. "Male care and life history traits in mammals." *Nature Communications* 7, (2016): 1-10.

Whitaker, Harry. "History of Neurolinguistics." In *The Handbook of Neurolinguistics*, edited by Harry Whitaker, and Brigitte Stemmer, 27-57. San Diego: Academic Press, 1998.

White, Laurence. "Segmentation of Speech." In *The Oxford Handbook of Psycholinguistics (2st edn)*, edited by Shirley-Ann Rueschemeyer, and M. Gareth Gaskell, 5-30. Oxford: Oxford University Press, 2018.

Whitfield, D. Philip. "Behaviour and ecology of a polyandrous population of Grey Phalaropes Phalaropus fulicarius in Iceland." *Journal of Avian Biology*, (1995): 349-352.

Whitham, Jessica C., Melissa S. Gerald, and Dario Maestripieri "Intended receivers and functional significance of grunt and gurney vocalizations in free-ranging female rhesus macaques." *Ethology* 113, (2007): 862-874.

Wilson, Edward O. 1975. *Sociobiology. The New Synthesis*. Cambridge: Harvard University Press.

Wittgenstein, Ludwing. 1975. *Philosophische Untersuchungen*. Berlin: Suhrkamp Verlag.

Wittgenstein, Ludwing. 2012. *The Big Typescript: TS. 213*. New York: John Wiley & Sons.

Wittman, Anna B., and Lewis L. Wall. "The evolutionary origins of obstructed labor: bipedalism, encephalization, and the human obstetric dilemma." *Obstetrical & Gynecological Survey* 62, no. 11 (2007): 739-748.

Wray, Alison. 2002. *The Transition to Language. Studies in the Evolution of Language*. Oxford: Oxford University Press.

Wray, Alison. "Protolanguage as a holistic system for social interaction." *Language & Communication* 18, no. 1 (1998): 47-67.

Xian-Ming, Y. "The Talking Musical Instruments of the Province of Yunnan." *Ethnomusicology Research Seminars*. London: Goldsmiths University.

Yamaguchi, Chieko, and Akihiro Izumi. "Vocal learning in nonhuman primates: Importance of vocal contexts." In *The Origins of Language*, edited by Nabuo Masataka, 75-84. Tokyo: Springer, 2008.

Zahavi, Amotz, and Avishag Zahavi. 1975. *The Handicap Principle: A Missing Piece of Darwin's Puzzle*. New York: Oxford University Press.

Zahavi, Amotz. "The cost of honesty (Further remarks on the Handicap Principle)." *Journal of Theoretical Biology* 67, (1977): 603-605.

Zanoli, Anna, Chiara De Gregorio, Daria Valente, Valeria Torti, Giovanna Bonadonna, Rose Marie Randrianarison, Cristina Giacoma, and Marco Gamba. "Sexually dimorphic phrase organization in the song of the indris (Indri indri)." *American Journal of Primatology* 82, no. 6 (2020): e23132.

Zatorre, Robert J. "Music and the brain." *Annals of the New York Academy of Sciences* 999, no. 1 (2003): 4-14.

Zatorre, Robert J., and Andrea R. Halpern. "Identification, discrimination, and selective adaptation of simultaneous musical intervals." *Perception & Psychophysics* 26, no. 5 (1979): 384-395.

Zatorre, Robert J., and Isabelle Peretz (eds.). *The Biological Foundations of Music*. New York: The New York Academy of Science, 2001.

Zatorre, Robert J., Pascal Belin, and Virginia B. Penhune. "Structure and function of auditory cortex: music and speech." *Trends in Cognitive Sciences* 6, no. 1 (2002): 37-46.

Zimmermann, Elke, Lisette M. C. Leliveld, and Simone Schehka. "Toward the evolutionary roots of affective prosody in human acoustic communication: a comparative approach to mammalian voices." In *Evolution of Emotional Communication: From Sounds in Nonhuman Mammals to Speech and Music in Man*, edited by Eckart Altenmüller, Sabine Schmidt, and Elke Zimmermann, 116-132. Oxford: Oxford University Press, 2013.

Zoloth, Stephen R., Michael R. Petersen, Michael D. Beecher, Steven Green, Peter Marler, David B. Moody, and William Stebbins. "Species-specific perceptual processing of vocal sounds by monkeys." *Science* 204, no. 4395 (1979): 870-873.

Zuberbühler, Klaus. "Linguistic prerequisites in the primate lineage." In *Language Origins. Perspective on Evolution*, edited by Maggie Tallerman, 262-282. Oxford: Oxford University Press. 2005.

Zuberbühler, Klaus. "Survivor signals: the biology and psychology of animal alarm calling." *Advances in the Study Behavior* 40, (2009): 277-322.

Zuidema, Willem. "Language in nature: on the evolutionary roots of a cultural phenomenon." In *The Language Phenomenon. Human Communication from Milliseconds to Millennia*, edited by Philippe Binder, and Kenny Smith, 163-189. Berlin: Springer, 2013.

Zwitserlood, Pienie, Herbert Schriefers, Aditi Lahiri, and Wilma van Donselaar. "The role of syllables in the perception of spoken Dutch." *Journal of Experimental Psychology: Learning, Memory, and Cognition* 19, (1993): 260-271.

INDEX

A

alarm barks, 80
alarm calls, 25, 56, 57, 100, 102
allomothering, 45
analogy, 11, 49, 69, 78, 106
Area X, 77
Asian elephants (*Elaphus maximus*), 62
auditory cortex, xv, 20, 25
Australian magpie-larks (*Grallina cyanoleuca*), 67

B

babbling, 43, 49, 50, 76, 105, 106
baboons (*Papio ursinus*), 80
baby talk, 30, 47, 50
biological constraints, xii, xx, 34, 44, 79, 91, 92, 112
birdsong, 66, 67, 69, 78, 97
Broca's area, 12, 23, 25

C

calls, 8, 9, 25, 31, 41, 49, 50, 56, 57, 68, 80, 82, 100, 101, 102
cercopithecus (*Cercopithecus*), 25
chimpanzees (*Pan troglodytes*), 42, 73, 79
chuck calls, 80
clownfish (*Amphiprion ocellaris*), 40
contact barks, 80
convergent evolution, xx, 69, 75
cooperative breeding, xxii, 41
cotton-haired tamarins (*Saguinus oedipus oedipus*), 26
cotton-top tamarins (*Saguinus oedipus oedipus*), 40
courtship calls, 57, 102

D

Darwin, xix, xx, xxi, 18, 29, 30, 31, 33
distant calls, 27
dorsal pathway, 59
duet-splitting, 71

E

embodied, xi, 22, 44, 87, 88, 89, 90
embodied cognition, 90
embodied language, 87
embodied music, 88, 89
embodied music cognition, 88, 89
Evo-Devo, xii, 21, 49
exaptation, 103

F

fireflies (*Luciola*), 83
foregrounding, 51
formant frequencies, 67, 93, 94, 95, 99, 104

G

gelada baboons (*Theropithecus gelada*), 58
gibbons of Southeast Asia (*Hylobatidae*)., 70

gobies (*Gobiidae Cuvier*), 40
Great Crested Grebe (*Podiceps cristatus*), 62
grounded cognition, 89
GTTM, 11, 12

H

HCV, 77
Homo sapiens, xi, xii, xvi, 21, 47, 97
homology, 56
HVC, 77
HVCX, 77, 78

I

imitation, xxiii, 30, 54, 74, 78, 79, 81, 82, 92
Indri (*Indri indri*), 72
infant-directed communication, 43

J

Japanese macaques (*Macaca fuscata*), 48
Japanese sparrow (*Lonchura striata domestica*), 69

K

kin selection, 98, 100

L

larynx, 5, 43, 51, 81, 93, 94, 99, 103

M

mandarin diamond (*Taeniopygia guttata*), 76
marmoset monkeys (*Callithrix jacchus*), 40, 49

marsh sparrow (*Melospiza georgiana*), 68
mating calls, 30
meerkats (*Suricata suricatta*), 102
monk parakeets (*Myiopsitta monachus*), 81
motherese, xiii, xvii, xviii, xxii, 8, 29, 35, 41, 45, 46, 47, 48, 50, 51, 52, 54, 55, 92, 103, 111, 112
moving calls, 102
musical protolanguage, xvii, xviii, xx, xxiii, 24, 32, 47, 60, 70, 96, 97, 98, 103, 111, 112, 113
musilanguage, 58, 59, 60, 70, 102

N

natural selection, xix, 30, 34, 67, 70, 85, 92, 97, 99, 104, 110, 112

O

ontogenetic, xvi, xx, xxi, 50, 81, 103, 109

P

pant-hoot, 73
phalarope (*Phalaropus fulicarius*), 40
phylogenetic, xvi, xx, 81, 103
primary auditory cortex, 25, 59
Prince Albert's lyre bird (*Menura alberti*), 78
propositional rhythm, 26
prosodic bootstrapping, xiii, xix, 51
prosody, xix, xxii, 17, 18, 19, 28, 29, 31, 32, 41, 51, 53, 54, 56, 92, 105, 110
protolanguage, xiii, xvii, xxi, xxiv, 6, 29, 33, 45, 100, 102, 110, 112

Pygmy marmosets (*Cebuella pygmaea*), 106

R

red-bellied lemurs (*Eulemer rubriventer*), 25
rhesus monkeys (*Macaca mulatta*), xvii

S

semiological tripartition, 14
sexual selection, 65, 66, 70, 72, 96, 97, 98
shining blue wren (*Malurus splendens*), 67
song-splitting, 71
squirrel monkeys (*Saimiri sciureus*), 80
superb lyre bird (*Menura novaehollandiae*), 78
SVT, 93, 95, 99, 103, 105
 supralaryngeal vocal tract, 93
syrinx, 63, 75, 76, 81

T

TMI

talking musical instruments, 28
turn-taking system, 106

V

ventral pathway, 59
vocal communication, xv, xxiii, 23, 32, 40, 45, 48, 65, 73, 76, 78, 82, 83, 84, 85, 87, 92, 101, 103, 106
vocal learning, xvi, 30, 67, 68, 69, 74, 75, 76, 77, 79, 80, 81, 82, 83, 84

W

winter wren (*Troglodytes troglodytes*), 68

Y

yellow-crested cockatoo (*Cacatua sulphurea*), 83

Z

zoomusicology, 64
zoosemiotics, 63, 64

www.ingramcontent.com/pod-product-compliance
Lightning Source LLC
Chambersburg PA
CBHW061836300426
44115CB00013B/2411